Learning SolidWorks®

Learning SolidWorks®
SECOND EDITION

Richard M. Lueptow
Northwestern University, Evanston, IL

Michael Minbiole
*Northrop Grumman Corporation,
Rolling Meadows, IL*

Pearson Education, Inc.
Upper Saddle River, New Jersey 07458

Library of Congress Cataloging-in-Publication Data

Lueptow, Richard M.

    Learning SolidWorks / Richard M. Lueptow, Michael Minbiole.—2nd ed.

      p. cm.

    ISBN 0-13-140974-3

     1. SolidWorks. 2. Computer graphics. 3. Computer-aided design. I. Minbiole, Michael.

    II. Title.

    T385.L85 2003

    620'.0042'02855369—dc21

                                    2003044005

Vice President and Editorial Director, ECS: *Marcia J. Horton*
Acquisitions Editor: *Eric Svendsen*
Vice President and Director of Production and Manufacturing, ESM: *David W. Riccardi*
Executive Managing Editor: *Vince O'Brien*
Managing Editor: *David A. George*
Production Editor: *Scott Disanno*
Director of Creative Services: *Paul Belfanti*
Creative Director: *Jayne Conte*
Art Editor: *Greg Dulles*
Manufacturing Manager: *Trudy Pisciotti*
Manufacturing Buyer: *Lisa McDowell*
Marketing Manager: *Holly Stark*

© 2004 by Pearson Education, Inc.
Upper Saddle River, New Jersey 07458

SolidWorks is a registered trademark of the SolidWorks Corporation, 300 Baker Avenue, Concord, MA 01742.

Printed in the United States of America
10 9 8 7 6 5 4 3

ISBN 0-13-140974-3

Pearson Education Ltd., *London*
Pearson Education Australia Pty. Ltd., *Sydney*
Pearson Education Singapore, Pte. Ltd.
Pearson Education North Asia Ltd., *Hong Kong*
Pearson Education Canada, Inc., *Toronto*
Pearson Educación de Mexico, S.A. de C.V.
Pearson Education—Japan, *Tokyo*
Pearson Education Malaysia, Pte. Ltd.
Pearson Education, Inc., *Upper Saddle River, New Jersey*

Contents

Preface

The latest version of SolidWorks can be learned quickly and easily using *Learning Solid-Works* as a guide. SolidWorks has quickly become one of the leading computer-aided design (CAD) programs available. It is used around the world in a wide range of industries. The success of SolidWorks results from its ability to provide sophisticated solids modeling capability on low-priced PC computers.

Unlike some books for learning CAD software, we do not provide a CD-ROM with modeled parts ready to be modified nor do we use tedious exercises drawing simplistic shapes or adding useless features to a simple part. Instead, we model a real-life product as an engineer would in practice. Our approach is to model a pizza cutter from start to finish by using increasingly more sophisticated modeling techniques as the design progresses. First, we model six parts of a pizza cutter using extrusions, revolves, cuts, rounds, patterns, and many other features. Then we assemble the parts to create a virtual pizza cutter. Finally, we create standard engineering drawings of one of the parts and the entire assembly. After completing these basics of SolidWorks, we redesign the pizza cutter's handle to make it suitable for injection molding and then we design a stylized, ergonomic handle introducing many advanced features.

Learning SolidWorks uses a progressive self-learning method to effectively teach the basics of SolidWorks as well as advanced solids modeling concepts. The descriptions of the SolidWorks commands are quite detailed early in the tutorial, but as concepts are learned, the SolidWorks commands become second nature. Of course, whenever a new concept or command is introduced, it is explained completely.

Each tutorial chapter should take two to four hours to successfully complete. In Chapter 1, "Solids Modeling with SolidWorks," computer-aided graphics are introduced and the basics of the solids modeling approach used in SolidWorks are described. Chapter 2, "Getting Started in SolidWorks," begins the CAD process by modeling three parts of the pizza cutter as simple extrusions with additional features added using cuts, chamfers, fillets, and rounds. Chapter 3, "Modeling Parts in SolidWorks: Revolves," adds three more parts using revolves as well as introducing advanced sketching and feature creation capabilities. In Chapter 4, "Modeling an Assembly: The Pizza Cutter," the parts modeled in the previous two chapters are assembled to create an entire pizza cutter assembly. Corrections are made to the parts to avoid interference between components and an exploded view is created. In Chapter 5, "Creating Working Drawings," a sheet format is generated that can be used as the starting point for any drawing. Then, engineering drawings of one of the pizza cutter parts and the entire pizza cutter are created. Chapter 6, "Modeling the Handle as a Plastic Injection-Molded Part," introduces sweeps and shells to create an advanced part that could be easily injection molded. Chapter 7, "Redesigning the Handle," uses lofts and other advanced features of Solid-Works to create an ergonomic, smoothly contoured handle for the pizza cutter that integrates with the other parts that were modeled earlier. By the end of the book, the user has implemented nearly all of the capabilities that SolidWorks has to offer. Not only is the tutorial complete in its coverage, it is fun to work through it as the pizza cutter takes form and evolves.

Learning SolidWorks was written for students who have never studied CAD before. Each chapter begins with an overview and a list of objectives. Many figures show the menus and dialog boxes, as well as the pizza cutter as it takes shape. Problems at the end of the chapters focus on modifying the pizza cutter to change or improve it. Special boxes describe advanced capabilities of SolidWorks or explain useful modeling or engineering concepts.

We want to thank the editorial staff at Pearson Prentice Hall, particularly Eric Svendsen, for working with us on this book. In addition, the SolidWorks Corporation has provided us with prerelease versions of SolidWorks so that this book could be published in a timely manner for use with the latest version. RML thanks Northwestern University for time to work on this book and his loving wife, Maiya, and his children, Hannah and Kyle, for their support in this endeavor. MM is grateful to his parents for their continuing love and support.

RICHARD M. LUEPTOW
MICHAEL MINBIOLE

Learning SolidWorks®

1

Solids Modeling with SolidWorks

OVERVIEW

SolidWorks is the state of the art in computer-aided design (CAD). SolidWorks represents an object in a virtual environment just as it exists in reality, that is, having volume as well as surfaces and edges. This, along with exceptional ease of use, makes SolidWorks a powerful design tool. Complex three-dimensional parts with contoured surfaces and detailed features can be modeled quickly and easily with Solid-Works. Then, many parts can be assembled in its virtual environment to create a computer model of the finished product. In addition, traditional engineering drawings can be easily created from the solids models of both the parts and the final assembly. This approach opens the door to innovative design concepts, speeds product development, and minimizes design errors. The result is the ability to bring high-quality products to market very quickly.

SECTIONS

OBJECTIVES

After reading this chapter, you will be able to

- Explain how a cross section is extruded or revolved to create a solids model,
- Explain the analogy between creating a solids model of a part, and machining the part,
- Explain feature-based modeling,
- Explain constraint-based modeling, and
- Explain history-based modeling.

1.1   CONSTRAINT-BASED SOLIDS MODELING

The *constraint-based solids modeling* used in SolidWorks makes the modeling process intuitive. The process begins with the creation of a two-dimensional sketch of the profile for the cross section of the part. Here "sketch" is the operative word. The sketch of the cross section begins much like the freehand sketch of the face of an object. The only difference is that SolidWorks draws straight lines and perfect arcs.

The initial sketch need not be particularly accurate; it needs only to reflect the basic geometry of the part's cross-sectional shape. Details of the cross section are added later. The next step is to constrain the two-dimensional sketch by adding enough dimensions and parameters to completely define the shape and size of the two-dimensional profile. The name *constraint-based modeling* arises because the shape of the initial two-dimensional sketch is "constrained" by adding dimensions to the sketch. Finally, a three-dimensional object is created by *revolving* or *extruding* the two-dimensional sketched profile. Figure 1.1 shows the result of revolving a simple L-shaped cross section by 270° about an axis and extruding the same L-shaped cross section along an axis. In either case, these solid bodies form the basic geometric solid shapes of the part. Other features can be added subsequently to modify the basic solid shape.

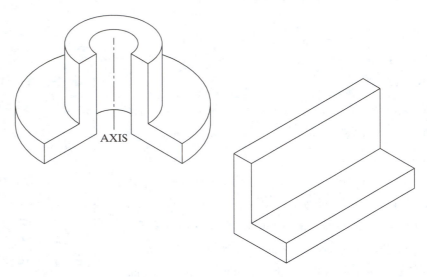

AXIS

Figure 1.1. Revolved solid and extrusion of an L-shaped cross section.

Once the solids model is generated using SolidWorks, all of the surfaces have been automatically defined, so it is possible to shade it in order to create a photorealistic appearance. It is also easy to generate two-dimensional orthographic views of the object. One might look at solids modeling as the sculpting of a virtual solid volume of material. Because the volume of the object is properly represented in a solids model, it is possible to slice through the object and show a view of the object that displays the interior detail. Once several solid objects have been created, they can be assembled in a virtual environment to confirm their fit and to visualize the assembled product.

Solids models are useful for purposes other than visualization. The solids model contains a complete mathematical representation of the object, inside and out. This mathematical representation is easily converted into specialized computer code that can be used for stress analysis, heat-transfer analysis, fluid-flow analysis, and computer-aided manufacturing.

1.2   THE NATURE OF SOLIDS MODELING

Solids modeling grew steadily in the 1980s, but it was not until the 1990s that solids modeling software like SolidWorks delivered on the promise of gains in productivity. These gains result from five characteristics of the software: feature based, constraint based, parametric, history based, and associative modeling.

Feature-based modeling using SolidWorks makes the modeling process more efficient by creating and modifying geometric *features* of a solids model in a way that represents how geometries are created using common manufacturing processes. Features in a part have a direct analogy to geometries that can be manufactured or machined. A *base feature* is a solids model that is roughly the size and shape of the part that is to be modeled. The base feature is the three-dimensional solid created by revolving or extruding a cross section, such as those shown in Figure 1.1. It can be thought of as the initial work block. All subsequent features directly or indirectly reference the base feature. Additional features shape or refine the base feature. Examples of additional features include holes or cuts in the initial work block.

The analogy between feature-based modeling and common manufacturing processes is demonstrated in Figure 1.2, which shows how to make the handle for a pizza cutter. Beginning at the top of the figure, we follow the steps on the left that an engineer would use with SolidWorks to create a solid model, or a virtual part, and the steps on the right that a machinist would take to create the same physical part in a machine

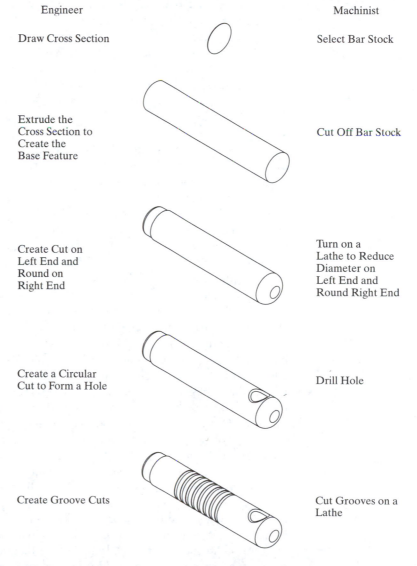

Figure 1.2.   Analogy between feature-based modeling and the manufacturing process.

shop. The engineer using SolidWorks begins by creating a two-dimensional profile, or *cross section*, of a part, in this case a circle (shown in isometric projection). The analogous step by a machinist is to choose a circular bar stock with the correct diameter. Next, the engineer *extrudes*, or stretches, the circular cross section along the axis perpendicular to the plane of the circle to create a three-dimensional base feature (a cylinder in this case). The equivalent action by a machinist is to cut off a length of bar stock to create an initial work block. Now the engineer adds features by cutting away material on the left end to reduce the diameter and by rounding the right end of the cylinder. The machinist performs similar operations to remove material from the cylinder on a lathe. Then the engineer creates a circular cut to form a hole through the cylinder on the right end. The machinist drills a hole in the right end of the cylinder. Finally, the engineer creates a pattern of groove cuts around the handle. Likewise, the machinist cuts a series of grooves using a lathe. In similar fashion, a geometric shape could be added to the base feature in the solids model, analogous to a machinist welding a piece of metal to the work block. Feature-based techniques give the engineer the ability to easily create and modify common manufactured features. As a result, planning the manufacture of a part is facilitated by the correspondence between the features and the processes required to make them.

Constraint-based modeling permits the engineer or designer to incorporate "intelligence" into the design. Often, this is referred to as *design intent*. Unlike traditional CAD software, the initial sketch of a two-dimensional profile in constraint-based solids modeling, like SolidWorks, need not be created with a great deal of accuracy. It simply must represent the basic geometry of the part's cross section. The exact size and shape of the profile is defined by assigning enough parameters to fully "constrain" it. Some of this happens automatically. For example, if a line is within some preset tolerance range of horizontal (say five degrees), then the line is automatically constrained to be horizontal. As the part is resized, this line will always remain horizontal, regardless of what other changes are made. Likewise, if a hole is constrained to be a certain distance from an edge, it will automatically remain in that position with respect to the edge, even if the edge itself is moved. This differs from traditional CAD, in which both the hole and the edge would be fixed at a particular coordinate location. If the edge were moved, the hole location would need to be respecified so that the hole would remain the same distance from the edge. The advantage of constraint-based modeling is that the design intent of the engineer remains intact as the part is modified.

Another aspect of solids modeling in SolidWorks is that the model is *parametric*. This means that the parameters of the model may be modified to change the geometry of the model. A dimension is a simple example of a parameter. When a dimension is changed, the geometry of the part is updated. Thus, the *parameter drives the geometry*. This is in contrast to other CAD modeling systems in which the geometry is changed, say by stretching a part, and the dimension updates itself to reflect the stretched part. An additional feature of parametric modeling is that parameters can reference other parameters through relations or equations. For example, the position of the hole in the center of a plate could be specified with numerical values, say 40 mm from the right side of the plate. Or the position of the hole could be specified parametrically, so that the center of the hole is located at a position that is one-half of the total length of the plate. If the total length was specified as 80 mm, then the hole would be 40 mm from either side. However, if the length was changed to 100 mm, then the hole would automatically be positioned at half of this distance, or 50 mm, from either side. Thus, regardless of the length of the plate, the hole stays in the center. The power of this approach is that when one dimension is modified, all of the linked dimensions are updated according to specified mathematical relations, instead of having to update all related dimensions manually.

An additional aspect of solids modeling is that the order in which parts are created is critical. This is known as *history-based modeling*. For example, a hole cannot be created before a solid volume of material in which the hole occurs has been modeled. If the solid volume is deleted, then the hole is deleted with it. This is known as a *parent–child relation*. The child (hole) cannot exist without the parent (solid volume) first existing. Parent–child relations are critical to maintaining design intent in a part. Solids-modeling software such as SolidWorks recognizes that, if you delete a feature with a hole in it, you do not want the hole to remain floating around without being attached to a feature. Consequently, careful thought and planning of the base feature and initial additional features can have a significant impact on the ease of adding subsequent features and making modifications.

The *associative* character of solids-modeling software causes modifications in one object to "ripple through" all associated objects. For instance, suppose that you change the diameter of a hole on the engineering drawing that was created based on your original part's solid model. The diameter of the hole will automatically be changed in the solid model of the part, too. In addition, the diameter of the hole will be updated on any assembly that includes the part. Similarly, changing the dimension in the part model will automatically result in updated values of that dimension in the drawing or the assembly incorporating the part. This aspect of solids-modeling software, such as SolidWorks, makes the modification of parts much easier and less prone to error.

As a result of being feature based, constraint based, parametric, history based, and associative, SolidWorks captures "design intent," as well as the design. This comes about because SolidWorks incorporates engineering knowledge into the solids model with features, constraints, and relationships that preserve the intended geometrical relationships in the model.

Problems

1. Sketch the cross section that should be revolved to create the objects shown in Figure 1.3. Include the axis about which the cross section is revolved in the sketch.

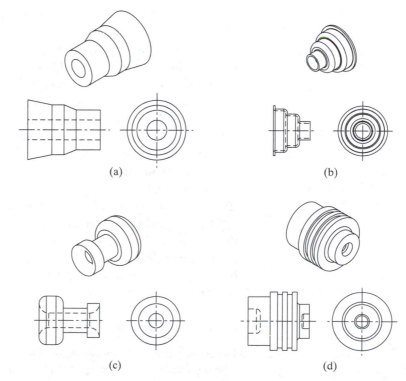

(a) (b)

(c) (d)

Figure 1.3.

2.   Sketch at least two cross sections that could be extruded to form a base feature of the objects shown in Figure 1.4. Use cross sections that can be extruded into a base feature from which material is only removed, not added. Make sure that the cross sections you propose minimize the number of additional features necessary to modify the base feature. (The hole in Figure 1.4(a) is only through the face shown, not the back face. The holes in Figures 1.4(b), 1.4(c), and 1.4(e) are through holes.)

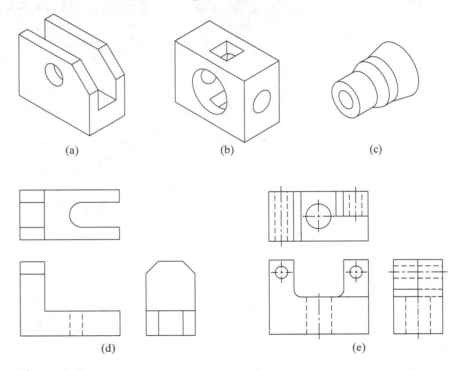

(a)   (b)   (c)

(d)   (e)

Figure 1.4.

3.   Consider the following objects. Sketch what the base feature would look like. List what features would be added to model the object. The type of base feature to be used (extrude, revolve, or both) is noted.
  (a) Hexagonal cross section of a wooden pencil that is sharpened to a point (do not include eraser)—extrude.
  (b) Plastic 35-mm film container and cap—extrude and revolve.
  (c) Nail—extrude and revolve.
  (d) Push pin—revolve.
  (e) Baseball bat—revolve.
  (f) Broom handle—revolve and extrude.
  (g) Ceiling-fan blade—extrude.
  (h) Cinder block—extrude.
  (i) Compact disk—revolve and extrude.
  (j) Single staple (before being deformed)—extrude.
  (k) Automobile tire—revolve.
  (l) Gear—extrude.
  (m) Round toothpick—revolve.

4.   Describe parametric modeling and give an example of a family of parts for which parametric modeling would be useful.

5.   Describe constraint-based modeling and explain how it relates to design intent.

2

Getting Started in SolidWorks

OVERVIEW

In this chapter, you will begin modeling a pizza cutter. The guard, arm, and blade of the pizza cutter are modeled first, since they are the easiest parts to create. For all of these parts, you will sketch a two-dimensional section and then extrude it into the third dimension to create a base feature. Other features, such as rounds, cuts (holes), and chamfers, will be added to the base feature. You will also learn to rotate a part in order to view it from different angles.

2.1 INTRODUCTION AND REFERENCE

SolidWorks Corporation developed SolidWorks® as a three-dimensional, feature-based, solids-modeling system for personal computers. Solids modeling represents objects on a computer as volumes, rather than just as collections of edges and surfaces. Features are three-dimensional geometries with direct analogies to shapes that can be machined or manufactured, such as holes or rounds. Feature-based solids modeling creates and modifies the geometric shapes of an object in a way that represents common manufacturing processes. This makes SolidWorks a very powerful and effective tool for engineering design.

You are about to model an object that you have probably seen many times—a pizza cutter, as shown in Figure 2.1. The pizza cutter consists of six different parts. You will model each of these parts, learning various commands along the way. Each concept that you learn will be applied again as you model subsequent parts and work on practice exercises. Once all of the individual parts are modeled in Chapters 2

SECTIONS

OBJECTIVES

After working through this chapter, you will be able to

- Set both the grid and units for a part,
- Open, close, and save a part file,
- Sketch lines and circles,
- Sketch a two-dimensional section of a part,
- Dimension a part,
- Extrude a two-dimensional sketch,
- Use the PropertyManager to create features,
- Create chamfers, fillets, and rounds,
- Create a circular cut (hole),
- Use the FeatureManager design tree to edit features,
- Mirror features about a plane to create a symmetric part,
- Undo or correct errors,
- Use relations to define a part's geometry, and
- View the part in various orientations.

Figure 2.1.   Finished pizza cutter.

and 3, you will assemble those parts in Chapter 4 to create the pizza cutter model. In Chapter 5, you will create two-dimensional engineering drawings of one of the parts and of the pizza cutter assembly. In Chapters 6 and 7, new versions of the handle will be modeled using advanced features of SolidWorks, such as shells, sweeps, and lofts.

As with other computer programs, SolidWorks organizes and stores data in files. Each file has a name followed by a period (dot) and an extension. The extension is a string of three letters that denote the type of file. For instance, a "part" file related to a handle could be named "handle.prt". The first part of the file name (handle) describes the contents of the file. The extension (.prt) indicates the type of file. There are several file types used in SolidWorks, but the most common file types and their extensions are

Part files	.prt or .sldprt
Assembly files	.asm or .sldasm
Drawing files	.drw or .slddrw.

Part files are the files of the individual parts that are modeled. Part files contain all of the pertinent information about the part. Because SolidWorks is a solids-modeling program, the virtual part on the screen will look very similar to the actual manufactured part. *Assembly files* are created from several individual part files that are virtually assembled (on the computer) to create the finished product. *Drawing files* are the two-dimensional engineering drawing representations of both the part and assembly files. The drawings should contain all of the necessary information for the manufacture of the part, including dimensions, part tolerances, and so on.

The part file is the *driving* file for all other file types. The modeling procedure begins with part files. Subsequent assemblies and drawings are based on the original part files. One advantage of SolidWorks files is the feature of dynamic links. Any change to a part file will automatically be updated to any corresponding assembly or drawing files. Therefore, both drawing and assembly files must be able to find and access their corresponding part files in order to be opened. SolidWorks uses information embedded within the file and the filename to maintain these links automatically.

2.1.1   Starting SolidWorks

SolidWorks runs on computers running the Microsoft Windows® operating system. You open SolidWorks in the same way that you would start any other program:

> Using the left mouse button, click **Start** (lower left corner of the screen), click **Programs**, click **SolidWorks**, and then click on **SolidWorks** in the submenu;
>
> or
>
> Double click on the **SolidWorks** icon on the screen with the left mouse button.

If the methods listed here do not work on your system, contact your system administrator for system-specific instructions.

2.1.2   Checking the Options Settings

The SolidWorks window that appears on the computer screen looks similar to the standard Microsoft Windows interface, as shown in Figure 2.2. The top line of the window is the Menu bar, from which menus of various operations can be opened. Below the Menu bar are the toolbars, which provide a variety of commonly used operations, or tools, with a single click of the mouse button. Toolbars can also extend down the right and left sides of the window. They may or may not be shown on your screen. At this point, most items within the toolbars are grayed out. This indicates that they are not presently available for use. The main part of the window is the Graphics Window. This is where the model is displayed. Just below the Graphics Window is the Status bar, which displays information about the current operation. The Status bar should now indicate "Ready", since SolidWorks is ready to proceed. The **Welcome to SolidWorks** dialog box may or may not be present.

Figure 2.2.   SolidWorks window.

This book will follow some basic conventions when presenting information and commands. All commands and tools will be in **bold**. Arrows (⇒) denote a move between menus or menu windows. Commands and tools can be in the Menu bar at the top of the window, in the toolbars at the top or sides of the window, or in the menus or windows that pop up on the screen. Commands and tools will be differentiated by the text style:

Bold text indicates tools (accessible from either the toolbars or the Menu bar) or commands in the Menu bar.

<u>**Underlined**</u> text indicates buttons in the toolbars.

Italic text indicates commands or inputs in the windows or dialog boxes.

Before you begin, be sure that the SolidWorks settings match the ones used in this tutorial. This is done by setting up the appropriate options:

1. If the ***Welcome to SolidWorks*** dialog box is open, close it by clicking on the **X** in its upper right corner.

2. Click **Tools** in the Menu bar. Next, select **Options** (that is, **Tools ⇒ Options**).

   • The ***System Options*** dialog box appears with the ***System Options*** tab visible, as shown in Figure 2.3.

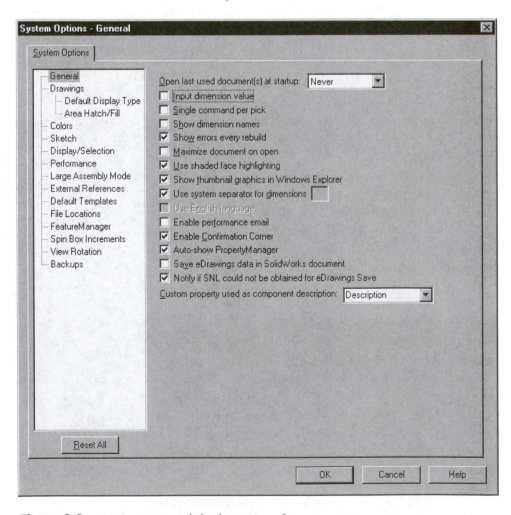

Figure 2.3. *System Options* dialog box: *General*.

3. Reset all of the preferences to the factory default by clicking ***Reset All*** followed by ***Yes*** in the confirmation dialog box.

4. Click on the check mark next to ***Input dimension value*** to remove the check mark. This changes the way that dimensions are added to sketches. Click ***OK*** to close the dialog box.

5. To specify which toolbars are displayed on the screen, select **View** ⇒ **Toolbars** (i.e., select **Toolbars** from the **View** menu). Be sure that the **Features**, **Sketch**, **Sketch Relations**, **Sketch Tools**, **Standard**, **Standard Views** and **View** toolbars are checked, as shown in Figure 2.4. If they are not, click on each of these items until all are checked. If other toolbars are checked, click on them to uncheck them. It may be necessary to select **View**, then **Toolbars** again to display the menu after checking (or unchecking) an item to confirm that the desired change was made. The **Standard Views** toolbar may appear as a dialog box in the Graphics Window instead of as a toolbar. If so, click the blue bar at the top of the dialog box with the left mouse button and drag it to the toolbar at the upper right of the Graphics Window. Release the mouse button. The dialog box should change to a toolbar.

Figure 2.4.   Toolbars menu.

The selected toolbars are frequently used in SolidWorks.

-   The **<u>Features</u>** toolbar contains tools that modify sketches and existing features of a part.
-   The **<u>Sketch</u>** toolbar contains tools to set up and manipulate a sketch of a cross section.

- The **Sketch Relations** toolbar contains tools for constraining elements of a sketch by using dimensions or relations.
- The **Sketch Tools** toolbar contains tools to draw lines, circles, rectangles, arcs, and so on.
- The **Standard** toolbar contains the usual commands available for manipulating files (Open, Save, Print, and so on), editing documents (Cut, Copy, and Paste), and accessing Help.
- The **Standard Views** toolbar contains common orientations for a model.
- The **View** toolbar contains tools to orient and rescale the view of a part.

You can find these toolbars around the Graphics Window by checking and unchecking them in the **View** ⟹ **Toolbars** menu. The toolbars will appear as you check them and disappear as you uncheck them. Currently, most of the items in the toolbars are grayed out, since they are unusable. They will become active when they are available for use. Be sure that the **Toolbars** menu looks like the one in Figure 2.4 before continuing. Click any open spot in the Graphics Window to close all menus.

2.1.3 Getting Help

If you have questions while you are using SolidWorks, you can find answers in several ways:

- Click **SolidWorks Help Topics** in the **Help** Menu bar.
- Move the cursor over a toolbar button to see the ToolTip, which indicates the name of the tool.
- Move the cursor over buttons or click menu items. The Status bar at the bottom of the SolidWorks window will provide a brief description of the function.
- Click the *Help* button in a dialog box.
- Refer to the *SolidWorks User's Guide*, by SolidWorks Corporation, for detailed information.

2.2 MODELING THE GUARD

The first part that you will model is the guard of the pizza cutter, shown in Figure 2.5. The guard is between the handle and the cutting blade of the pizza cutter. It is designed to prevent the user's hand from slipping from the handle onto the sharp blade while slicing a pizza. The guard would be fabricated from stainless steel sheet metal. Do not begin working on this part until you have set the *System Options* as described in the previous section.

2.2.1 Creating a New Part

1. With the SolidWorks window open, select **File** ⟹ **New** in the Menu bar, or click the **New** button (a blank-sheet icon) in the **Standard** toolbar.
2. The *New SolidWorks Document* dialog box appears. You will be modeling a new part. If *Part* is already highlighted, click *OK*. If it is not highlighted, click *Part*, then *OK*. A new window appears with the name **Part1**, as shown in Figure 2.6. On the left side of the window is the FeatureManager design tree. It contains a list of the features that have been created so far. Every

Figure 2.5. Finished guard.

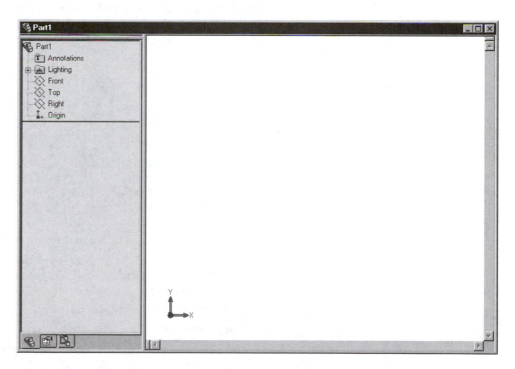

Figure 2.6. New part window.

new part starts with six features: annotations, lighting, three datum planes, and an origin. The datum planes are three mutually perpendicular planes that are created in space as references for constructing features of the part that you are modeling. You might think of them as the x–y, y–z, and x–z planes in a three-dimensional Cartesian coordinate system. The planes are used to locate the features of the part within the virtual environment of SolidWorks. The three planes intersect at the origin, which is in the center of the Graphics Window. The arrows in the lower left corner of the Graphics Window show the coordinate directions. As the part is modeled, the features that are created will appear in the FeatureManager design tree. These features can be highlighted or modified by clicking on them in the FeatureManager design tree. For example, click on a plane or the origin in the FeatureManager design tree to highlight these items. **Front** is the plane of the screen, **Top** is the horizontal plane perpendicular to the screen, and **Right** is the vertical plane perpendicular to the screen. Finish by clicking on **Part1** in the FeatureManager design tree, so that no plane is highlighted.

2.2.2   Sketching

Every part begins as a cross section sketched on a two-dimensional plane. Once a sketch is made, it is extruded or revolved into the third dimension to create a three-dimensional object. This is the base feature of the part. For the guard, a series of lines representing the shape of the guard's edge will be sketched. Then, a depth will be specified to extrude the guard perpendicular to the sketching plane.

1. The **Sketch** toolbar, shown in Figure 2.7, has tools to set up and manipulate a sketch of a cross section. Find the **Sketch** toolbar. Move the cursor over each of the tools, but do not click on any of the tools. The ToolTips should appear, displaying the name of each tool.

Figure 2.7.   <u>Sketch</u> toolbar.

- **Select** highlights sketch entities, drags sketch entities and endpoints, and modifies dimension values.
- **Grid** activates the **Grid/Snap** field of the **Document Properties** dialog box to change the sketching environment.
- **Dimension** adds dimensions to sketch entities.
- **Sketch** opens and closes sketches as a part is created.

2. To set the units and grid size to be used, click the **Grid** toolbar button with the left mouse button.

- Click **Units** on the left side of the dialog box to set the units. This tutorial will use inches, so set the **Linear units** to inches. To do this, click on the inverted triangle to the right of the box that says "Inches", as shown in Figure 2.8, so that the possible units are listed. Click on **Inches** so that it appears in the box. This tutorial will work with three decimal places. If necessary, change the **Decimal places** to "3" by clicking just after the number in the **Decimal places** box. Use the Backspace key to delete the number that is shown, and then type in "3". The dimensions will be displayed as fractions, so click the button next to **Fractions**. The

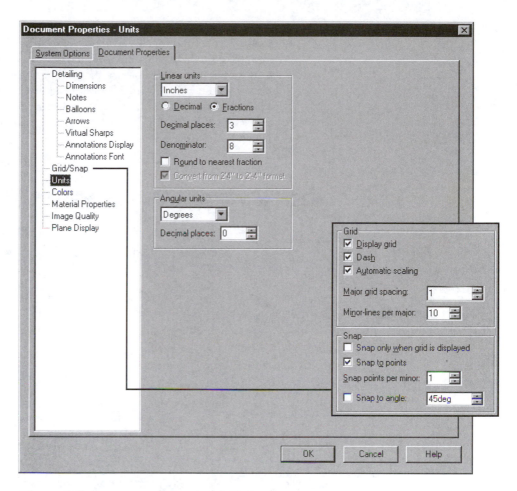

Figure 2.8. *Document Properties* dialog box: *Units*.

Denominator should be set to "8" so that fractions as small as 1/8 will be displayed. Set the *Angular units* to *Degrees* with "0" *Decimal places*.

- Click *Grid/Snap* on the left side of the dialog box to control the grid that will appear on the screen when a cross-section is sketched. Be sure that all three of the boxes under *Grid* are checked, as shown in Figure 2.8. Adjust the grid spacing to *1* by typing in the value to the right of the *Major grid spacing* box. The spacing will be 1 inch between major lines of the grid.

- Snap controls the way in which sketched lines are related to the grid. The points that are sketched should "snap" to the nearest intersection of grid lines when they are close. Be sure the *Snap to points* box is checked. If not, click the box to check it.

- Click *Detailing* on the left side of the dialog box. If necessary, change *Dimensioning standard* to *ANSI* to match the dimensioning style used in this tutorial. Then, click *OK* at the bottom of the dialog box to accept the values.

3.   Open a new sketch by selecting **Insert** ⇒ **Sketch**, or by clicking the **Sketch** button (a pencil drawing a line) in the **Sketch** toolbar. (Note that, for most commands in SolidWorks, it is possible to implement the command from either the Menu bar or the toolbars.) A grid should appear on the screen, as shown in Figure 2.9, indicating that the sketch mode is active. The window's name changes to **Sketch1 of Part1**. In the bottom right corner of the screen, the Status bar reads *Editing Sketch1*. You are now ready to sketch in the **Front** plane.

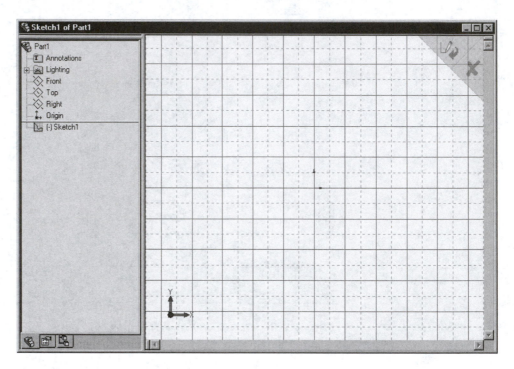

Figure 2.9.   New sketch window.

4.   The **SketchTools** toolbar, shown in Figure 2.10, contains tools to create and modify two-dimensional features, called Sketch Entities. Sketch Entities are items that can be drawn on the sketch. The following Sketch Entities and Sketch Tools are available:

- **Line** creates a straight line.
- **CenterpointArc** creates a circular arc from a centerpoint, a start point, and an end point.
- **TangentArc** creates a circular arc tangent to an existing sketch entity.
- **3 Pt Arc** creates a circular arc through three points.
- **Circle** creates a circle.
- **Spline** creates a curved line that is not a circular arc.
- **Polygon** creates a regular polygon.
- **Rectangle** creates a rectangle.
- **Point** creates a reference point that is used for constructing other sketch entities.

Figure 2.10. <u>**SketchTools**</u> toolbar.

- <u>**Centerline**</u> creates a reference line that is used for constructing other sketch entities.
- <u>**Convert Entities**</u> creates a sketch entity by projecting an edge, curve, or contour onto the sketch plane.
- <u>**Sketch Mirror**</u> reflects entities about a centerline.
- <u>**Sketch Fillet**</u> creates a tangent arc between two sketch entities by rounding an inside or an outside corner.
- <u>**Offset Entities**</u> creates a sketch curve that is offset from a selected sketch entity by a specified distance.
- <u>**Sketch Trim**</u> removes a portion of a line or curve.
- <u>**Construction Geometry**</u> creates entities that aid in sketching.
- <u>**Linear Sketch Step and Repeat**</u> creates a linear pattern of sketch entities.
- <u>**Circular Sketch Step and Repeat**</u> creates a circular pattern of sketch entities.

Move and hold the cursor over each of the tools to display its function but do not click on the tool. Note the description of each tool in the Status bar at the bottom of the SolidWorks window. Some of these tools may not be included in the toolbar or other tools may be available, depending on the way in which it was previously set up. All tools are available in the **Tools** Menu.

5. Begin by sketching a line. Select the **Line** tool (an angled line) in the **SketchTools** toolbar by clicking on it, or select **Tools** ⇒ **Sketch Entity** ⇒ **Line** in the Menu bar. Bring the cursor over the grid. Notice that the cursor has changed to a pencil with a straight line next to it, indicating that the **Line** tool is active.

6. When you bring the cursor directly over the origin (at the tails of the two red arrows in the center of the grid), a square replaces the line near the cursor. This means that SolidWorks will snap one end of the line to the origin if you click there. With the square visible on the cursor, click *and hold* the left mouse button. Then, drag a line to the right, as shown in Figure 2.11. As you move away from the origin, the "H" below the pencil signifies that the line is horizontal. When the line looks similar to the one in the figure, release the mouse button. The line does not need to be exactly the same length as the line in the figure. If the line does not look like the one in the figure, click the **Select** button (an arrow) in the **Sketch** toolbar. Then, select the line by clicking on it with the left mouse button. (It will turn green.) On the keyboard, hit the Delete key to delete the line. Using the **Line** tool, redraw the horizontal line from the origin. At this point, you need not dimension the line nor draw it exactly the length shown in the figure. All of the sketch entities will be created first, and later the appropriate dimensions will be added. This is known as constraint-based modeling.

Figure 2.11.   Horizontal line drawn.

7. The **Line** tool should still be active. If it is not, click the **Line** button in the **SketchTools** toolbar. Draw a second line that starts from the right end of the first line and is angled upward and to the right. To do this, bring the cursor over the right endpoint of the first line so that the square on the cursor appears. Click and hold the left mouse button and drag the line up and to the right, as shown in Figure 2.12. This time the "H" will not appear, since this is not a horizontal line. Let go of the mouse button to finish the line.

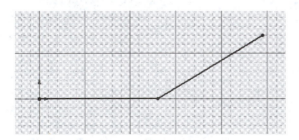

Figure 2.12.   Angled line drawn.

8. Complete the sketch, as shown in Figure 2.13, by repeating Steps 6 and 7 to draw two lines on the left side of the origin. The first line drawn should be horizontal, and the second should go down and to the left. The sketched lines represent the contour of the guard's edge. These lines will be extruded into the sketching plane to create the three-dimensional base feature of the guard.

Figure 2.13.   Other lines drawn.

2.2.3   Dimensioning the Sketch

1. As noted on the right side of the Status bar at the bottom of the window, the sketch is *Under Defined*, because the dimensions have not been specified. The sketch will be *Fully Defined* when dimensions are added to "constrain" the geometry. The simplest dimension is the length of a line. Dimensions in SolidWorks can extend from any sketch entity to another. For example, the length of a line can be defined by dimensioning from one endpoint of the line to the other. Dimensions can also be assigned to a particular sketch entity. For example, a line can be dimensioned by specifying its length, and a circle can be dimensioned by specifying its diameter. Click on the **Dimension** button (a dimensioned line) in the **Sketch** toolbar or **Tools** ⇒ **Dimensions** ⇒ **Parallel**.

2. With the **Dimension** tool active, bring the cursor over the right endpoint of the first horizontal line that was drawn. Notice that a circle appears next to the cursor. Click the point. The point turns to a small square.

3. Click on the origin point. It also turns to a small square, and a blue dimension box appears. The dimension box moves with the cursor. Use the mouse to move the dimension box to the position shown in Figure 2.14, and click with the left mouse button to place it in that position. At this time, the value of the dimension is not critical. The number in the dimension box represents the current length of the line. The number is probably not the same as the dimension in the figure, but it will be changed shortly.

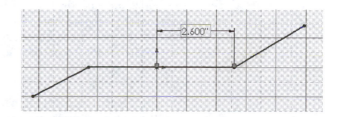

Figure 2.14.   Horizontal dimension placed.

4. The **Dimension** tool should still be active. Now, dimension the other horizontal line in the same manner as the first. Place the dimension at a convenient location above the line. Figure 2.17 shows this dimension and the other dimensions that will be created shortly.

5. With the **Dimension** tool active, click on the two endpoints of the angled line on the right side. It does not matter which endpoint is selected first. Before you place the dimension box, move the cursor around. Depending on where the cursor is positioned, three different choices for the dimension appear. These different types of dimensions are shown in Figure 2.15.

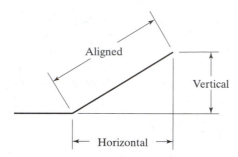

Figure 2.15. Different ways to dimension an angled line.

- A *vertical* dimension, which defines the vertical distance between two points, appears when the cursor is to the right or left of both endpoints *and* vertically between them.
- A *horizontal* dimension, which defines the horizontal distance between two points, appears when the cursor is above or below both endpoints *and* horizontally between them.
- An *aligned* dimension, which represents the actual length of the line, appears when the cursor is close to the line and at several other positions.

Create a *vertical* dimension by placing the dimension box both between and to the right of both points. This dimension should be similar to the one shown in Figure 2.17, although the numerical value may not match exactly. If you place a dimension that you do not want, use the **Select** tool (**Select** button in **Sketch** toolbar) to highlight the dimension. Then, delete it using the Delete key on the keyboard. Redo the dimension with the **Dimension** tool.

6. Make another vertical dimension for the left angled line.

7. Dimensions can also be used to define angular values. Be sure that the **Dimension** tool is still active. Click on the angled line on the right, and then on the horizontal line that it touches. When placing an angular dimension, there are three options to choose from, as shown in Figure 2.16. Place the dimension representing the angle of the line above the horizontal (Φ in the figure). To do this, click the mouse button when the dimension appears where Φ is shown in the figure. An angular dimension will appear, with degrees as the units.

8. Once you have placed the dimension, activate the **Select** tool. Click and drag the angular dimension value to move it to a more convenient location, as shown in Figure 2.17.

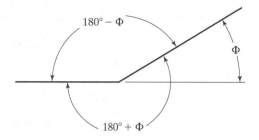

Figure 2.16. Different ways to dimension an angle.

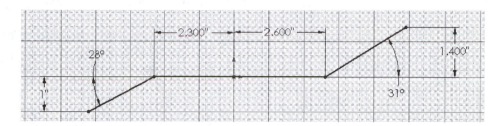

Figure 2.17. Dimensions placed.

9. At this point, the bottom right corner of the Status bar displays *Under Defined*, because more dimensions are needed in order to unambiguously represent the shape in the sketch. SolidWorks helps the user to know what dimensions are still needed by highlighting undefined sketch entities in blue. In this case, the left angled line is blue, because the angle must still be dimensioned with respect to the horizontal. Use the **Dimension** tool to dimension the angle of the blue angled line. After adding this dimension, all of the lines should be black. This color change indicates that the sketch is fully defined. That is, the dimensions and constraints completely describe the geometry of the sketch. The bottom right corner of the Status bar displays *Fully Defined*. The screen should look similar to that shown in Figure 2.17. The values of the dimensions may be different, however.

2.2.4   Changing the Values of the Dimensions.

In SolidWorks, changing the value of a dimension changes the properties of the sketch entity to which the dimension refers. Dimensions, along with constraints (e.g., parallel and horizontal), define the sketch. At this point, you must change the values of the dimensions to those that describe the shape of the edge of the guard.

1. Activate the **Select** tool by clicking the <u>**Select**</u> button in the <u>**Sketch**</u> toolbar. Double click the left mouse button on one of the linear dimensions that define the length of one of the horizontal lines. In the *Modify* dialog box, shown in Figure 2.18, type in the value *1.25*. Then, click the green check button in the *Modify* dialog box, or hit Enter on the keyboard. The length of the line is changed and the value shows "1 1/4". The units need not be specified while changing a dimension. The units were already set in the *Document Properties* dialog box. In SolidWorks, you can enter equations that represent dimension values. For example, the above dimension could be entered as "1 + 1/4" or "1 1/4" instead of 1.25.

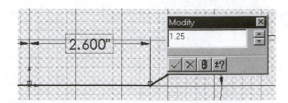

Figure 2.18. *Modify* dialog box.

2. Angular dimensions can be changed in the same way as linear dimensions. With the **Select** tool active, double click on one of the angular dimensions. Set the value to **30**. After you hit Enter, the angle automatically updates to 30 degrees.

3. Dimension the other values so that the sketch matches that shown in Figure 2.19. Use the **Select** tool to drag the position of the dimensions to match the figure. Arrows for some dimensions may look different from those in Figure 2.19.

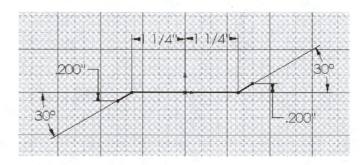

Figure 2.19. Dimensions updated.

4. A handy feature in the *Modify* dialog box is the stoplight button, which regenerates (redraws) the model with the new value. The stoplight button can be used to test the value in the dialog box. This is often helpful in determining what value looks reasonable as a design is modified. Using the **Select** tool, double click one of the "1 1/4" dimensions. Change the value to **2** and click the stoplight button in the *Modify* dialog box. The length of the horizontal line is increased in the sketch. If the green check button is clicked, the new value of **2** is used. If the red **X** button is clicked, the sketch reverts back to the original value of "1 1/4". In this case, click the red **X** button.

5. After moving the dimensions, "shadows" of the dimension values might remain on the grid. Click **View** ⇒ **Redraw** to update the screen.

2.2.5 Adding Fillets to a Sketch

The guard's bends are rounded. Fillets are rounded corners that will be used to round the sharp, angled bends on the guard's sketch.

1. While still in sketch mode, activate the **Fillet** tool by clicking the <u>**Sketch Fillet**</u> button (a rounded corner) in the <u>**Sketch Tools**</u> toolbar, or **Tools** ⇒ **Sketch Tools** ⇒ **Fillet**.

2. The *Sketch Fillet* PropertyManager appears on the left side of the screen, as shown in Figure 2.20. Type in **.3** to set the fillet radius to .3 inches.

Figure 2.20. *Sketch Fillet* PropertyManager.

3. Bring the cursor over the angled line on the right side. Notice that the line becomes highlighted and an icon of a line appears next to the cursor. Click the line. It turns green, signifying that it is selected.

4. Click the horizontal line that touches the angled line you just selected. A fillet appears at the intersection of the two lines with a .3 dimension attached. A small cross also appears, showing the location of the center of the fillet's radius. Do not close the *Sketch Fillet* PropertyManager.

5. Repeat Steps 3 and 4 to add a fillet to the left side of the guard. Notice that a dimension did not appear next to the second fillet. That is because the first dimension refers to both fillets.

6. Close the *Sketch Fillet* PropertyManager by clicking the green check mark (**OK**) near the top of the PropertyManager window. With the **Select** tool, move the .3 dimension to an appropriate location. Your sketch should look similar to the one shown in Figure 2.21.

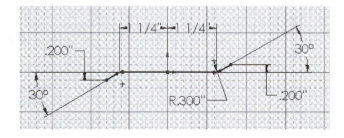

Figure 2.21. Fillets added.

2.2.6   Extruding the Cross Section

Now that the sketch is both *Fully Defined* and properly dimensioned, it can be extruded into the third dimension. An extrusion "creates" material in the direction perpendicular to the plane of the sketch. For example, an extrusion of a circle would be a cylinder. In this case, the contour of the guard will be extruded to form the base feature of the guard. Now, the guard sketch shows line segments forming the edge of the guard. You will add thickness to these line segments and extrude the sketch to model the guard as a sheet metal part.

1. While still in sketch mode, click on the **Extruded Boss/Base** button in the **Features** toolbar, or select **Insert** ⇒ **Base** ⇒ **Extrude**. This is one of the only buttons in the **Features** toolbar on the left side of the screen that is highlighted. It causes a sketched section to be extruded perpendicular to the screen to create a three-dimensional part.

2. The view changes to an isometric view (the grid is at a 30-degree angle to the horizontal). On the left side of the Graphics Window the FeatureManager design tree is replaced by the PropertyManager, which displays the options for the **Base-Extrude**, as shown in Figure 2.22. The guard is considered a **Thin Feature** because its sketch is a series of connected line segments rather than a closed polygon. Thin features have both a depth into the drawing plane and a thickness, which can be thought of as the thickness of the lines of the sketch. In the **Direction 1** field of the PropertyManager, click on the small inverted triangle next to **Blind**. This displays the **End Condition** menu. Select **Mid Plane**. This places the sketched lines at the mid plane of the extrusion. In other words, the base feature will be extruded on both sides of the lines you have sketched to the front and back of the **Front** plane. Bring the cursor over the dimension symbol with D1 next to it just below **Mid Plane**. The ToolTip displays **Depth** indicating that the depth of the extrusion is specified in the adjacent box. Set the **Depth** to **1**. This extrudes the sketched cross section 1/2 inch on both sides of the mid plane.

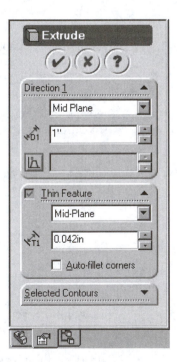

Figure 2.22. *Extrude* PropertyManager.

3. In the **Thin Feature** field, select **Mid Plane** in the upper **Type** pull-down menu to indicate that the sketched lines will be at the mid plane of the part's thickness. Type in a **Thickness** of **.042** in the lower field and hit Enter on the Keyboard. This makes a thin part with its surfaces .021 inches above and below the lines that you have sketched. The PropertyManager should look like Figure 2.22, and a preview of the extrusion should appear in the Graphics

Window. Click the green check mark at the top of the PropertyManager to accept the settings. In the Menu bar, click **View** ⇒ **Display** ⇒ **HLR Edges In Shaded Mode** to remove the lines on the edges of the part. The screen should look similar to that shown in Figure 2.23. If it does not, you can remove the extrusion by clicking the **<u>Undo</u>** button (a curved arrow) in the **<u>Standard</u>** toolbar, or **Edit** ⇒ **Undo Base**. Then repeat Steps 1–3.

Figure 2.23. Extruded guard.

2.2.7 Viewing the Guard

Once you have extruded the sketch, several things in the SolidWorks environment will change.

- The sketch mode is no longer active. (No grid is shown on the screen.)
- The FeatureManager design tree on the left-hand side of the screen shows a new feature, **Extrude-Thin1**, which is the base feature that you just created.

Now is a good time to use some of capabilities that SolidWorks has for orienting and viewing the part. Viewing options are available in the **View** menu and the **<u>Standard Views</u>** toolbar, as shown in Figure 2.24.

Figure 2.24. **<u>Standard Views</u>** toolbar.

1. Since you have made a three-dimensional representation of an object, you can view the part from any angle. The **<u>Standard Views</u>** toolbar, shown in Figure 2.24, is used to change the display of the model to one of several views. To see which views are available, bring the cursor over each of the buttons in the toolbar to see the ToolTips.

2. Click the **<u>Front</u>** button. The guard rotates to display the front edge of the guard. Click the **<u>Select</u>** button in the **Sketch** toolbar so that nothing is selected. Experiment with the other standard views by clicking on the active buttons in the toolbar.

3. The **Normal To** orientation requires you to specify the part's planar face that the view will be "normal to." To use **Normal To**, first click the

Isometric button, so that the view looks like that shown in Figure 2.23. Next, select the guard's large planar face by clicking on it one time. The face becomes highlighted, and the **Normal To** button becomes active. Now, click on the **Normal To** button to show the part as viewed "normal to" this face. Return to the **Isometric** view.

Figure 2.25.   <u>View</u> toolbar.

4. The **View** toolbar, shown in Figure 2.25, has tools that can be used to view the model at any angle, or to zoom in and out. Becoming accustomed to these tools will be helpful with orienting more complex parts. Click on the **Rotate View** button (two arrows forming a circle) and rotate the piece dynamically by moving the mouse while holding down the left mouse button. To translate the part on the screen, click on the **Pan** button (two crossed arrows) and drag while holding down the left mouse button. Use the **Zoom In/Out** button (magnifying glass with an arrow next to it) by clicking and dragging the cursor up to zoom in or down to zoom out. Return to the **Isometric** view. Click the **Zoom To Area** button (magnifying glass with a plus sign) to zoom in on a particular area of the Graphics Window. Note that the cursor changes to the same icon shown on the button. Move the cursor over the Graphics Window above the left end of the guard. Hold down the left mouse button as you drag the cursor downward and to the right. A box appears on the screen. When you release the mouse button, the view zooms to the area in the box. To get back to the standard view, click on the **Zoom To Fit** button (a magnifying glass with a box inside). Finally, you can zoom to a particular selected item using the **Zoom To Selection** button (a magnifying glass with two horizontal lines). To do this, return to the **Isometric** view and click on the **Select** button. Now, select the flat angled face of the guard at either the right or the left end. The face should now be highlighted. Next, click on the **Zoom To Selection** button to zoom in on the face. Return to the **Isometric** view and click the **Select** button so the face is not highlighted.

5. Also in the **View** toolbar are the **Wireframe**, **Hidden Lines Visible**, **Hidden Lines Removed**, **Shaded**, and **Shadows In Shaded Mode** buttons. Click each of these buttons to see the guard in wireframe, hidden lines shown in gray, hidden lines not shown at all, and shaded displays. The shaded view of the model is the most realistic, but the other types of display can be helpful to see hidden faces of the part.

2.2.8   Cutting a Hole in the Guard

The next feature to model is the hole at the center of the guard. This is done by extruding a circular solid cut through the guard at the origin.

1. In the **Standard Views** toolbar, click **Isometric** to orient the view. Use the **Shaded** display.

2. With the **Select** tool, click on the large top face of the guard. The face becomes highlighted, indicating that it is selected.

3. Open a sketch on that face by clicking the **Sketch** button in the **Sketch** toolbar, or **Insert ⇒ Sketch**. A grid appears, indicating that you are in sketch

mode. Notice that **Sketch2** has appeared in the FeatureManager design tree. Also, note that the new grid is in the plane of the top face of the guard, which is the face that you just selected.

4. To orient the view so that it is facing the sketch plane, click <u>**Normal To**</u> in the <u>**Standard Views**</u> toolbar. This sets the view so that you look along a line normal to the surface just selected. Now, viewing the top face of the guard, you are ready to start sketching.

5. Select the **Circle** tool by clicking on the <u>**Circle**</u> button in the <u>**Sketch Tools**</u> toolbar, or **Tools ⇒ Sketch Entity ⇒ Circle**. Notice that the cursor has changed to a pencil with a circle below it.

6. Move the cursor to the origin. A small square appears next to the pencil cursor, indicating that the cursor is over the origin. Click at the origin and hold the mouse button down to drag the radius of the circle outward from the origin. Release the mouse button when the circle is close to the size shown in Figure 2.26. The grid is not shown on this figure for clarity. If the circle is not quite the way you want it to be, it can be easily undone using the **Undo Circle** command in the **Edit** menu. The circle can then be redrawn using the **Circle** tool.

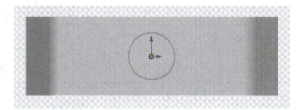

Figure 2.26. Circle drawn.

7. To dimension the circle, click the <u>**Dimension**</u> button in the <u>**Sketch**</u> toolbar, or select **Tools ⇒ Dimensions ⇒ Parallel**. Click somewhere on the arc of the circle. Click again to place the diameter dimension, as shown in Figure 2.27. The dimension appears with the lowercase Greek letter phi (ϕ) in front of the value. This indicates that the value refers to the diameter of the circle. A dimension beginning with **R** would indicate the radius of an arc or a circle.

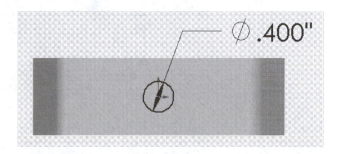

Figure 2.27. Circle dimensioned.

8. Use the **Select** tool to double click on the dimension. Set the value to **.4**. The screen should look like Figure 2.27.

9. Material can be removed by extruding a cut. Click on the **<u>Extruded Cut</u>** button (cube with a square hole) in the **<u>Features</u>** toolbar, or select **Insert ⇒ Cut ⇒ Extrude**.

10. The *Cut-Extrude* PropertyManager appears, as shown in Figure 2.28. In the *End Condition* pull-down menu for *Direction 1*, select *Through All*. This option results in all of the material below the circle being cut away through all of the object. Other options include *Up To Next*, which makes a cut up to the next feature, and *Blind*, which makes a cut with a specified depth.

Figure 2.28. *Cut-Extrude* PropertyManager.

11. Click the green check button in the PropertyManager or the large green check in the upper right corner of the Graphics Window. Using the **Rotate View** tool, rotate the part to see the newly created hole. In the **Isometric** view, the part should look like that shown in Figure 2.29.

Figure 2.29. Hole cut.

2.2.9   Creating Rounds on the Corners

A round on each corner is the last feature to add to the model of the guard. There are four corners that need to be rounded. This can be done one corner at a time or as a group. In this case, the rounds will be added one at a time. To do this, a feature called a **Fillet** will be created. When the bends of the guard were rounded, a fillet was created in the sketch mode. Here, the fillet will be applied as a feature rather than as a sketch entity.

1. Start in the **Isometric** view using the **Hidden Lines Removed** display. Zoom in to the corner closest to you by using the <u>**Zoom to Area**</u> button in the <u>**View**</u> toolbar. To do this, drag the **Zoom to Area** tool from the hole diagonally to the lower right corner to create a rectangular box. The result should look similar to what is shown in Figure 2.30. If you zoom in too close, use either the **Zoom to Fit** or **Zoom In/Out** tool to change the viewing area.

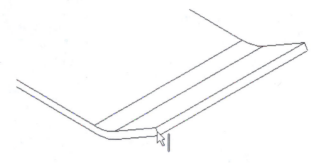

Figure 2.30.   Cursor on corner to be filleted.

2. All of the features created to this point started out as sketches. In this case, the fillet feature will modify the existing features without using a sketch. Using the **Select** tool, bring the cursor over the edge at the lower right corner of the guard, as shown in Figure 2.30. This is the edge that will be rounded. Notice that the cursor changes to a curvy plane, a vertical line, or a square, showing that it is over a surface, a line, or a point, respectively. Select the line that forms the edge to be rounded by clicking on it.

3. To round the edge, click on the <u>**Fillet**</u> button (a cube with one edge rounded) in the <u>**Features**</u> toolbar, or **Insert** ⇒ **Features** ⇒ **Fillet/Round**. The ***Fillet*** PropertyManager appears, as shown in Figure 2.31. The selected edge, ***Edge <1>***, is shown in the ***Items to Fillet*** list. If it is not there, you can select it while the PropertyManager is active. Set the ***Radius*** to **.35** and click the green check mark, which is equivalent to ***OK***. (In some cases, the green check mark in a PropertyManager has the ToolTip ***Close Dialog*** appear instead of ***OK***. For simplicity, we will use ***OK*** to refer to the green check mark in a PropertyManager in either case.)

4. Click on **Zoom To Fit**, set the display to **Shaded**, and use **Rotate View** to see the filleted edge. The part should look similar to that shown in Figure 2.32.

5. Set the display to **Hidden Lines Removed**. Add **.35** fillets to the other three corners by rotating the part, zooming in, selecting the edge, and using the **Fillet** tool. Note that SolidWorks assumes that the new fillets have the same radius as the previous fillets. Return to the **Isometric** view and click on **Shaded** after rounding all of the corners.

Figure 2.31. *Fillet* PropertyManager.

Figure 2.32. Corner rounded.

Congratulations! You have completed the model of the guard. The part should look similar to the one shown in Figure 2.5. Click the **Save** button in the **Standard** toolbar, or **File ⇒ Save**. The name of the file and where it will be saved are specified in the **Save As** dialog box, as shown in Figure 2.33. Depending on your system settings, the **Save As** dialog box may look different. Type in *guard* for the *File name*. The type of file, .sldprt, is automatically added to the specified filename. Navigate through the file system by clicking in the *Save in* field. Typically, you will save the part either to the hard drive (C:) or to your own floppy disk (A:). Click *Save* after specifying both the filename and the folder.

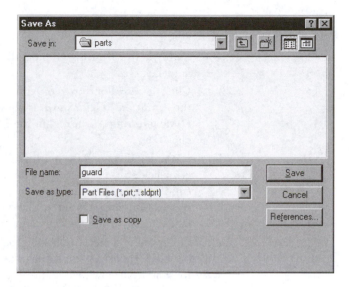

Figure 2.33. *Save As* dialog box.

It is also possible to print the image of the guard that appears in the Graphics Window. To do this, click on the **Print** button in the **Standard** toolbar (an icon of a printer near the left end of the toolbar), or **File ⇒ Print**. Printing is somewhat computer–printer system specific, so you may need more detailed printing instructions from your computer system administrator.

Close the guard model using **File ⇒ Close**.

2.3   MODELING THE ARM

The next component to model is the arm, which would be fabricated from stainless steel sheet metal of uniform thickness. One end of the arm is inserted into the handle, while the other end holds the blade. The pizza cutter has two arms. Since the arms are identical, you will model one arm and use it twice in the assembly procedure outlined in Chapter 4. The finished arm is shown in Figure 2.34. The arm is modeled much like the guard was modeled, although a few new concepts will be introduced.

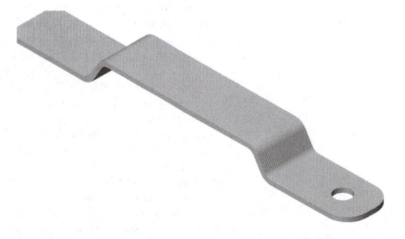

Figure 2.34. Finished arm.

2.3.1 Creating a New Part and a New Sketch

1. The arm will require a new part file. Select **File** ⇒ **New**, or click the **New** button in the **Standard** toolbar. Be sure *Part* is highlighted in the dialog box and click *OK*.

2. Click the **Grid** button to open the **Document Properties** dialog box. Set up the **Units** and **Grid/Snap** as shown in Figure 2.8. Also, be sure that the **Dimensioning Standard** in the **Detailing** dialog box is set to **ANSI**. Then click *OK*.

3. Instead of changing the settings for every new part, a template can be created. Click **File** ⇒ **Save**. In the **Save As** dialog box, click in the **Save as type** field to open the pulldown menu. Select **Part Templates**. Save the part as *tutorial part* and click *Save*. This template with new settings can be loaded easily when new parts are modeled.

4. Open a new sketch by clicking the **Sketch** button from the **Sketch** toolbar, or select **Insert** ⇒ **Sketch**. The sketching grid appears. The first sketch for a new part always defaults to the **Front** plane as the sketching plane. To see this, click **Front** in the FeatureManager design tree on the left-hand side of the screen. A rectangle appears, signifying that you are facing the **Front** plane. The other two planes appear as lines, since you are viewing only their edges.

2.3.2 Sketching the Lines

The initial sketch of the arm is similar to that of the guard, although the sketching method will be somewhat different. You will first draw several lines, which indicate the shape of the arm's edge, shown in Figure 2.35. Then, the sketch will be extruded into the third dimension as a thin feature. This creates the base feature for the arm.

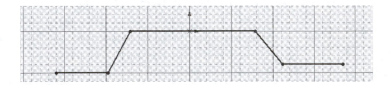

Figure 2.35. Lines sketched.

1. In the base sketch of the guard, lines were drawn by clicking and dragging endpoints, known as *click-drag* sketching. The base sketch of the arm will use a different method, *click-click* sketching. *Click-click* sketching does not require you to hold the mouse button down as sketch entities are created. The first line of the arm sketch is a horizontal segment that passes through the origin. To create this line, activate the **Line** tool (the **Line** button in the **SketchTools** toolbar), then click and release the left mouse button even with the origin and to its left. Bring the cursor to the right, past the origin, look for the "H" next to the cursor, and click the mouse button again to complete the line. Be sure that the line extends from the left of the origin to the right of it and passes through the origin. If it does not, or if the line is not horizontal, delete it. This can be done by selecting it (**Select** button in the **Sketch** toolbar) and then hitting the Delete key. Alternatively, you could undo the line using **Undo Line** in the **Edit** menu, or by clicking the **Undo** button in the **Standard** toolbar.

2. Now move the cursor downward and to the right of the first line. You will notice that the next line is in the process of being drawn. Finish this second line by clicking down and to the right of the right endpoint of the first line. This time you should *not* see an "H" next to the cursor.

3. From the right endpoint of the angled line, draw a horizontal line that extends to the right. Click to specify the right endpoint of this line. To finish the "chain" of line segments, double click anywhere in the Graphics Window.

4. Start a new chain by clicking on the left endpoint of the upper horizontal line. In a similar manner as before, draw two line segments using the click-click method. One segment should be angled, downward and to the left from the left endpoint of the first line. The second segment should be horizontal extending to the left. Finish the chain by double clicking anywhere in the Graphics Window. The sketch should look like the one in Figure 2.35. The origin in the sketch should be on the upper horizontal line.

2.3.3   Dimensioning the Sketch

1. Activate the **Dimension** tool by clicking on the <u>**Dimension**</u> button in the <u>**Sketch**</u> toolbar, or by selecting **Tools** ⇒ **Dimensions** ⇒ **Parallel**.

2. Dimension the middle horizontal line by clicking on the line itself. This is an alternative to clicking on both endpoints of the line. When the blue dimension box appears, place it above the line. At this time, the value of the dimension does not matter.

3. With the **Dimension** tool still active, dimension the two lower horizontal lines the same way you dimensioned the first line. Use Figure 2.36 as a guide.

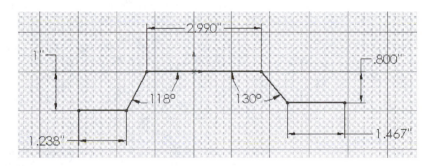

Figure 2.36. Dimensions placed.

4. Add a vertical dimension to the angled line on the right side of the origin by clicking on its endpoints. Remember that there are several ways in which this dimension can be placed, so be sure that you have chosen the vertical distance between the two endpoints as the dimension, and not the horizontal or the aligned dimension.

5. To add the vertical dimension to the left angled line, first, click on the leftmost horizontal line segment. Next, click on the upper horizontal line segment and place the dimension. By choosing these line segments instead of the endpoints of the angled line, SolidWorks automatically assumes that this is a vertical dimension.

6. Next, you need to add a dimension that defines the angle of the angled line on the right side. With the **Dimension** tool active, click on the angled line to the right of the origin, then click on the upper horizontal line. The position of the dimension box is important, so look at Figure 2.36 before placing the dimension.

7. In the same manner, dimension the angle of the angled line on the left side. Except for the dimension values, the sketch should look similar to the one shown in Figure 2.36. If necessary, delete a dimension by selecting it with the **Select** tool and hitting the Delete key.

2.3.4 Adding a Relation

The Status bar at the bottom of the SolidWorks window indicates that the sketch is still *Under Defined*, even though all of the line segments have been dimensioned. The position of all five lines relative to the origin has not been defined. In other words, the entire sketched section needs to be horizontally located with respect to the origin. To add this constraint, you could dimension the distance from the origin to any point on the sketched section. Instead, a relation will be added that keeps the origin at the midpoint of the upper horizontal line.

1. Click the **Add Relation** button (perpendicular lines) in the **Sketch Relations** toolbar, or **Tools** ⇒ **Relations** ⇒ **Add**. The *Add Relations* PropertyManager appears. This defines the relationships for entities in the sketch.

2. Click on the origin point at the intersection of the tails of the perpendicular red arrows. Notice that the cursor has an asterisk next to it when it is near the origin. Once the origin is selected, *Point1@Origin* appears in the *Selected Entities* list. Since you want to orient the upper horizontal line with respect to the origin, click on the upper horizontal line to add it to the *Selected Entities* list. *Line1* appears in the *Selected Entities* list.

3. Select the *Midpoint* relations button in the *Add Relations* field in the lower part of the PropertyManager. By selecting this button, *Midpoint1* is added to the *Existing Relations* field, and the origin moves to the midpoint of the selected line. Notice that the *Coincident0* relation already exists, since it was created when the line was drawn through the origin. The screen should look similar to that shown in Figure 2.37.

4. Click the green check (*OK*) button. The origin is now the midpoint of the upper horizontal line, regardless of its length or orientation. The sketch is now *Fully Defined*, as indicated in the Status bar.

5. You may check all of the existing constraints for a particular sketch entity by clicking on the sketch entity in the Graphics Window and examining the PropertyManager. The constraints are listed in the *Existing Relations* field. Click on any of the horizontal lines and you will see that the *Horizontal* constraint is satisfied. This constraint occurred automatically when the "H" appeared as the line was sketched. Click on the upper horizontal line. The *Existing Relations* field indicates that this line has six relations. Clicking on any of the relations listed produces a callout box in the Graphics Window displaying the relation and highlighting the related sketch entities. In addition to the origin being at the midpoint of the upper horizontal line, the other relations are that it is horizontal, coincident with the origin, a specified distance above the left horizontal line segment, and at an angle other than 90 degrees with respect to the angled lines (one relation for each angled line).

Figure 2.37. *Add Relations* PropertyManager.

Notice that it is possible to change any of the parameters of the sketch entity (such as the length of the line) within the PropertyManager.

6. Using the **Select** tool, double click on the dimension that defines the length of the upper horizontal line. In the *Modify* dialog box, type in *1.6* and hit Enter. The line length changes to the new dimension.

7. Do the same for the other dimensions using the values shown in Figure 2.38. Arrange the dimensions by clicking and dragging the dimension box with the **Select** tool. Redraw the screen by selecting **View** ⇒ **Redraw** to clean up the sketch. Click the **Zoom to Fit** button to make the sketch easier to read.

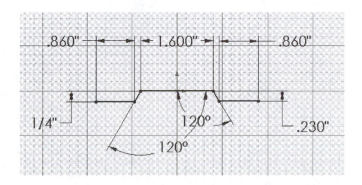

Figure 2.38. Dimensions updated.

2.3.5   Extruding the Arm

Now that the sketch is *Fully Defined*, you can extrude the sketched section into the third dimension.

1. To extrude the sketched section, click **Extruded Boss/Base** in the **Features** toolbar. This changes the view to isometric and the *Extrude* PropertyManager appears. This is the same feature that was used to create the base feature of the guard. Again, the sketch in this case is a series of connected line segments rather than a closed polygon, indicating that the part is thin. This means that the part will have a uniform thickness along the sketched line segments, as well as a depth into the sketching plane.

2. In the *Direction 1* field, set the *End Condition* to *Mid Plane* so that the sketching plane is located at the mid plane of the extruded section. Set the *Depth* to *1/2*. This extrudes the arm 1/4 inch on each side of the sketch plane to obtain a total depth of 1/2 inch.

3. In the *Thin Feature* field, set the *Type* to *Mid Plane* and the *Thickness* to *.048*. This creates a thin sheet .048-inches thick, with the lines of the sketch at the center of the thickness. This thickness is a standard thickness for a type of stainless-steel sheet metal referred to as 18 gauge.

4. The sharp bends at the intersections between the lines need to be rounded. This is because, in a real fabricated sheet-metal part, bends are always rounded, not sharp. The rounded bends can easily be created using the *Auto-fillet corners* checkbox. Check the *Auto-fillet corners* box in the *Thin Feature* field and set the *Fillet Radius* to *.075*. This produces the same results as inserting the fillets in the sketch of the guard.

5. Click **OK** (the green check mark). Examine the part by rotating and zooming to be sure that it looks like that shown in Figure 2.39. Change the view to **Isometric** by clicking the **Isometric** button in the **Standard Views** toolbar. Note that the origin is at the center of the part's thickness and at the center of its width. (This is most evident when displaying the arm as **Wireframe** and rotating it, or when using the **Front** view.) Also, note that the bends in the arm are rounded as they would be if the part were formed out of sheet metal. If the arm does not look like the one shown in Figure 2.39, use **Edit** ⇒ **Undo Base** and start the extrusion again.

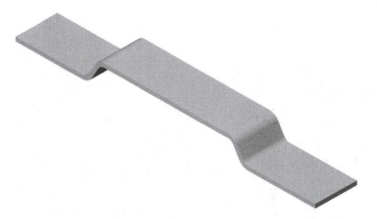

Figure 2.39. Arm extruded.

2.3.6   Rounding the End of the Arm

The right end of the arm is rounded. This feature can be added to the base feature by using a fillet feature.

1.   While in **Isometric** view with **Shaded** display, zoom in to the right end of the arm by using the **Zoom To Area** tool. Figure 2.40 shows the two corners to be rounded. Switch to the **Hidden Lines Removed** display.

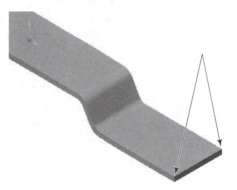

Figure 2.40.   Corners to be rounded.

2.   Several lines can be selected at one time. Click on the line forming the left-corner edge with the **Select** tool to select it. Remember to look for the icon of a line next to the cursor when selecting. The selected line will become highlighted, signifying that it is selected. To add another line to the selection, hold down the Control key on the keyboard while selecting the line forming the right-corner edge. Both lines should be highlighted.

3.   Click the **Fillet** button in the **Features** toolbar, or **Insert** ⇒ **Features** ⇒ **Fillet/Round**. The *Fillet* PropertyManager appears. Both lines are listed in the *Items to Fillet* as *Edge <1>* and *Edge <2>*. If both lines are not listed there, select the edge to be rounded, and it will be added to the list.

4.   Set the *Radius* to *.2* and click **OK**. This creates two rounds, one on each edge selected. In **Shaded, Isometric** view, the part should look similar to that shown in Figure 2.41. Be sure that the rounded edges are the ones at the right end. If not, use **Edit** ⇒ **UndoFillet** to start rounding the correct end again.

Figure 2.41.   Corners rounded.

2.3.7 Adding Chamfers to the End of the Arm

The opposite end of the arm will have chamfers. A chamfer is an angled cutoff of a corner.

1. Click the **Left** button in the **Standard Views** toolbar. This shows the arm from the left side, which does not have the rounded corners. If necessary, click the **Hidden Lines Removed** button in the **View** toolbar to make the view a little clearer.

2. To better understand what you are viewing, it is a good idea to slightly rotate the part in order to orient yourself. Use the **Rotate View** tool to slightly rotate the part so that it looks like that shown in Figure 2.42. Use the **Zoom In/Out** button in the **View** toolbar to zoom out. Be sure that you can still see the entire end of the arm.

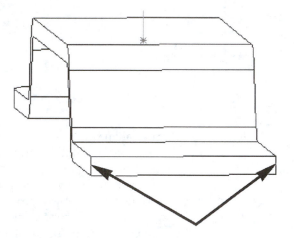

Figure 2.42. Corners to be chamfered.

3. To add the chamfer, click the **Chamfer** button (cube with one edge chamfered) in the **Features** toolbar, or **Insert** ⇒ **Features** ⇒ **Chamfer**. The *Chamfer* PropertyManager appears.

4. Select both of the edges, as shown in Figure 2.42, by clicking each one. Each edge is added to the list in the PropertyManager. Note that it is not necessary to *control click* the second edge as was done for the round. This is because the **Chamfer** PropertyManager was opened before the edges were selected. Once the feature is chosen, several edges can be selected. In the case of the fillet, the edges were selected before clicking the **Fillet** button. Prior to activating a feature, *control clicking* must be used to select more than one entity.

5. Be sure the *Angle distance* button is selected. Set the *Distance* to *.1* and the *Angle* to *45* degrees. This will cut off the edge at a 45-degree angle so that the side of the triangle is .1 inch long.

6. Click *OK* to finish the chamfers. This creates two chamfers, one on each edge that you selected. Click the **Shaded** button in the **View** toolbar. In the **Isometric** view, the part should look similar to that shown in Figure 2.43. Be sure that the chamfers are on the left end of the arm, as shown in the figure.

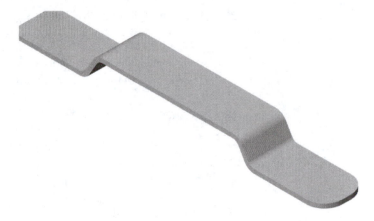

Figure 2.43. Corners chamfered.

7.   To see the surfaces defined by the chamfer, click on **Chamfer1** in the FeatureManager design tree on the left side of the window. Both of the chamfers will be highlighted in green. Double clicking on **Chamfer1** in the FeatureManager design tree will display the chamfers' dimensions. If the dimensions are difficult to read, drag them to a better position. Use **Zoom to Fit**, if necessary. Click any open space in the Graphics Window so the dimensions are not displayed. Double clicking on **Fillet1** or **Extrude-Thin1** in the FeatureManager design tree will display the dimensions of these features. You could modify the dimensions by double clicking on the values, but do not do this now. The dimensions can be displayed in any view. Activate the **Select** tool to hide the dimensions, and use **Redraw** to repaint the screen, if necessary.

2.3.8   Adding a Hole in the Arm

The last feature to add to the arm is the hole at the rounded end. This can be accomplished by extruding a circular cut through the arm.

1.   Return to the **Isometric** view and click on the top face (the one with the rounded edges at the right end of the arm) using the **Select** tool. The face becomes highlighted. Open a sketch on the face by clicking the **Sketch** button in the **Sketch** toolbar. Click **Top** in the **Standard Views** toolbar so that the view is directed toward the selected face. The screen should look similar to that shown in Figure 2.44, although the guard might be perpendicular to that shown in the figure.

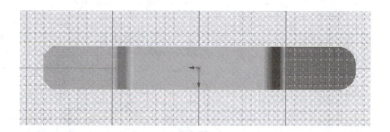

Figure 2.44. Face selected.

2. Click the <u>**Circle**</u> button in the <u>**Sketch Tools**</u> toolbar, or **Tools** ⟹ **Sketch Entity** ⟹ **Circle**. The circle next to the cursor signifies that the **Circle** tool is active. Draw a circle near the end of the arm by clicking and dragging the cursor with the left mouse button. At this point, neither the diameter nor the location of the center is important. However, if the center of the circle is on an edge, delete the circle and redraw it.

3. Activate the **Dimension** tool by clicking the <u>**Dimension**</u> button in the <u>**Sketch**</u> toolbar, or **Tools** ⟹ **Dimensions** ⟹ **Parallel**. Dimension the diameter of the circle by clicking on the circle and then clicking again to place the dimension box.

4. The center of the circle must be located relative to the arm. In this sketch, the center of the circle will be dimensioned from existing features (the edges of the arm). With the **Dimension** tool active, click on the center point of the circle. Next, click on the upper edge of the arm (as oriented in Figure 2.45).

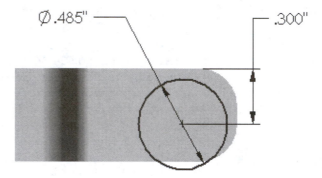

Figure 2.45. Circle with dimensions placed.

Click again to place the dimension. The sketch should look similar to that shown in Figure 2.45. The dimension values may be different than those in the figure.

5. The circle center point needs a second dimension in order to locate it with respect to the arm. The **Dimension** tool should still be active, so click on the center of the circle. Click on the edge of the arm that is between the two rounds at the rounded end. Before you click the line, be sure that an icon of a line appears next to the cursor. Zoom in, if you have trouble selecting the line. Click again to place the dimension.

6. Activate the **Select** tool to change the values of the dimensions to match the ones shown in Figure 2.46.

7. The circle will become a hole when it is extruded as a cut. Click <u>**Extruded Cut**</u> in the <u>**Features**</u> toolbar. In the ***Cut-Extrude*** PropertyManager, set the ***End Condition*** to ***Through All***, so that the cut goes all the way through the thickness of the arm. Click ***OK*** to finish the cut.

8. Rotate the part to be sure that the hole was created correctly. It should look like the arm shown in Figure 2.34.

9. Click **Save** in the **File** menu, or click the <u>**Save**</u> button in the <u>**Standard**</u> toolbar. The ***Save As*** dialog box appears, with ***tutorial*** in the ***Save in*** field. This is because the most recently saved item, the ***tutorial part*** template, was automatically saved

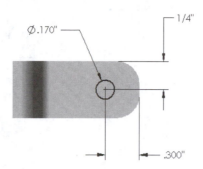

Figure 2.46. Dimensions updated.

to the **tutorial** folder in the SolidWorks directory, so that it could be accessed later. Your part should be saved in the same location as the **guard** was saved. Navigate to the appropriate directory and save the part as *arm*.

Congratulations! This completes the arm. Now, close the arm window.

ADDING HOLES

The hole in the guard was modeled by sketching a circle and then using an **Extruded Cut** to remove the material within it. Holes can also be modeled without using the sketch mode. To do this, select the point on the surface on which the hole is to be created. Then, use either the **Simple Hole** feature or the **Hole Wizard** tool, found in the **Features** toolbar, or in the **Insert** ⇒ **Features** ⇒ **Hole** menu.

The **Simple Hole** feature creates a sketch of a circle on the selected surface. Using the *Hole* Property-Manager, the diameter is specified and the material is removed using a *Blind, Through All*, or other method of cut. After the hole is cut, *right click* **Hole1** in the FeatureManager design tree and select **Edit Sketch**.

Then, add dimensions to position the hole's centerpoint using the **Dimension** tool. Finish by clicking the **Sketch** toolbar button. To delete the hole, *right click* on **Hole1** in the FeatureManager design tree and click **Delete Feature**.

The **Hole Wizard** tool can create more complex holes, such as countersunk, counterbored, and tapped holes. After selecting the point on the surface on which the hole is to be created, activate the **Hole Wizard** tool. Select the tab for the desired hole type and modify its parameters in the dialog box. Click *Next* and locate the hole with the **Dimension** tool. Modify the dimensions to the desired values and click *Finish*. Using the **Hole Wizard** tool can save time in the design process, especially when many special holes are needed in a model. To delete the hole, *right click* it in the FeatureManager design tree and click **Delete Feature**.

2.4   MODELING THE BLADE

The third component of the pizza cutter to be modeled in this chapter is the blade, shown in Figure 2.47. The blade could be modeled using an extruded circular section as the base feature, with a circular cut for the hole as an additional feature. But in this case, you will include the circular hole at the center of the blade in the base feature. This avoids adding the hole later as a separate feature. The chamfered edges are then added to the base feature.

2.4.1   Sketching the Blade

The initial sketch for the blade consists of two concentric circles. The larger circle is the edge of the blade. The smaller circle is for the hole at the center of the blade.

Figure 2.47. Finished blade.

1. Click the **New** button in the **Standard** toolbar, or **File** ⇒ **New**. The *New SolidWorks Document* dialog box appears. The template saved in the previous section, ***tutorial part***, should be listed. Click on ***tutorial part*** followed by *OK*. The new part uses all of the settings that were saved in the previous section.

2. Open a new **Sketch**. Activate the **Circle** tool and draw a small circle that is centered at the origin. Be sure that you see the square next to the cursor before you place the center of the circle, signifying that the center is coincident with the origin.

3. Draw a larger circle that is also centered at the origin. The sketch should look similar to that shown in Figure 2.48.

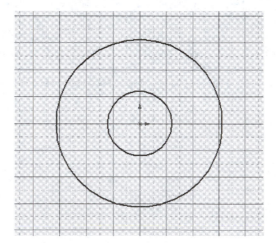

Figure 2.48. Circles drawn.

4. **Dimension** the inner circle to have a diameter of **.170** by clicking on the arc of the circle and placing the dimension. Dimension the outer circle to have a diameter of **3 1/2**. Use the **Select** tool to modify the values. The sketch should look similar to that shown in Figure 2.49.

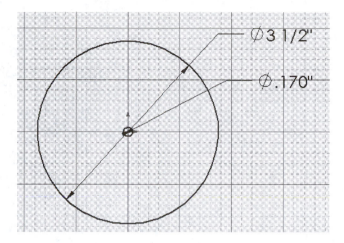

Figure 2.49. Dimensions placed and updated.

2.4.2   Extruding the Sketch

The sketch is extruded perpendicular to the screen to create a cylinder with a hole through it. The extrusion depth is the thickness of the blade.

1.   Turn off the sketching grid by clicking the **Grid** button in the **Sketch** tool-bar. Click on *Display Grid* to remove the check mark. Click **OK** to close the dialog box.

2.   Open the ***Base-Extrude*** PropertyManager by clicking the **Extruded Boss/Base** button in the **Features** toolbar.

3.   The two circles form a closed geometric shape. Since the shape is closed, it is not a thin feature, having only a wall thickness and a depth. Instead, it is a solid feature in which the sketched geometric shape is extruded perpendicular to the sketching plane. Thus, only the ***Direction 1*** field appears in the PropertyManager. Be sure the ***End Condition*** is set to ***Blind***. Then move the cursor into the Graphics Window and click the large conical arrow that is highlighted when you move the cursor over it. As the cursor is moved, the depth of the extrusion changes, and the numeric value of the depth is displayed in the Graphics Window and in the PropertyManager. The arrow along the axis of the circles points the direction of the extrusion. Bring the extrusion depth to about $\frac{1}{2}''$ with the arrow pointing left. Click the left mouse button to accept the depth.

4.   Click **OK** in the PropertyManager to finish the extrusion. The extruded part should look similar to that shown in Figure 2.50. The final blade will be quite thin. However, larger objects are easier to work with, so a very thick blade was extruded. The thickness of the blade will be changed later.

2.4.3   Adding a Chamfer to Form the Edge of the Blade

1.   To create a chamfer, the edge indicated in Figure 2.51 must be selected. This edge is opposite the face of the extrusion that lies in the **Front** plane. To see where the **Front** plane is, select it in the FeatureManager design tree on the left side of the screen. Its location is easier to see from the right side. Click **Right** in the **Standard Views** toolbar. Set the display to **Hidden**

Figure 2.50. Blade extruded.

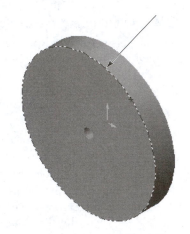

Figure 2.51. Edge to be chamfered.

Lines Visible. Click on the vertical edge that does *not* lie in the **Front** plane. Return to the **Isometric** view and **Shaded**. The edge should be highlighted, as shown in Figure 2.51.

2. Add a chamfer to the highlighted edge by clicking the **<u>Chamfer</u>** button in the **<u>Features</u>** toolbar, or **Insert** ⇒ **Features** ⇒ **Chamfer**.

3. Be sure that ***Edge <1>*** is listed in the ***Chamfer*** PropertyManager.

4. Activate the ***Distance distance*** button. This removes a triangular section with its sides defined by two distances. Set the display to **Hidden Lines Visible**. The chamfer dimensions are shown in the callout box in the Graphics Window and in the PropertyManager. In the PropertyManager set ***Distance 1*** to *.02* and set ***Distance 2*** to *.12*.

5. Click ***OK*** to create a chamfer around the entire edge. Be sure that the long side of the chamfer is on the flat face of the extrusion. Double click on **Chamfer1** in the FeatureManager design tree to show the chamfer dimensions, as in

Figure 2.52. You may need to move the dimensions using the **Select** tool in order to see them better. If the chamfer is not as desired, click on **Chamfer1** in the FeatureManager design tree to highlight it. Hit the Delete key on the keyboard to delete the chamfer feature. Redo the feature, making sure that the settings are the same as those stated previously.

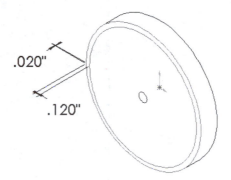

Figure 2.52. Chamfer dimensions shown.

2.4.4   Mirroring a Feature

In many cases, a feature is symmetric about a plane of the part. Symmetric features are easily modeled by creating a mirror image of the feature. Mirroring both the extrusion and the chamfer will create a new set of features on the other side of the **Front** plane. This will form the other half of the blade.

1. The two features that will be mirrored—the cylindrical base feature and the chamfer—must both be selected. To select these two features, click on **Extrude1** in the FeatureManager design tree. If the FeatureManager design tree is not shown, it can be activated using the tabs at the bottom of the FeatureManager/PropertyManager window. The extrusion is high-lighted to show that it is selected. Then, *control click* **Chamfer1** in the FeatureManager design tree, adding it to the selection.

2. Click the **Mirror** button in the **Features** toolbar or **Insert** ⇒ **Pattern/Mirror** ⇒ **Mirror** in the Menu bar. The *Mirror* PropertyManager appears.

3. The two features, *Extrude1* and *Chamfer1*, should appear in the *Features to Mirror* list. These features will be mirrored about the **Front** plane. Be sure that the *Mirror/Face Plane* field is highlighted in pink. If it is not highlighted, click on the field. Click the FeatureManager tab (leftmost tab at the bottom of the PropertyManager) to display the FeatureManager design tree. Click on **Front** in the FeatureManager design tree, adding it to the *Mirror/Face Plane* list. The **Front** plane and the mirrored features now appear, as shown in Figure 2.53.

4. In the *Options* field, check the *Geometry Pattern* checkbox to ensure that the chamfer dimensions will be oriented the same way on both sides of the mirror plane.

5. Click *OK* to accept the settings. Rotate the part to be sure that both the extrusion and the chamfer were copied. If there is a problem with the mirror operation, select **Mirror1** in the FeatureManager design tree, delete it, and repeat the previous steps.

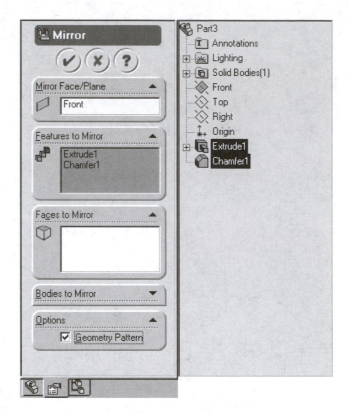

Figure 2.53. *Mirror* PropertyManager and Flyout FeatureManager design tree.

2.4.5 Changing the Definition of the Extrusion

You may now go back and change the extrusion depth for the blade. Since the chamfer and the mirror operation were done *after* the extrusion, they will be updated to reflect the new blade thickness.

1. In the FeatureManager design tree, *right click* **Extrude1**. Using the right mouse button activates a menu. Choose **Edit Definition** in the menu. The **Extrude1** PropertyManager appears, with the settings that were originally specified for the extrusion of the blade's base feature.

2. Change the **Depth** to **.02** by typing the value in the PropertyManager. This changes the thickness of the blade to exactly the width of the chamfer. Leave the other settings as they were.

3. Click **OK**. SolidWorks rebuilds all of the part's features, including the mirror operation with the new depth. The final blade should look like that shown in Figure 2.47. If an exclamation point appears next to **Chamfer1** in the FeatureManager design tree, *right click* **Chamfer1** and select **Edit Definition**. Be sure that the settings match those described above.

Congratulations! This completes the blade. Save the part as **blade** and close the window. If you are going to quit now, use **File** ⇒ **Exit**.

PARENT–CHILD RELATIONSHIPS

The concept of parent–child relationships is important in solids modeling. A "child" is a feature that depends on another feature, namely the parent feature. For example, the chamfer created on the blade is a child of the base extrusion for the blade, since the chamfer cannot exist without the base extrusion. Therefore, the base extrusion is a "parent" of the chamfer. A parent can have multiple children (if several different features are dependent upon it), and a child can have multiple parents (if it is dependent on several different features).

To see the parent–child relationships in Solid-Works, *right click* a feature in the FeatureManager design tree and select **Parent/Child**. The parents and children of that feature are shown. These relationships are important, because features within SolidWorks maintain their dependencies if the parent features are changed. This was demonstrated when the blade was modeled. When the thickness of the blade was changed, the chamfers (children) remained on the edge of the blade base feature (parent), as defined earlier on the thicker blade. It is important to keep track of parent–child relationships, since altering or deleting a parent feature might adversely affect the children of that feature.

Problems

1. Model the guard by making both ends bend 30 degrees in the same direction, rather than in opposite directions.

2. Model the guard so that it is extruded only to one side of the **Front** plane, using **Blind** instead of **Mid Plane** in the **Extrude** PropertyManager. Make the radius of the round **.15** instead of **.35**.

3. Model the arm by using a **Blind** depth extrusion instead of a **Mid Plane** extrusion, so that it is extruded to one side of the **Front** plane. Change the chamfer to a **.15** fillet.

4. Create the blade by first creating a **3 1/2** solid disk with a **Blind** depth of **1/2**. Add the **.170** hole at the center. Then, mirror both the extrusion and the hole. Create the chamfers using **Angle distance**. The angle size is that necessary to create the same chamfer as described earlier in this chapter. Note that the chamfer distance is in the direction of the arrow shown when the **Chamfer** PropertyManager is open. Modify the definition of the extrusion to provide the correct blade thickness.

5. Model the blade by creating a **3 1/2** disk with a **.170** hole, but for the **End Condition**, use **Mid Plane** with the actual final blade thickness of .040 inches. Finally, add a chamfer on both sides of the **Front** plane to form the cutting edge of the blade.

3

Modeling Parts in SolidWorks: Revolves

OVERVIEW

In this chapter, you will learn how to create a three-dimensional model of a solid by revolving a two-dimensional cross section. Revolving is ideal for creating axisymmetric models, such as the pizza cutter cap, handle, and rivet. Modeling a revolved solid begins in the sketch mode. But, unlike an extrusion, a centerline is added to the sketch to indicate the axis about which the cross section is revolved. After the revolved base feature is created, additional features, such as fillets, holes, and other cuts, can be added, including features that are repeated in a pattern. In addition, parts can be colored to look much like the actual part.

3.1 MODELING THE CAP

The cap covers the end of the handle, where the two arms of the pizza cutter are inserted into the handle. The cap, shown in Figure 3.1, has a uniform thickness and is axisymmetric. The cap can be modeled as a thin feature by revolving a single sketch of a cross section around a centerline.

3.1.1 Sketching the Cap
You will begin by sketching the thin section that will be revolved.

SECTIONS

3.1   Modeling the Cap
3.2   Modeling the Handle
3.3   Modeling the Rivet

OBJECTIVES

After working through this chapter, you will be able to

- Sketch centerlines,
- Revolve a sketch to model a solid body,
- Revolve a sketched geometry to add a revolved feature to a base feature,
- Use the Fillet, Rectangle, and Trim sketch tools,
- Create an axis from the intersection of two planes,
- Create multiple identical features,
- Color a part,
- Sketch arcs, and
- Change detailing settings to make a sketch clearer.

Figure 3.1. Finished cap.

1.   Open a new part using **File ⇒ New** and selecting **tutorial part** as the template. Create a new sketch by clicking the <u>**Sketch**</u> button, or **Insert ⇒ Sketch**.

2.   With the **Line** tool, draw a horizontal line that starts to the right of the origin and extends further to the right, as shown in Figure 3.2. Remember to look for an "H" next to the cursor when drawing horizontal lines.

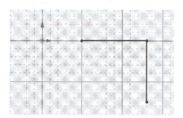

Figure 3.2. Lines sketched.

3.   The **Line** tool should still be active. Draw a vertical line that starts at the right endpoint of the horizontal line and continues downward. Look for two things when drawing this line. First, when you start the line, a square should appear next to the cursor. This signifies that the line will start at the endpoint of the horizontal line. Then, as you draw the line, look for a "V", indicating that a vertical line is being drawn. If you need to correct a mistake, use <u>**Undo**</u>, or **Edit ⇒ Undo Line**, to remove the line. Then, draw the line again. The sketch should look like that shown in Figure 3.2.

4.   Activate the **Dimension** tool. Dimension the distance from the origin to the left endpoint of the horizontal line to **.3**. To do this, click on each point and then click again to place the dimension. Use the **Select** tool to modify the value by double clicking on the dimension.

5.   Dimension the horizontal line to **.2** by clicking on the line, placing the dimension, and then modifying the value.

6.   In a similar manner, dimension the vertical line to **3/8**. The sketch is now fully defined. The screen should look similar to that shown in Figure 3.3. Use the **Select** tool to place the dimensions like those in the figure. It may help to **Zoom to Fit** to see a close-up view of the sketch.

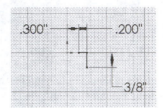

Figure 3.3.   Dimensions placed and updated.

7.   Now, round the corner between the two line segments by clicking on the **Sketch Fillet** button in the **Sketch Tools** toolbar, or **Tools ⇒ Sketch Tools ⇒ Fillet**.

8.   The **Sketch Fillet** PropertyManager appears. Type in **.075** as the **Radius**.

9.   With the dialog box still open, click the horizontal line, and then click the vertical line. The corner is rounded, and a dimension is automatically placed on the sketch.

10.   Click **OK** (green check mark) or **Close** (red X) to close the **Sketch Fillet** dialog box. Using the **Select** tool, move the fillet dimension to a location in which it can be seen clearly.

3.1.2   Adding a Centerline

Centerlines are frequently used in SolidWorks. Centerlines are considered to be *construction geometry*—they aid in creating a sketch of a part, but are not the part itself. Centerlines are used in mirroring objects, revolving sketches, and constraining endpoints to be collinear. You will create a vertical centerline through the origin that will serve as an axis of revolution for the shape that has been sketched.

1.   Activate the **Centerline** tool by clicking the **Centerline** button in the **Sketch Tools** toolbar, or **Tools ⇒ Sketch Entity ⇒ Centerline**.

2.   Centerlines are drawn just like any other line. With the **Centerline** tool, click on the origin and drag the centerline upward. Release the mouse button when a "V" appears next to the cursor. A centerline extends infinitely (even though it has a finite length on the sketch), so it does not need to be dimensioned. Be sure that the centerline is vertical and begins at the origin. The sketch should look similar to that shown in Figure 3.4.

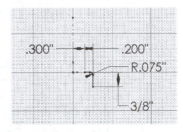

Figure 3.4.   Fillet and centerline added.

3.1.3   Revolving the Sketch

You are now ready to revolve the sketch around the centerline in order to model a three-dimensional, axisymmetric part.

1. Now that a centerline exists in the sketch, the **Revolved Boss/Base** button (half of a ring) in the **Features** toolbar is active. Click this button, or select **Insert ⇒ Boss/Base ⇒ Revolve**.

2. The dialog box shown in Figure 3.5 will appear, since the sketch is not a closed outline. The cap is a thin feature, so the sketch outline should not be closed. If you answered "yes" to the question in the dialog box, SolidWorks would automatically draw a line between the left end of the horizontal line and the bottom end of the vertical line, creating a closed triangle with a rounded corner. Then, SolidWorks would revolve this triangle around the centerline axis. Instead, you should revolve the thin shape that was sketched, so click **No** to continue.

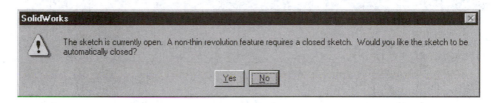

Figure 3.5. Open sketch dialog box.

3. The **Revolve** PropertyManager appears and a preview of the revolved section is displayed in the Graphics Window. In the **Revolve Parameters** field, set the **Revolve Type** to **One-Direction**. This causes the revolved section to extend in one direction from the sketch plane. Using the **Two-Direction** type revolves the sketch a specified angle on one side of the sketch plane and a different specified angle on the opposite side of the sketch plane. **MidPlane** revolves the sketch a specified angle, but places the sketch plane so that it bisects the angle.

4. Set the **Angle** to **360** degrees. This revolves the sketch completely around the centerline, which creates a body of revolution.

5. In the **Thin Feature** field, set the **Type** to **Mid Plane**. Set the **Direction 1 Thickness** to **.02**. This creates a thin feature .02 inches thick, with the sketch lines at the middle, or midplane, of the thickness.

6. Click **OK** to accept the settings. Rotate the part using **Rotate View** to see all sides of the cap. Notice that it is symmetric about the centerline and has a uniform wall thickness of .02 inches. To return to the **Isometric** view, click the **Isometric** button in the **Standard Views** toolbar.

Congratulations! This completes the cap. The part should look like the one in Figure 3.1. **Save** the part as **cap**. Close the cap window using **File ⇒ Close**, or by clicking the **X** in the upper right corner of the **cap** window (not the SolidWorks window).

Revolving a section can transform a simple sketch into a relatively complex part. The cap could have been modeled using an extrusion of a circle to create a cylinder, followed by various cuts and fillets to remove material. But this would have required several features. By using a revolved section, the cap was modeled using just one feature. In fact, the blade could have been made with a revolve in only one step using the sketch shown in Figure 3.6. When modeling in three dimensions, there are usually several different ways to create parts. Some are more efficient than others. As a result, it is helpful to visualize the part and think about the options available before modeling it.

Figure 3.6. Revolved blade sketch.

WHAT IS THE BEST APPROACH FOR MODELING A PART?

Many different approaches are possible for modeling the same part. Which is the best approach? The answer to this question depends on the skill of the CAD user, the complexity of the part, the potential for redesign of the part, the design intent, and the preferences of the user. Unskilled users may prefer to "carve up" a solid block of material by using rounds, cuts, and chamfers, whereas skilled users may extrude or revolve a cross section that already includes many of these features. Simple parts can often be modeled with only a few strategic features, but complex parts may require hundreds of features. For a simple part, the order in which features are modeled is unlikely to be critical. For a complex part, it may be necessary to model one feature before another one can be created. If the redesign of the part is likely, several features may be separately added to the model, so that each could be individually removed or modified. If redesign is unlikely, these features could be combined. Design intent can play a key role in both how a feature is created and which features

are modeled first. The parent–child relationships, how features are dimensioned with respect to other features, and what features are likely to be modified all play a role. Finally, some users prefer to model using the fewest features possible by extruding or revolving very detailed sketches. Others prefer to mimic the operations that a machinist might use in making a part. They begin with a stock shape of material (a simple base feature) and add cut features and detail features, such as holes and rounds, just as a machinist would to the initial block of material.

The bottom line is that there are always several ways, and rarely one best way, to model a part. Think ahead about the easiest way to visualize the part, the most efficient method to extrude or revolve the cross section, the best way to add details, the critical dimensions of the part, what might be redesigned in the part, and how the part fits with other parts. Then proceed, understanding that there are many approaches that may work equally well.

3.2 MODELING THE HANDLE

The handle, shown in Figure 3.7, is a more complex part than the cap. The handle is generally cylindrical in shape with a circular hole at one end and a rectangular hole to accept the arms at the other end. Grooves on the handle provide a better grip. One end is rounded and the other end has a reduced diameter. The handle could be made in several different ways. For instance, a circle could be extruded to form a cylindrical base feature, and then cuts could be added for the reduced diameter, the rounded end, the two holes, and the grooves (a total of six features). Instead, you will model the handle by revolving a section that already includes the reduced diameter and the rounded end. Then, you will add the grooves and the holes (a total of four features).

Figure 3.7.   Finished handle.

3.2.1   Sketching the Base Feature of the Handle

You will begin by sketching the cross section of the handle to be revolved.

1. Open a new **Sketch** for a new part using the **tutorial part**.
2. Activate the **Rectangle** tool by clicking the <u>**Rectangle**</u> button in the <u>**Sketch Tools**</u> toolbar, or **Tools** ⇒ **Sketch Entity** ⇒ **Rectangle**.
3. Bring the cursor over the origin and look for the square next to the cursor, indicating you are on the origin. Click and drag up and to the right. Release the mouse button. This creates a rectangle with its bottom left corner coincident with the origin.
4. Activate the **Line** tool. In the lower right corner of the rectangle, draw two lines, one horizontal and one vertical, to form a small rectangle (as shown in Figure 3.8). These two lines should start on the lines of the large rectangle and their endpoints should meet. Note that the symbol next to the pencil cursor changes when the cursor is over a line or a point.

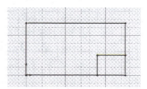

Figure 3.8.   Lines sketched.

5. Activate the **Trim** tool by clicking the <u>**Sketch Trim**</u> button (a scissors icon) in the <u>**Sketch Tools**</u> toolbar, or **Tools** ⇒ **Sketch Tools** ⇒ **Trim**. The **Trim** tool clips away a part of the sketch entity. The bottom right corner of the rectangle will be clipped away.
6. With the **Trim** tool active, bring the cursor over the horizontal line segment on the right side of the rectangle, as indicated in Figure 3.9. The segment will be highlighted, indicating which part of the line will be trimmed away. Click on this segment to trim the line. Repeat the trim for the vertical line segment indicated in the figure.

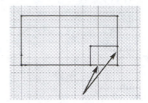

Figure 3.9. Segments to be trimmed.

7. Dimensioning a complex sketch can be challenging. In a sketch like this, you should place all of the dimensions first, and then change the values afterward. Activate the **Dimension** tool. Insert dimensions, as shown in Figure 3.10, by clicking on each line and placing it into the dimension box. The dimensions will probably be different from those shown in the figure. Do not change the dimensions. After adding these four dimensions, the sketch is *Fully Defined*.

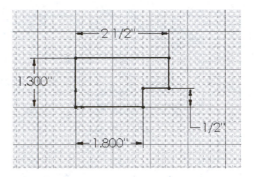

Figure 3.10. Dimensions placed.

8. Activate the **Select** tool, and modify each of the four dimensions to correspond to the values shown in Figure 3.11. As you change the dimensions, the aspect ratio of the sketch will change substantially. You might need to **Zoom In/Out** or **Zoom to Fit** to see the entire sketch.

9. Now the round at the top right corner is added. Open the ***Sketch Fillet*** PropertyManager by clicking the **Sketch Fillet** button in the **Sketch Tools** toolbar, or **Tools** ⇒ **Sketch Tools** ⇒ **Fillet**. Enter *.3* for the ***Radius***.

10. Move the cursor over the point at the upper right corner of the rectangle. Note that, as the cursor is positioned over the corner, a circle appears next to the cursor. Click on the point. The corner is rounded and the .3-inch dimension is added. This is an alternate method available for adding a fillet. For previous fillets, the two line segments that intersected at the corner were selected instead of the corner point.

11. Click ***OK*** or ***Close*** and move the fillet dimension to a convenient position.

3.2.2 Revolving the Cross Section

Since this sketch will be revolved, you must create an axis about which it will be revolved.

1. Activate the **Centerline** tool.

2. Create a vertical centerline that starts at the origin and extends vertically upward. This completes the base sketch. Before continuing with the revolve, be sure that the screen looks similar to that shown in Figure 3.12.

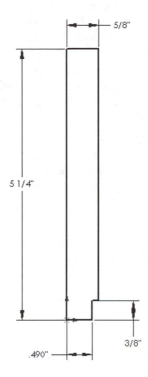

Figure 3.11. Dimensions updated.

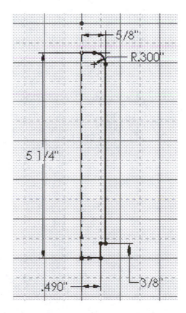

Figure 3.12. Fillet and centerline added.

3. Now that a centerline is in the sketch, the **<u>Revolved Boss/Base</u>** button becomes active in the **<u>Features</u>** toolbar. Click it to activate the ***Revolve*** PropertyManager.

4. This is a closed sketch, so the revolve is a solid feature, not a thin feature. Only the ***Revolve Parameters*** field appears and the ***Thin Feature*** field is not active. Set the ***Revolve Type*** to ***One-Direction*** and the ***Angle*** to ***360*** degrees.

This revolves the sketch 360 degrees in one direction from the plane of the sketch.

5. SolidWorks displays an outlined preview of the revolved section in the Graphics Window. Click **OK** to accept the settings. Rotate the part and zoom in to see the part from all sides. In the **Isometric** view, the part should look similar to that shown in Figure 3.13.

Figure 3.13. Handle base feature.

3.2.3 Sketching and Cutting a Single Groove

Since the basic shape, or base feature, of the handle is complete, details may now be added. The grooves in the handle are the first details to be added. Although the grooves appear to require many steps, they can be easily modeled by using a pattern feature. First, a single groove will be sketched and cut. Then, a pattern of grooves will be created based on this first groove.

1. Try to open a sketch by clicking on the **Sketch** button in the **Sketch** toolbar. A message appears in the PropertyManager informing you that you need to select a planar face before sketching. Click the FeatureManager design tree tab (the leftmost tab at the bottom of the PropertyManager). The Feature-Manager design tree is displayed. The groove will be sketched on the **Front** plane, so select it in the FeatureManager design tree.

2. A new sketch opens and a grid appears. If the sketch plane is skewed in the **Isometric** orientation, click the **Normal To** button in the **Standard Views** toolbar. To see the sketch more clearly, click the **Hidden Lines Visible** button in the **View** toolbar.

3. In the first quadrant (above and to the right of the origin), draw a box using the **Rectangle** tool, as shown in Figure 3.14. This rectangle will become the groove once you modify its shape, move it to the correct position, and revolve it as a cut.

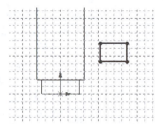

Figure 3.14. Rectangle drawn.

4. First, position the groove vertically. With the **Dimension** tool, select the origin followed by the lower horizontal edge of the rectangle. Click again to place the dimension. With the **Select** tool, modify the dimension to *1.5*.

5. Dimension both the height and width of the rectangle to be *.1*. Use **Zoom to Area** to zoom in on the rectangle, as shown in Figure 3.15.

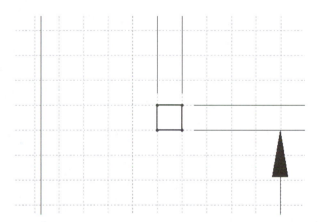

Figure 3.15. Zoomed in on rectangle.

6. Open the *Sketch Fillet* PropertyManager by clicking the <u>**Sketch Fillet**</u> button in the <u>**Sketch Tools**</u> toolbar. Set the *Radius* to *.04*. Click the upper horizontal line of the rectangle, followed by the left vertical line. A fillet appears with a dimension. Before closing the *Sketch Fillet* PropertyManager, add another fillet to the lower left corner of the rectangle by clicking on that corner point. The second fillet appears without a dimension, because the first dimension refers to both fillets. Click **OK** to close the *Sketch Fillet* PropertyManager. **Zoom to Fit** and then move the fillet dimension to a convenient location with the **Select** tool.

7. Activate the **Centerline** tool. Draw a vertical centerline that starts at the origin. This centerline is the axis about which the cut for the groove will be revolved. You cannot use the centerline that was drawn for the previous sketch, since it is now part of the parent feature, **Revolve1**, listed in the FeatureManager design tree. With the **Select** tool, click anywhere on a blank space in the sketch to ensure that nothing is currently selected.

8. The last thing to do is to place the rectangle on the sketch with respect to the handle base feature. This could be done by making the dimension from the

centerline to the right side of the rectangle the same as the radius of the handle. But if you cannot remember the radius of the handle, there is another way to position the rectangle. You can use a relation to align the right side of the rectangle to the handle's outer edge. Use **Zoom To Area** to zoom in on the small rectangle. To add the relation, click the **Add Relation** button in the **Sketch Relations** toolbar, or **Tools ⇒ Relations ⇒ Add**. The *Add Geometric Relations* PropertyManager appears. Then, click on the right side of the small rectangle. **Zoom to Fit** and click on the right edge of the handle. Both lines appear in the *Selected Entities* field of the dialog box, and both are highlighted. The edge of the handle is called *Silhouette Edge <1>*, because the selection is really the silhouette of a curved surface of the handle. The selected items should be collinear, so click the *Collinear* button. The relation is added to the *Existing Relations* field. With this relation, the groove will always be collinear with the edge of the handle, even if the handle's radius is changed. The sketch should be similar to the one in Figure 3.16. Click *OK* to close the *Add Relations* PropertyManager.

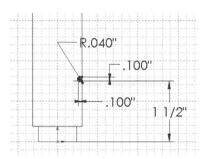

Figure 3.16. Groove sketch completed.

9. The groove can be made by revolving the small rectangle as a cut to remove material around the handle. Click the **Revolved Cut** button in the **Features** toolbar, or **Insert ⇒ Cut ⇒ Revolve**. Since material is being removed from the part, a **Revolved Cut** is used, not a **Revolved Boss/Base**, which creates material.

10. The *Cut-Revolve* PropertyManager appears. This is the same PropertyManager that appears for a **Revolved Boss/Base**, except that material is removed with a **Revolved Cut**.

11. Set the angle to revolve the sketch all the way around the centerline. Click *OK* to accept the settings. Be sure the display is set to **Tangent Edges Visible** by selecting **View ⇒ Display**. If **Tangent Edges Visible** is not checked, click it to show tangent edges between surfaces as solid curves (such as the edge of the round at the top of the handle). **Tangent Edges as Phantom** displays the edges as dashed lines. **Tangent Edges Removed** does not display the edges at all. In the **Isometric** view, the part should look similar to that shown in Figure 3.17.

Figure 3.17. Groove cut.

3.2.4   Modeling More Grooves: Inserting a Linear Pattern

Instead of re-creating the previous sketch again and again to make more grooves, you can use a linear pattern to repeat the revolved cut several times along the length of the handle to create a pattern of grooves.

1.   The pattern of grooves must be repeated along a defined direction. To do this, an axis will be created from the intersection of two planes. Click on **Front** in the FeatureManager design tree and then *control click* **Right** to select both planes. The intersection of the **Front** plane and the **Right** plane is a vertical line.

2.   Click **Insert** ⇒ **Reference Geometry** ⇒ **Axis** to create an axis at the intersection of the two planes. The ***Reference Axis*** dialog box appears, as shown in Figure 3.18.

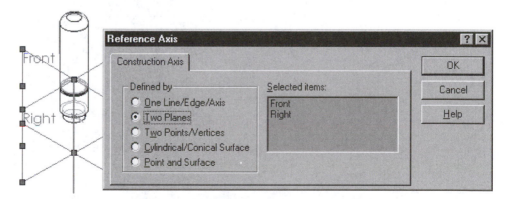

Figure 3.18. *Reference Axis* dialog box.

3.   The ***Two Planes*** button should already be selected. **Front** and **Right** should appear in the ***Selected Items*** list. Click ***OK*** to create the axis. Verify that **Axis1** is the axis of the handle by rotating the handle.

4. A pattern will be made from the revolved cut that created the first groove. Click on **Cut-Revolve1** in the FeatureManager design tree to select it. The cut becomes highlighted.

5. Click the <u>**Linear Pattern**</u> button (a 2 × 3 array) in the <u>**Features**</u> toolbar, or **Insert** ⇒ **Pattern/Mirror** ⇒ **Linear Pattern**, to create a pattern based on the highlighted feature. The *Linear Pattern* PropertyManager appears, as shown in Figure 3.19.

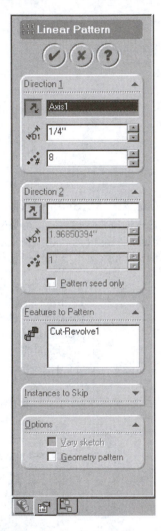

Figure 3.19. *Linear Pattern* PropertyManager.

6. *Cut-Revolve1* should appear in the *Features to Pattern* field. If it does not, activate the FeatureManager design tree and select **Cut-Revolve1**.

7. The *Pattern Direction* field under *Direction 1* should be highlighted in pink. If it is not, click in this box so that the next selection will indicate the direction. Click the FeatureManager design tree tab at the bottom of the PropertyManager. The FeatureManager design tree appears to the right of the PropertyManager. Click **Axis1** in the FeatureManager design tree to specify the direction in which the pattern will be created. The axis should be highlighted in green. A small conical arrow appears near the origin, showing the

direction of the pattern creation. The arrow should point upward, toward the rounded end of the handle. If the arrow is pointing downward to the squared-off end, check the ***Reverse Direction*** checkbox just below **Direction 1**.

8. Set the ***Spacing*** to ***.25***. This is the distance between each instance of the pattern.

9. Click the up arrow in the ***Number of Instances*** field until it shows **8**, for a total of eight grooves. A preview is shown as the number of cuts is increased. Be sure that the PropertyManager looks similar to that shown in Figure 3.19.

10. Click **OK** to accept the settings. Eight grooves are created along the length of the handle.

11. **Axis1** will no longer be needed, so *right click* it in the FeatureManager design tree. Select **Hide** from the menu so that **Axis1** is not shown. Shade the part and rotate it to see your progress. The handle should look like the one in Figure 3.20, in the **Front** orientation using the **Shaded** display.

Figure 3.20. Grooves patterned.

3.2.5 Modeling the Rectangular Hole

A rectangular hole at the bottom end of the handle holds the two arms. An extruded cut will be used to make this hole.

1. Open a sketch on the bottom surface of the handle by rotating it in the **Hidden Lines Visible** display until the flat end is visible. Select the bottom face (not the edge), as indicated in Figure 3.21. Click the <u>**Sketch**</u> button in the <u>**Sketch**</u> toolbar to open a sketch in the plane of the bottom face of the handle.

2. Set the view to **Normal To** and use the **Hidden Lines Removed** display.

3. Draw a rectangle that surrounds the origin. Be careful: If any of the vertices lie on the origin or on the arc of the circle, you may have created an undesirable constraint that will cause problems when dimensioning later. If necessary, delete the rectangle and draw a new one.

4. Dimension both the geometry and the location of the rectangle, as shown in Figure 3.22. It may be necessary to **Zoom To Fit**.

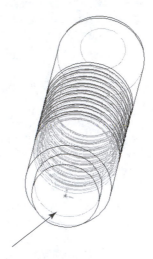

Figure 3.21. Bottom face of handle.

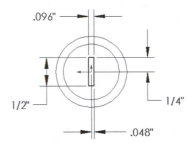

Figure 3.22. Rectangular hole sketch.

5. The grid sometimes makes it difficult to preview a new feature. Turn off the grid by clicking the **<u>Grid</u>** button and then clicking the ***Display Grid*** check-box to remove the check mark. Click ***OK***.

6. Cut a blind hole that extends **3/4** inch into the handle. Before clicking ***OK*** in the ***Cut-Extrude*** PropertyManager, ***Zoom to Fit*** and rotate the part. Be sure that the hole is going into the handle. If it looks as if you are cutting in the wrong direction, click the ***Reverse Direction*** button just below ***Direction 1*** in the PropertyManager. After clicking ***OK***, the part should look like the one in Figure 3.23.

3.2.6 Modeling the Circular Hole

The next feature to add is the circular hole at the rounded, top end of the handle. It is perpendicular to the widest dimension of the rectangular hole at the opposite end of the handle. The trick here is to determine which plane should be used as the sketch plane.

1. View the handle, using the **Hidden Lines Visible** display. Double click each plane in the FeatureManager design tree to see which plane is parallel to the long side of the rectangular cut. It may help to rotate the handle to look toward the flat end. You should find that the ***Front*** plane is parallel to the long side of the rectangular cut. Click **Front** in the FeatureManager design tree and open a sketch on it. Orient the sketch so that you are "normal to" the sketching plane by activating either the **Front** or the **Normal To** views.

Figure 3.23.   Rectangular hole cut.

2.   Centerlines are often useful in sketching. In this case, draw a vertical center-line extending from the origin to the top of the handle. Be sure that the lightbulb appears next to the cursor indicating that the centerline is coincident with a previous centerline.

3.   Draw a circle near the top of the handle with its center point on the center-line, as shown in Figure 3.24. This ensures that the circle is directly above the origin.

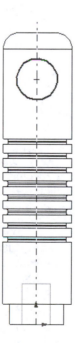

Figure 3.24.   Circle drawn.

4.   Dimension the diameter of the circle to be **1/2** and the distance between the center of the circle and the origin to be **4 1/2**.

5.   Open the ***Cut-Extrude*** PropertyManager. Set the ***End Condition*** for ***Direction 1*** to ***Through All***, so that the cut goes through all of the handle's material from the sketch plane, outward. Rotate the handle, using the **Rotate View** tool. Notice that a black circle appears at the center of the handle (where the sketch plane is located), and a light-colored circle appears on one side of the handle. The lighter circle indicates the side of the sketch plane to which the ***Through All*** setting applies. However, the cut must extend in two directions from the sketch plane. Click the checkbox next to ***Direction 2*** to activate the second direction. A second light-colored circle appears opposite the first and the ***End Condition*** for ***Direction 2*** is automatically set to ***Through All*** for the cut on the opposite side of the sketch plane. Note that different types of cuts can be applied on each side of the sketch plane. In this case, the material will be removed ***Through All*** on both sides of the **Front** plane.

6.   Click ***OK*** to accept the settings. The result should look like that shown in Figure 3.25. Rotate the part to be sure that the hole does indeed go all the way through the handle.

Figure 3.25.   Circular hole cut.

3.2.7   Adding the Finishing Touches to the Handle

Creating four rounds, or fillets, is all that is needed to complete the model of the handle. A round will be added on each side of the circular hole and on each of the edges at the flat bottom of the handle.

1.   The rounds on both ends of the circular hole are identical. Consequently, they will be added as a single feature. If the radius is ever changed, only one feature will need to be updated. In the **Hidden Lines Visible** display, rotate the handle, so that one end of the circular hole is visible. Since you are filleting a feature and not sketch entities, use the <u>**Fillet**</u> button in the <u>**Features**</u> toolbar. Type in the radius of **.050** and select the edge of the circular hole that is visible on one side of the handle. Then, click the edge of the circular hole that is shown as a hidden line on the other side of the handle. Both ***Edge <1>*** and ***Edge <2>*** should appear in the ***Items To Fillet*** field of the ***Fillet*** PropertyManager. If not, click the red X (***Cancel***) at the top of the PropertyManager and start over. Click ***OK*** to finish. The result should look like that shown in Figure 3.26.

Figure 3.26. Fillets added to circular hole.

2. Now, the edges at the flat bottom of the handle will be rounded. Rotate the view so that the bottom flat end is visible. Add a **.075** fillet to one of the edges at the bottom end of the handle, as indicated in Figure 3.27. Do not *control click* to round both edges at the same time. This permits the rounds to be altered separately later, if necessary.

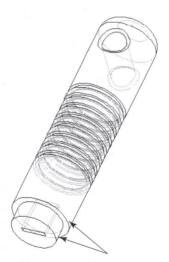

Figure 3.27. Edges to be rounded.

3. Add a **.075** fillet to the other edge, as indicated in Figure 3.27. The final results should look like that shown in Figure 3.28, in the **Hidden Lines Removed** display.

3.2.8   Changing the Color of the Handle

The color of a part can be changed to reflect its material or to make it appear more realistic. Set the view to **Shaded** to see the color of the handle. The default color is a metallike

Figure 3.28. Rounds added.

color. The color of the handle will be changed, since it would most likely be made of wood or plastic.

1. The color of any individual feature can be changed. However in this case, the color of the entire part should be changed, so select **Part1** (your part number may be different) at the top of the FeatureManager design tree.

2. To display color swatches, click the **Edit Color** button in the **Standard** toolbar. The **Edit Color** dialog box appears as shown in Figure 3.29.

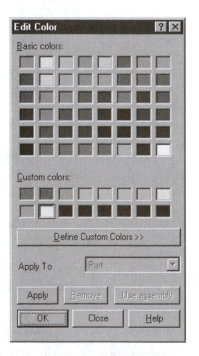

Figure 3.29. *Edit Color* dialog box.

3. Click any desired color and then click **OK**. The color of the handle changes to the new color. Experiment with other colors to find a color that looks realistic for the handle, selecting the part in the FeatureManager design tree each time. Be sure that the color is not too dark, so that the details of the part not will be difficult to see.

Congratulations! You have completed modeling the handle, a complicated part. Save the part as **handle**. Rotate the handle to see that it looks like the one shown at the beginning of this section. Close the window.

FILE TRANSFER BETWEEN CAD SYSTEMS

As the engineering world becomes more interconnected with e-mail and the Internet, engineering graphics are routinely transferred as electronic documents both within and outside of a company. Sometimes, this involves the need to import drawings created using one CAD system to a different CAD system. Each CAD system usually saves its files in its own format. Fortunately, several standard formats exist and can be used to transfer documents between different CAD programs. Translators are usually available within most CAD software to import and export data files that are in a standard format.

The most commonly used format for solids modeling applications is the Initial Graphics Exchange Specification, or IGES. Models may be imported to or exported from most CAD systems if the file is stored as an IGES transfer file (.igs). Unfortunately, IGES translators vary quite a bit and may sometimes give unexpected results, especially for the inexperienced user. Nevertheless, IGES is frequently used. Other standard file formats are available. STEP (.step) is capable of translating a solids model and maintaining it as such. DXF (.dxf) and DWG (.dwg) formats are intended for two-dimensional data, such as drawings.

SolidWorks can open a variety of file formats. In the **Open** dialog box, select the file format in the **Files of type** menu to show the different file types that SolidWorks can open. Files can be saved in standard formats using the **Save as type** menu in the **Save As** dialog box.

3.3   MODELING THE RIVET

The last part of the pizza cutter to model is the rivet, which secures the blade between the two arms. The rivet will be modeled to look as it would after being deformed to fasten the cutting blade to the arms. The rivet may look complicated in the three-dimensional views shown in Figure 3.30. However, its shape is more evident when shown in cross section, as in Figure 3.31. In the planning stages, imagining the cross section of a part helps in modeling complex shapes.

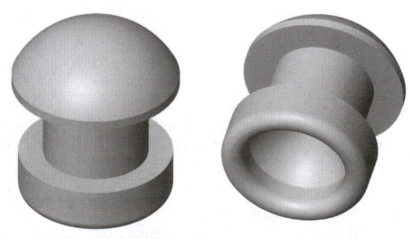

Figure 3.30. Finished rivet.

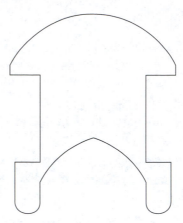

Figure 3.31.   Rivet cross section.

The rivet is symmetric about a vertical axis. Taking advantage of this symmetry makes the part easier to model. The rivet section shown in Figure 3.32 can be revolved about a vertical axis to model the part. You will add the round at the bottom of the rivet to complete the part using only two features (a revolved section and a fillet). This part could be modeled in a single feature, by adding the bottom round before the section is revolved. However, the section sketch to be revolved is already complicated, so the fillet will be added after revolving the section.

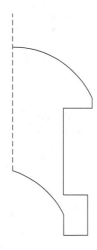

Figure 3.32.   Undimensioned rivet sketch.

3.3.1   Creating Arcs

The cross section of the rivet, shown in Figure 3.32, is based on arcs. There are three types of arc tools available in the **Sketch Tools** toolbar. Each arc tool uses a different geometric method to create an arc.

- A **Centerpoint Arc** starts with a point at the center of the arc. Then, both a radius and an angle are defined by selecting the start point and the endpoint of the arc.

- A **Tangent Arc** is tangent to an existing sketch entity.

- A **3 Point Arc** is defined by three points that lie on the arc (start point, endpoint, and midpoint).

You will be using a **3 Point Arc** and a **Centerpoint Arc** to sketch the cross section shown in in Figure 3.32, which will later be revolved to model the rivet. The first arc is the one at the bottom of the rivet.

1. Open a new sketch for a new part using the **tutorial part** template.
2. Click **3 Pt Arc** in the **Sketch Tools** toolbar, or **Tools** ⇒ **Sketch Entity** ⇒ **3 Point Arc**. A semicircle appears next to the cursor to indicate that an arc will be sketched.
3. Start the left end of the arc by clicking on the origin and dragging the cursor down and to the right as shown in Figure 3.33. Release the mouse button. This defines the location of the endpoints of the arc, but the arc is not yet finished. A third point must be defined. The screen should look like that shown in Figure 3.33, with a dashed arc and a point at the midpoint of the arc.

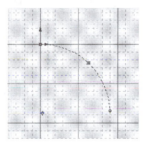

Figure 3.33. Arc drawn.

4. Click and drag the midpoint of the arc. As you drag the point, notice that both the angle and the radius of the arc are shown next to the cursor. Release the mouse button to finish the arc so that it is similar in shape to the arc shown in Figure 3.33. Be sure that the center of the arc (designated by a point at the center of the radius) is not directly below the origin. Also, be sure that the arc is not 90°. If either occurs, delete the arc and redraw it.

3.3.2   Drawing the Rest of the Sketch

1. Activate the **Line** tool and draw the seven line segments, as shown in Figure 3.34, to outline the shape of the rivet, starting at the bottom of the arc. You can use either the click-drag or click-click method of sketching. Be sure that each line is either horizontal or vertical, and that the endpoints of the lines are coincident.
2. If necessary, use the **Zoom In/Out** tool, so that there is space above the upper line segment that was just drawn. Then, draw a vertical **Centerline** that starts at the origin and extends vertically upward, well past the upper end of the line segments that were just sketched. This is the centerline for revolving the sketch.
3. The top arc of the sketch starts at the upper endpoint of the upper vertical line. The arc extends to the centerline and has a center point (denoted by the small cross) that lies on the centerline, as shown in Figure 3.35. Click the **Centerpoint Arc** button in the **Sketch Tools** toolbar, or

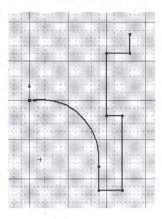

Figure 3.34. Lines added.

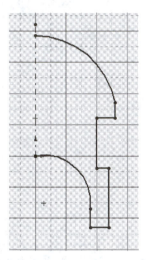

Figure 3.35. Second arc added.

Tools ⇒ **Sketch Entity** ⇒ **Centerpoint Arc**. Bring the cursor over the centerline. A lightbulb appears next to the cursor to indicate that it is pointing to the centerline. Click the left mouse button at a point that is both on the centerline and lies just above the origin. This places the center point.

4. Move the cursor to the upper endpoint of the upper vertical line. Look for the square indicating that the cursor is above the point. Click the left mouse button. This defines the first endpoint of the arc. **Zoom to Fit**, if necessary, in order to see the entire arc.

5. To define the second endpoint of the arc, click the left mouse button on the centerline when the light bulb appears at the cursor. This places the second endpoint on the centerline, directly above the origin. Be sure that the arc has one endpoint on the centerline and one endpoint on the upper end of the vertical line. Also, be sure that the arc's center point lies on the centerline. The sketch should look similar to that shown in Figure 3.35.

6. Create a closed sketch by drawing a vertical line that extends from the endpoint of the first arc (at the origin) to the endpoint of the second arc along the centerline. Since the section is a closed shape, it can be revolved to model a

solid object. Note that the sketch is *Under Defined*, since no dimensions have yet been added. You will add dimensions after revolving the sketch.

3.3.3 Revolving the Sketch

The rivet is modeled by revolving the sketch around the centerline. For previous parts, you were careful to constrain the sketch using dimensions and relations before revolving the section. In this case, the section will be revolved first, and the dimensions to fully define the model will be added later.

1. To revolve the sketch, click the **Revolved Boss/Base** button in the **Features** toolbar.

2. Revolve the sketch 360 degrees around the vertical centerline. The **Isometric** view of the part should look similar to that shown in Figure 3.36.

Figure 3.36. Undimensioned rivet.

3.3.4 Reopening the Sketch and Adding Dimensions

The revolve created a three-dimensional object without fully defining the sketch. You can go back and add dimensions to the sketch in order to constrain the geometry. The ability to make three-dimensional objects without fully defining a sketch is a useful tool for quickly displaying the approximate geometry of a part.

1. In the FeatureManager design tree, click on the plus sign (+) to the left of **Revolve1**. This displays the components of the revolve feature, namely **Sketch1**.

2. Right click **Sketch1** to highlight the sketched cross section that was revolved. Choose **Edit Sketch** from the menu. This hides the revolved feature and opens the sketch that was created before revolving the cross section.

3. Set the view to **Normal To**, so that the sketch plane is the plane of the screen.

4. With the **Dimension** tool, add dimensions to the radii of the arcs. This is done by clicking on each arc and then, clicking to place the dimension. The current radii should be similar to those in Figure 3.37. The "R" in front of the dimension indicates that the dimension describes the radius of the arc, not its diameter.

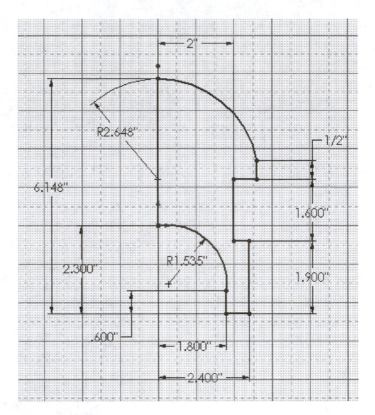

Figure 3.37.   Dimensions placed.

5.   With the **Dimension** tool still active, place the six vertical dimensions and the three horizontal dimensions, as shown in Figure 3.37. It may help to **Zoom In/Out** as you add dimensions. The values shown in the figure will probably be different than the values in your sketch. Do *not* change your dimensions to match the figure. When dimensioning, remember that you can dimension from point to point, line to line, or just dimension the length of the line. After placing the dimensions, the sketch should be *Fully Defined*.

6.   The dimension values that are now on the sketch are much larger than the ones necessary for the final part. For example, the height of the rivet is only .32 inches, but the present value is much larger (6.148 inches for the example in Figure 3.37). Changing all of the dimensions at once, rather than one at a time, keeps the sketch in proportion as the dimensions are modified. Uncheck the **Automatic Solve** feature in **Tools ⇒ Sketch Settings**. When this feature is unchecked, SolidWorks will not immediately change the length of the line when you modify the dimension value. Notice that the Status bar displays *Auto-Solve Mode Off*.

7.   Change each dimension as you normally would to match the values to those in Figure 3.38. With the automatic solve feature off, the geometry of the part does not change to correspond to the new dimensions.

8.   Be sure that all of the dimensions have been changed. Now that all of the dimensions reflect the desired values, click **Tools ⇒ Sketch Settings ⇒ Automatic Solve**, so that **Automatic Solve** is checked. The sketch adjusts itself to the smaller values. Zoom in to be sure that the part's geometry is similar to that shown in Figure 3.39. If it is not, undo the last operation and be sure that all of the dimensions are correct.

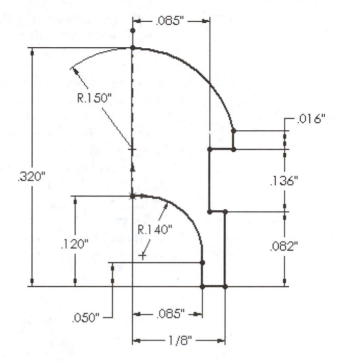

Figure 3.38. Dimensions updated.

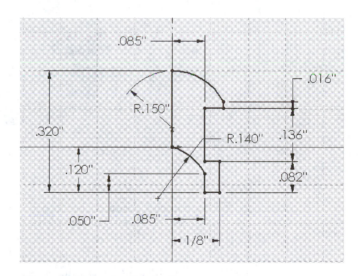

Figure 3.39. Sketch solved.

9. Since the final dimensions shown in Figure 3.38 are so different from the initially sketched dimensions, it will be necessary to move the dimensions closer to the sketched section using the **Select** tool and then **Zoom to Fit** or **Zoom In/Out** several times. It will also be necessary to shorten the centerline by dragging the endpoint with the **Select** tool. After several iterations of moving the dimensions closer to the section and zooming in, the sketch should look more like Figure 3.39. However, the font for the dimensions and the arrowheads may be much larger than in Figure 3.39. This is not a problem, as long as the sketch has the dimensions shown in the figure.

10. To exit the sketch, click on the **Sketch** button in the **Sketch** toolbar to turn off the sketch mode. The rivet is automatically rebuilt using the new sketch dimensions.

3.3.5 Rounding the Bottom of the Rivet

1. Previously, you had added fillets to round edges by selecting the edge. Fillets can also be used to round a face of a part. When a face is filleted, all of the edges that bound the face are rounded. To round the bottom of the rivet, rotate the part so that the bottom of the rivet can be seen.

2. Use the **Select** tool to highlight the flat face that forms the bottom of the rivet. The face becomes highlighted.

3. Click the **Fillet** button in the **Features** toolbar. *Face <1>* should appear in the *Fillet* PropertyManager.

4. Set the *Radius* to *.02* and click *OK*. The bottom of the rivet should look like the one in Figure 3.40. Return to the **Isometric** view.

Figure 3.40. Underside of finished rivet.

This completes the rivet. Save the part as *rivet* and close the window.

Congratulations! You have successfully modeled all six parts of the pizza cutter. The next chapter will take you through the assembly mode of SolidWorks to assemble these parts into a pizza cutter. Chapter 5 will describe how to create two-dimensional drawings of the parts and the assembly.

Problems

1. Model the blade using a revolve instead of an extrusion. Using the proper sketch, the entire blade can be modeled using a single revolve, with no other features needed.

2. Model the cap as a thin revolved section without the hole. Add the hole as a circular, extruded cut.

3. Measure the dimensions of a nail, and then, model it in two different ways:

    (a) Revolve a single cross section.

    (b) Extrude a cylinder the size of the head, and then revolve cuts to make the shaft of the nail and sharp point.

4. Model the handle by revolving a sketch of a rectangle. After revolving the section, revolve a cut at the bottom end of the handle to model the reduced diameter. Then, round the top end of the handle. Finish the handle by adding the holes and the grooves.

5. Model the handle by extruding a circle along its axis to create the base feature. Then, model the reduced diameter at the rectangular-hole end of the handle using a revolved cut. Add the grooves as a revolved feature, and finish by adding the holes and the rounds.

6. Model a hollow handle with an outer geometry identical to the handle in this chapter. The hollow core should have a uniform diameter of .5 inches. Omit the rectangular hole at the bottom of the handle.

4

Modeling an Assembly: The Pizza Cutter

OVERVIEW

A key feature of SolidWorks is the capability to assemble parts in a virtual environment. This feature allows an engineer to check fits and interference between parts and to visualize the overall assembly. Assembly involves orienting parts with respect to each other. Once assembled, the interference between parts can be checked. Then, errors in the design of individual parts can be corrected.

4.1 MODELING THE CUTTER SUB-ASSEMBLY

One of the great advantages of SolidWorks is that it allows engineers or designers to assemble modeled parts in order to create a virtual assembly. This helps the designer to work out problems with part interactions early in the design phase, before manufacturing has begun. SolidWorks has features that automatically check for both clearances and interference between parts in an assembly. It also permits the engineer or designer to get an idea of what the assembled object looks like before it is fabricated.

In SolidWorks, an assembly begins by bringing a single part into an assembly document and orienting it with respect to the planes of the assembly. Then, additional parts are brought into the document one at a time and oriented with respect to the first part. Once all of the parts have been assembled, the assembly can be checked for interference, or overlap, between parts.

In this chapter, you will use the parts modeled in the previous sections to make an assembly of the pizza cutter. Do not begin this section until all parts of the pizza cutter

OBJECTIVES

After working through this chapter, you will be able to

- Open a new assembly,
- Create a sub-assembly,
- Bring parts into an assembly or sub-assembly,
- Orient and constrain parts with respect to datum planes and other parts,
- Check for interference in an assembly,
- Correct errors in parts while assembling, and
- Create an exploded view of an assembly.

have been modeled. First, you will model the cutter sub-assembly, which consists of the blade, the rivet, and the two arms. The final cutter sub-assembly is shown in Figure 4.1.

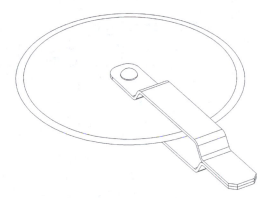

Figure 4.1. Finished cutter sub-assembly.

4.1.1   Creating a New Assembly Document

The assembly process begins with a new document, called an assembly document, which differs from a part document.

1. With the SolidWorks window open, click **File ⇒ New**.

2. Instead of choosing to make a new part at this point, select *Assem* in the dialog box and click *OK*.

3. A new assembly window opens, named **Assem1**. Note the seven items present in the FeatureManager design tree: annotations, lighting, three datum planes, the origin, and mates (related to mating parts together).

4. In the **View ⇒ Toolbars** menu, be sure that **Assembly**, **Selection Filter**, **Sketch**, **Standard**, **Standard Views**, and **View** are checked, so that these toolbars appear on the screen.

5. The **Selection Filter** toolbar, shown in Figure 4.2, is used to restrict the type of items that can be selected. If the toolbar appears as a dialog box, drag the blue bar at the top of the dialog box to just below the **Standard** toolbar to change it into a toolbar. If the entire toolbar is not visible, click on the double bars at the end of the toolbar, drag the toolbar to just below the **Standard** toolbar and release the mouse button. Each toolbar button represents a particular type of entity. When a part is clicked with the **Select** tool, only the types of items activated in the **Selection Filter** toolbar can be selected. This is helpful in selecting the desired item during assembly. For instance, if the **Filter Faces** button is active, the Select tool will only select faces (surfaces) of the part. Move the cursor over each button in the **Selection Filter** toolbar to see what items can be selected. One or several buttons can be activated at one time. Since faces are most commonly used to orient parts in an assembly, activate the **Filter Faces** button, to allow only faces to be selected. A filter icon appears next to the cursor, indicating that a filter is active. If the cursor is above a surface, the filter icon will change to an icon of a surface.

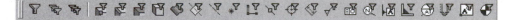

Figure 4.2.   **Selection Filter** toolbar.

6. In the **<u>View</u>** toolbar, click the **<u>Hidden Lines Removed</u>** button. This makes it easier to decipher the various components of the assembly. In addition, select **View ⇒ Origins**, so the origin of the assembly is visible.

4.1.2   Bringing the Rivet into the Sub-Assembly

Assemblies and sub-assemblies can consist of many parts. The first part inserted into the assembly is usually the foundation for all of the parts that are added later. In this case, you will use the rivet as the first part.

1. To insert the rivet into the assembly, select **Insert ⇒ Component ⇒ From File**.

2. Go through the file structure and find the rivet, as indicated in the dialog box that is shown in Figure 4.3. Be sure the ***Files of type*** pull-down menu is set to ***Part***, so that the rivet file is displayed. Highlight the file named **rivet** (which was modeled in the previous chapter) and click ***Open***.

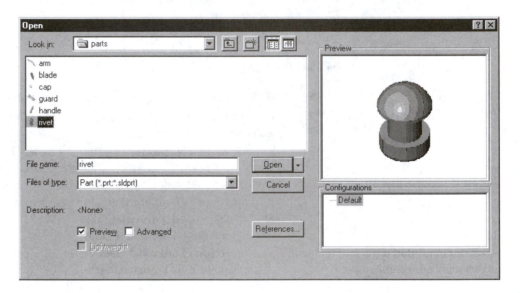

Figure 4.3.   ***Open*** dialog box.

3. A part symbol appears next to the cursor, signifying that the selected part will be placed in the assembly. Bring the cursor over the origin. Two right-angled sets of arrows appear at the cursor. This means that the planes of the assembly and the planes of the rivet will be matched. When this symbol appears, click on the origin to place the part. The rivet appears with its origin coincident with the origin of the assembly and its planes coincident with the planes of the assembly, as shown in Figure 4.4. You may need to **Zoom In/Out** to enlarge the rivet.

4. Notice that **(f) rivet<1>** has appeared in the FeatureManager design tree. The "f" means that the rivet is fixed in the assembly space. The "1" means that this is the first instance of the rivet in the assembly. Click the plus sign (+) next to **rivet** to show all of its features, just as when the part was being modeled. Click on the minus sign next to **rivet** in the FeatureManager design tree to hide the features of the rivet.

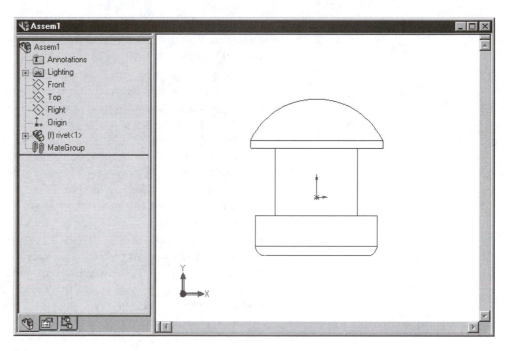

Figure 4.4.   Rivet placed in assembly environment.

5.   For clarity, uncheck **View** ⇒ **Origins**. This removes the arrows indicating the origin of the assembly.

4.1.3   Bringing the Arm into the Assembly and Orienting It

Now the second part, the arm, is brought into the assembly and oriented with respect to the rivet.

1.   To bring the arm into the assembly, click **Insert** ⇒ **Component** ⇒ **From File**. Find the arm part and *Open* it.

2.   Again, the cursor changes. In this assembly, only the rivet will be oriented with the origin of the assembly. Other parts will be oriented with respect to the rivet. Place the arm in the assembly by clicking anywhere on the screen. Notice that, in the FeatureManager design tree, (−), **arm<1>** appears. The minus sign indicates that the arm is free to move in space. **Zoom to Fit** to see both components of the assembly.

3.   With the **Select** tool, click on any face of the arm. You may need to rotate the view. The selected face becomes highlighted, and a box appears around the entire arm, signifying that the part is selected.

4.   The **Assembly** toolbar, shown in Figure 4.5, is used to control both the movement and the placement of parts in an assembly. The **Assembly** toolbar may be vertical rather than horizontal, as shown in the figure. You can

Figure 4.5.   **Assembly** toolbar.

move the toolbar to another position by dragging the double bars at the end of the toolbar. The rightmost tools in the **Assembly** toolbar shown in Figure 4.5 are used to move parts within an assembly:

- The **Move Component** button (a hand holding a part) translates a part relative to the other parts in the assembly.
- The **Rotate Component** button (a part with rotation arrows around it) rotates a part around its own centerpoint, or origin. To use the **Move Component** and the **Rotate Component** tools, select a face of the part that you want to move. Next, click on the **Move Component** or **Rotate Component** button in the **Assembly** toolbar. Then, click and drag to orient the part. These two tools can also be found under **Tools** ⇒ **Component** ⇒ **Move** and **Tools** ⇒ **Component** ⇒ **Rotate**.

5. Practice orienting the arm in various ways, using the **Move Component** and **Rotate Component** tools. If you select the rivet and try to move or rotate it, a dialog box alerts you that fixed components cannot be moved. Since the arm has not yet been fixed relative to the rivet, it can move and rotate freely. The PropertyManager window, which replaces the FeatureManager design tree when a part is moved or rotated, provides information about the position of the selected part. Orient the arm so that the hole in the arm is close to the rivet, similar to the orientation shown in Figure 4.6.

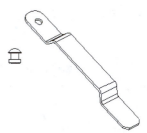

Figure 4.6. Arm positioned near the rivet.

4.1.4   Adding a Concentric Mate

After placing the first part, subsequent parts are oriented relative to other parts in the assembly using mates. For example, you will place the hole of the arm around the rivet with two mates: one concentric mate to match the hole's axis with the rivet's axis and another mate to match the top face of the end of the arm with the underside face of the head of the rivet.

1. Click the **Zoom to Area** button in the **View** toolbar and zoom in on the hole and the rivet.

2. Select the cylindrical surface of the rivet, shown in Figure 4.7, using the **Select** tool. It will become highlighted. Add the cylindrical surface of the hole in the arm to the selection by *control clicking* the surface. Notice that it is easy to select surfaces because the **Selection Filter** is set so that only surfaces can be selected. These two surfaces, which will be mated, are shown in Figure 4.7.

3. With the two surfaces selected, click the **Mate** button (a paper clip) in the **Assembly** toolbar, or select **Insert** ⇒ **Mate**.

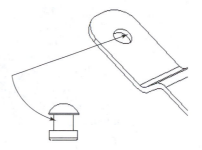

Figure 4.7.   Arm and rivet surfaces for the concentric mate.

4.   The *Mate* PropertyManager replaces the FeatureManager design tree, as shown in Figure 4.8. In the *Selections* field, the two faces that were selected are listed with their respective parts. Click the *Concentric* button (a circle) in the PropertyManager. A concentric mate constrains the parts so that circular features share the same axis.

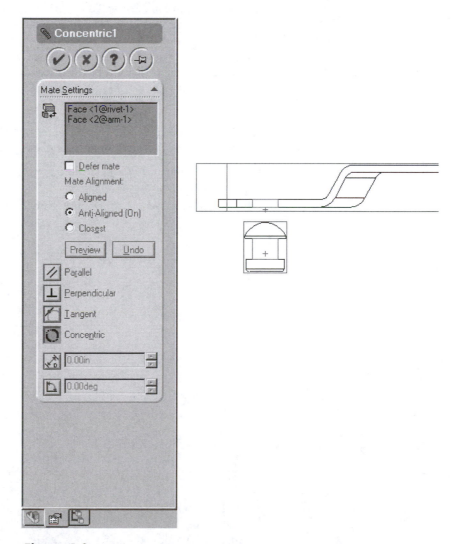

Figure 4.8.   *Concentric* PropertyManager.

5.   Click the ***Preview*** button in the PropertyManager. SolidWorks adjusts the position of the arm to show what the assembly will look like after the mate is created. The screen should look similar to that shown in Figure 4.8 in the **Front** orientation. Note that the shaft of the rivet and the hole in the arm are aligned. It does not matter if the arm is above or below the rivet. If the arm is upside down, click the ***Aligned*** button below ***Mate Alignment*** to flip the arm and ***Preview*** again. Click ***OK*** (the green check mark) to create the mate.

6.   In the FeatureManager design tree, click on the plus sign next to **Mates**. The mate that was just created, **Concentric1 (rivet <1>, arm <1>)**, is listed. You may need to move the border between the SolidWorks window and the FeatureManager design tree in order to see the entire name. To do this, move the cursor over the border between the FeatureManager design tree window and the Graphics Window until it becomes two vertical lines with horizontal arrows. Then, drag the border. As more and more mates are created, refer to the list under **Mates** to keep track of them.

7.   A part can be moved with respect to the other components using the **Move Component** tool. **Zoom To Fit** and select the arm. Move it with the **Move Component** tool. The concentric mate constrains the hole in the arm to be concentric with the rivet. As a result, the arm can only be moved along the axis of the rivet or rotated around the rivet's axis. Go to the **Front** view. Move the arm so that it is below the rivet.

4.1.5   Adding a Coincident Mate

The arm must be further constrained so that its top face is touching the underside face of the head of the rivet. This is called a *coincident* mate, since the plane of the arm's top face coincides with the plane of the underside of the rivet's head.

1.   Use the **Rotate View** tool in the **View** toolbar to rotate the view so that the top face of the arm is visible.

2.   Select the top face, as shown in Figure 4.9.

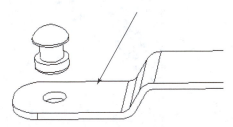

Figure 4.9. Arm surface for the coincident mate.

3.   Reactivate the **Rotate View** tool and rotate the view so that the underside of the head of the rivet is visible. Click the **Rotate View** button again. This turns off the **Rotate View** tool and activates the **Select** tool. *Control click* on the face, as shown in Figure 4.10, to add it to the selection. Be sure that both the top face of the arm and the underside face of the rivet head are highlighted, to indicate both are selected. If not, move the cursor to an open space away from both parts, click, and start over.

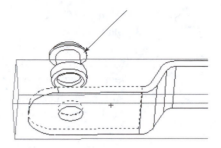

Figure 4.10.   Rivet surface for the coincident mate.

4.   Click the **<u>Mate</u>** button in the **<u>Assembly</u>** toolbar. The face of the arm and the face of the rivet should be listed in the ***Selections*** field. Click the ***Coincident*** button. A coincident mate simply places two surfaces against each other, so that the surfaces are in the same plane.

5.   ***Preview*** the mate. It might help to turn on the **Shaded** display and rotate the view. If the mate looks wrong, click the ***Close*** button (a red X) in the PropertyManager, and start over. Otherwise, click *OK* and return to **Hidden Lines Removed**.

4.1.6   Assembling the Blade

The blade is added next. It will have two mates in the assembly. The hole of the blade is concentric with the cylindrical shaft of the rivet, and one face of the blade is coincident with the bottom face of the arm.

1.   Go to the **Front** view.

2.   Bring the blade into the assembly and place it near the other parts.

3.   Select a surface of the blade. Use **Move Component** and **Rotate Component** to position the blade so that you can see both the hole in the blade and the shaft of the rivet. Select both of these surfaces, as indicated in Figure 4.11. Be sure to *control click* the second surface.

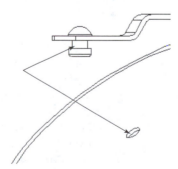

Figure 4.11.   Blade and rivet surfaces for the concentric mate.

4.   With the two surfaces selected, create a concentric mate. It may help to **Redraw** the screen after the mate.

5.   Click on the blade, and use the **Move Component** tool to move the blade below the arm and the rivet.

6. With the **Rotate View** tool, rotate the view so that the top surface of the blade can be seen. Then, rotate the view to see the bottom surface of the arm. If the blade obstructs the view of the arm, use the **Move Component** tool to move the blade further below the arm. This will make it easier to select the two surfaces. Rotate the view and select the top surface of the blade.

7. Reactivate the **Rotate View** tool and rotate the view so that the bottom face of the arm is visible. Click the <u>**Rotate View**</u> button again to turn off the **Rotate View** tool. *Control click* the bottom face of the arm. The two surfaces to be mated are shown in Figure 4.12.

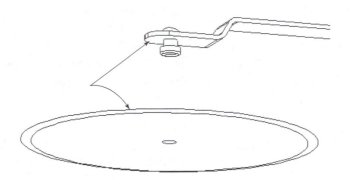

Figure 4.12. Blade and arm surfaces for the coincident mate.

8. Create a coincident mate between the selected surfaces and *Preview* the mate. It may help to turn on **Shaded** display and to rotate the view. Click *OK* and return to **Hidden Lines Removed**.

4.1.7 Assembling the Second Arm

Although the assembly has two arms, only one part was modeled, because the two arms are identical. Now, a second arm is brought into the assembly and added to the other side of the blade.

1. Bring the arm into the assembly and place it below the existing components. Notice that a **<2>** appears next to **arm** in the FeatureManager design tree. This means that it is the second arm brought into the assembly.

2. Use the **Move Component** and **Rotate Component** tools to move and rotate the second arm. Place the second arm so that it closely mirrors the first arm and the hole is close to the rivet, as shown in Figure 4.13. It may help to use the **Shaded** display as you orient the arm. Then, return to **Hidden Lines Removed** display.

3. Apply a mate so that the hole of the arm is concentric with the shaft of the rivet. *Preview* the mate before clicking *OK*. If the second arm does not mirror the first, click the *Aligned* or the *Anti-Aligned (On)* button in the *Mate Alignment* field to flip it. *Preview* the mate again and click *OK*.

4. Select the bottom surface of the blade and the facing surface of the arm, as indicated in Figure 4.13. Create a coincident mate between the two selected surfaces.

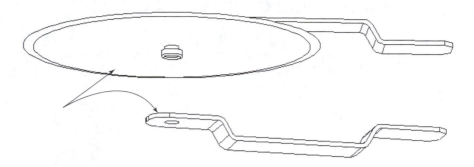

Figure 4.13. Second arm and blade selections for the coincident mate.

4.1.8   Adding a Parallel Mate

The arms can still rotate relative to each other, so they are probably not parallel to one another at this point. A parallel mate will constrain the arms so that they are aligned with each other.

1.   Move one of the arms with the **Move Component** tool so that the two arms are approximately aligned with each other.

2.   Select the side face (edge) of both arms, as indicated in Figure 4.14.

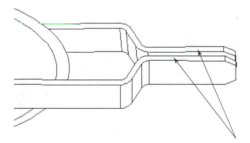

Figure 4.14. Arms surfaces for parallel mate.

3.   Click the **Mate** button in the **Assembly** toolbar. In the *Mate* Property-Manager, click the *Parallel* button. This makes the two edge surfaces parallel to each other, removing any angle between the two arms.

4.   When you are satisfied with the *Preview*, click *OK* to create the mate.

5.   With the parallel mate applied, one arm moves with the other. Try this using the **Move Component** tool. Turn off the **Move Component** tool by clicking its toolbar button or the green check mark.

Congratulations! This completes the cutter sub-assembly. The assembly should look like the one shown in Figure 4.1. **Save** the assembly as *cutter sub-assembly*. SolidWorks may ask you if you want to rebuild the assembly. Answer *Yes*, so that the changes that you have made will be implemented before saving. Since you will be using this sub-assembly in the next section, leave the **cutter sub-assembly** window open.

4.2   MODELING THE PIZZA CUTTER ASSEMBLY

In this section, the cutter sub-assembly will be joined with the handle, the cap, and the guard to complete the pizza cutter assembly. The final pizza cutter assembly is shown in Figure 4.15.

Figure 4.15.   Finished pizza cutter assembly.

4.2.1   Creating a New Assembly and Inserting the Handle

A new assembly is created for the entire pizza cutter.

1.   Click the **New** toolbar button or **File ⇒ New** to model a new assembly. Select **Assem** and **OK**. Select **View ⇒ Origins** to display the origin.

2.   Select the **Grid** button in the **Sketch** toolbar. In the **Document Properties** tab, select **Units**. Set **Linear Units** to **Inches** to match this tutorial.

3.   Bring the handle into the assembly by clicking **Insert ⇒ Component ⇒ From File**. Remember to set the **Files of type** pull-down menu to **Part files**. Bring the cursor over the origin so that the two right-angled sets of arrows appear. Place the handle at the origin. This orients the planes of the handle with the planes of the assembly, so that the origins coincide.

4.   Be sure that the **Filter Faces** toolbar button is selected, so that only faces of parts can be selected. Turn off **Origins** in the **View** menu to hide the origin. Set the view to **Hidden Lines Removed**. Now you are ready to begin assembling the rest of the pizza cutter.

4.2.2   Assembling the Cap

The next part added to the assembly is the cap. It is placed on the end of the handle with the reduced diameter.

1.   Bring the cap into the assembly and place it near the bottom of the handle.

2.   Select the cap and rotate it using **Rotate Component Around Centerpoint**, so that the concave side faces the bottom of the handle.

3.   Select the two surfaces, as shown in Figure 4.16.

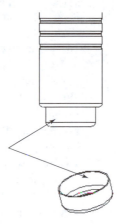

Figure 4.16.   Handle and cap surfaces for the concentric mate.

4.   Click the <u>**Mate**</u> button in the <u>**Assembly**</u> toolbar, or click **Insert** ⇒ **Mate**, to mate the two cylindrical surfaces.

5.   In the *Mate* PropertyManager, click the *Concentric* button. If the *Preview* shows the cap facing the wrong direction, click *Aligned* in the *Mate Alignment* field to flip the cap. Click *OK* to create the mate. Check the constraint by selecting the cap and using the **Move Component** tool. The cap should only move along the axis of the handle.

6.   A second constraint is needed to position the cap at the end of the handle. Select the inside flat surface of the cap and the bottom surface at the end of the handle. You will need to rotate the view to select both surfaces. The inside surface of the cap that should be selected is shown in Figure 4.17.

Figure 4.17.   Cap surface for the coincident mate.

7.   Create a coincident mate between the two surfaces in order to bring the inside of the cap up to the bottom surface at the end of the handle. Switch to the **Shaded** view to see the cap on the handle clearly. If the preview appears to be correct, click *OK*. Then, return to **Hidden Lines Removed**.

4.2.3   Assembling the Guard

The guard is placed on the bottom face of the cap and aligned so that the axis of the hole in the guard coincides with the axis of the handle.

1. Insert the guard into the assembly and place it near the cap.

2. Mate the surface of the guard to the bottom surface of the cap using a coincident mate. Be sure to select the surface of the cap, rather than the handle. When the **Select** tool is over the correct surface of the cap, a box should pop up near the cursor, indicating **Revolve-Thin1 of cap<1>**. The guard may not actually touch the cap after the mate has been created. The planes of the surfaces, which have infinite length, have been mated. To see this, go to the **Front** view. Then, move the guard from side to side. Although it can move left or right, the plane of the upper surface of the guard will always remain coincident with the lower surface of the cap, as shown in Figure 4.18. Click **OK** to turn off the **Move Component** tool.

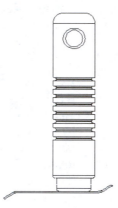

Figure 4.18.   Guard mated to cap.

3. To fully constrain the position of the guard, you can match the planes of the guard with the fixed planes of the assembly. Click on the plus sign next to **guard** in the FeatureManager design tree. It should look similar to Figure 4.19. The features of the guard are displayed, including its three planes. Move the cursor over each of the planes to view their location. Similarly, view the planes of the assembly in the FeatureManager design tree. You will be mating the **Front** plane and the **Right** plane of the guard to the **Front** plane and the **Right** plane of the assembly, respectively.

4. Click on the **Front** plane of the **guard** in the FeatureManager design tree. The plane becomes highlighted.

5. Control click the **Front** plane of the assembly in the FeatureManager design tree (under **Assem2** in Figure 4.19) to add it to the selection.

6. Click the **Mate** button in the **Assembly** toolbar. Both planes should be listed in the **Selections** field. Set the mate type to be a **Coincident** mate and click **OK**. This aligns the **Front** plane of the guard to the **Front** plane of the assembly.

7. Mate the **Right** plane of the guard to the **Right** plane of the assembly in the same way. This completely constrains the position of the guard relative to the handle. Click the minus sign next to the **guard** in the FeatureManager design tree.

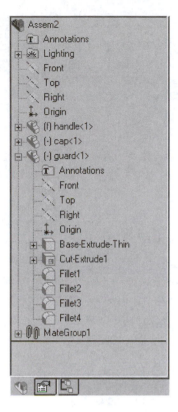

Figure 4.19.   FeatureManager design tree.

4.2.4   Hiding an Object

The next component to be added to the assembly is the cutter sub-assembly. The arms of the cutter sub-assembly will be inserted into the rectangular hole at the end of the handle. Since the guard partially covers the view of the hole, you will temporarily hide the guard, so that the mate between the handle and the cutter sub-assembly can be created more easily.

1. *Right click* **guard** in the FeatureManager design tree.
2. Select **Hide components** from the menu that appears. The guard is now hidden. The outlined part icon to the left of **guard** in the FeatureManager design tree indicates that the guard is not shown on the screen.

4.2.5   Inserting the Sub-Assembly into the Assembly

A sub-assembly can be mated, moved, and rotated just like any part in an assembly. Here, the cutter sub-assembly will be added to the main assembly.

1. If necessary, maximize the SolidWorks window by clicking the <u>**Maximize**</u> button in the upper right corner of the Graphics Window, to provide enough space for the assembly. Then, select **Window** ⇒ **Tile Horizontally** to see all of the active windows. If the cutter sub-assembly has been closed, click **File** ⇒ **Open** to open it. Then, select **Window** ⇒ **Tile Horizontally** again. The screen should look similar to that shown in Figure 4.20.
2. In the FeatureManager design tree of the cutter sub-assembly window, click and drag **cutter sub-assembly** to the main assembly window (above the sub-assembly window). The component icon appears next to the cursor, signifying

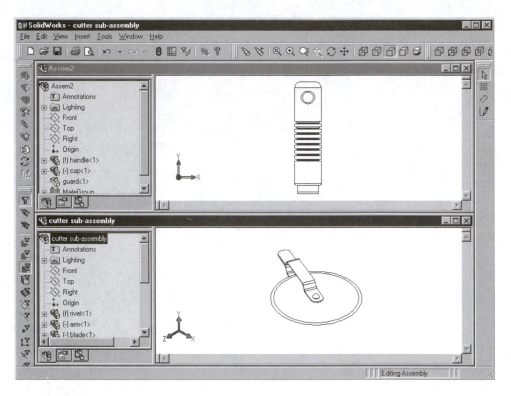

Figure 4.20. Assembly and sub-assembly windows.

that a component is being brought into the assembly. Release the mouse button to place the cutter sub-assembly in the main assembly window.

3. Maximize the main assembly window, so that you have more room to work. If necessary, **Zoom to Fit** to show both the cutter sub-assembly and the handle.

4. Move and rotate the cutter sub-assembly, so that the ends of the arms are close to the rectangular hole at the end of the handle. Be sure that the **<u>Filter Faces</u>** toolbar button is selected.

5. Zoom in as shown in Figure 4.21. Select the flat face of one of the arms and the long side of the inside of the rectangular hole of the handle. You will need to rotate the view to select both surfaces. To ensure a correct mate, the surfaces should be facing each other.

6. Use a coincident mate to make the two faces coplanar. While previewing the mate, go to the **Left** view and turn on **Hidden Lines Visible** to see the hidden lines. If the arm looks like it will interfere with the handle instead of fitting into the hole, flip the cutter sub-assembly by clicking either ***Aligned*** or ***Anti-Aligned (On)*** in the ***Mate*** PropertyManager. Click ***Apply***. Return to **Hidden Lines Removed**.

7. Rotate the view and zoom in as necessary to see the short side of the inside surface of the rectangular hole in the handle. Select the short side, as shown in Figure 4.22. Rotate the view and add the edge of the arm to the selection, as shown in Figure 4.22.

8. Add a coincident mate between these two surfaces so that they are coplanar. ***Preview*** the position in the **Front** view. Click ***OK***.

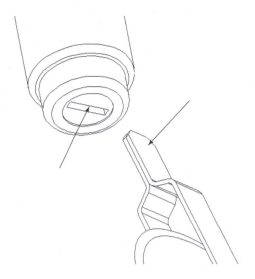

Figure 4.21.   Arm and handle surfaces for the coincident mate.

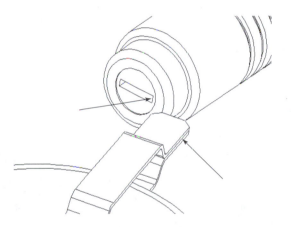

Figure 4.22.   Short side of the arm and handle for the coincident mate.

4.2.6   Showing the Guard and Finishing the Assembly

The cutter sub-assembly can still move along the axis of the handle. To fully constrain the sub-assembly, it will be mated to the guard.

1. Make the guard visible by *right clicking* on **guard** in the FeatureManager design tree and selecting **Show components**. The guard reappears.

2. In the following steps, you will mate an edge of the arm to the face of the guard. Rotate the view of the assembly, zoom in, and select the face of the guard closest to the cutter sub-assembly, as shown in Figure 4.23.

3. Since an edge will be selected next, turn on the **Filter Edges** button and turn off the **Filter Faces** button in the **Selection Filter** toolbar. Add the edge of the bend in the arm to the selection, as shown in Figure 4.23. This edge is the line along which the curved corner meets the flat face of the arm. If you cannot see the edge, be sure that **View** ⇒ **Display** ⇒ **Tangent Edges Visible** is checked.

Figure 4.23.   Arm and guard selections for the coincident mate.

4. Click the **Mate** button in the **Assembly** toolbar and add a coincident mate. This makes the line forming the edge of the arm coincident with the plane of the face of the guard. In other words, the line of the edge of the arm is constrained to be in the plane of the face of the guard. Click **Preview** and then **OK**. The assembly should look like the one in Figure 4.24.

Figure 4.24.   Finished assembly.

5. Because you have finished creating the assembly, you will not need the selection filters from now on. Click the **Clear All Filters** toolbar button to turn off the filters.

Congratulations! This completes the assembly. Rebuild your assembly by clicking the **Rebuild** button (a stoplight) in the **Standard** toolbar, or **Edit** ⇒ **Rebuild**. Save your work as *pizza cutter*. Leave the **pizza cutter** window open for the next section, in which you will check the assembly for interference. Close the **cutter sub-assembly** window by clicking on it in the **Window** menu, followed by **File** ⇒ **Close**.

4.3   CHECKING THE ASSEMBLY FOR INTERFERENCE

Now that you have successfully assembled the pizza cutter, the next task is to determine whether the parts fit together properly. SolidWorks simply assembles the parts using the specified placements. It does not immediately check to determine whether any part interferes with another part. However, SolidWorks has built-in functionality to check for these types of design errors. This is done by comparing the solid volumes and placements of every part in the assembly to find interference between components.

4.3.1   Checking for Interference Volumes

The interference-detection feature of SolidWorks will be used to determine whether any of the components of the pizza cutter interfere.

1.   Be sure that the **pizza cutter** window is open. Click on **Tools ⇒ Interference Detection**. The ***Interference Volumes*** dialog box appears.

2.   If the ***pizza cutter*** assembly does not already appear on the ***Selected components*** list, select it in the FeatureManager design tree. The position of each part in the assembly will be checked in relation to its neighboring components.

3.   Click the ***Check*** button to have SolidWorks check for interference. Solid-Works generates a list of the interferences in the assembly. ***Interference1*** and ***Interference2*** should appear under the ***Interference results*** box. Change the display to **Hidden Lines Visible**, and zoom in to the cap of the pizza cutter. Click on each item on the ***Interference results*** list to see the location of each highlighted interference on the assembly, as shown in Figure 4.25. When you click on any interference on the ***Interference results*** list, its

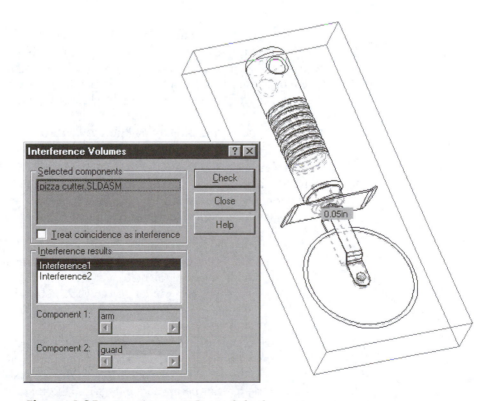

Figure 4.25. ***Interference Volumes*** dialog box.

volume is highlighted on the assembly. The components that are interfering are shown next to **Component 1:** and **Component 2:** just below the *Interference Results* box. In this case, each interference is between the guard and one of the arms. A close-up of one of the interferences is shown in Figure 4.26.

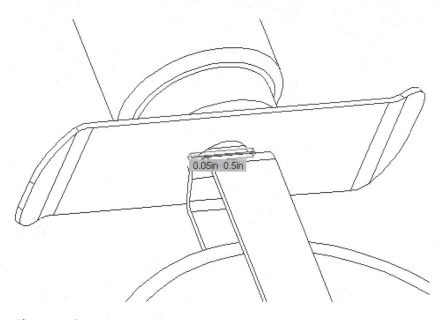

Figure 4.26.   Interference close-up.

After clicking each interference, it becomes evident that the rectangular arms are too wide to fit through the circular hole in the guard. To remedy this, you will reopen the guard part file and change the circular hole to a rectangular hole. The assembly will be rebuilt once the guard is modified to incorporate the redesigned hole. To continue, close the *Interference Volumes* dialog box by clicking *Close*.

4.3.2   Opening a Sketch Within the Guard

Two options are available to edit the geometry of the guard. The first option, **Edit Part**, permits changes in the properties of the part while still in the assembly window. This is useful for changing the values of dimensions and making other minor changes. The second option, **Open guard.sldprt**, opens the **guard** file in a new window. It is easier to make major changes to an individual part using this option.

1.   Bring the **Select** tool over the guard in the Graphics Window and *right click* on it. Select **Open guard.sldprt** from the menu. You may need to click the double arrows at the bottom of the menu to see all of the options. The guard opens in its own window. If you click on the **Window** menu, you can see that the pizza cutter assembly is still available. The assembly window is behind the **guard** window.

2.   The features that were modeled in the guard are listed in the FeatureManager design tree. **Cut-Extrude1** represents the hole. Click on the plus sign to the left of **Cut-Extrude1**. **Sketch2** is the sketch of the circular hole. This sketch can be opened and revised, so that a rectangle replaces the circle.

When you exit the sketch, the model of the guard will be "rebuilt" and the hole will be rectangular.

3. Right click **Sketch2** and select **Edit Sketch** from the menu. This opens the sketch. Set the view **Normal To** the guard's face.

4.3.3 Creating the Rectangular Hole

Now that the circular cut is visible in its sketch plane, you can change the hole to a rectangular one.

1. With the **Select** tool, click on the circle. It will become highlighted in green. Hit the Delete key on the keyboard, or **Edit ⇒ Delete**, to remove the circle. The dialog box shown in Figure 4.27 appears. This dialog box is referring to the dimension on the circle which will be removed when the circle is deleted. You need to delete this dimension, so click **Yes**. The circle and the dimension are removed from the sketch.

Figure 4.27. *Sketcher Confirm Delete* dialog box.

2. Activate the **Rectangle** tool in the **Sketch Tools** toolbar, or **Tools ⇒ Sketch Entity ⇒ Rectangle**. Draw a rectangle that surrounds the origin by clicking to the bottom left of the origin and dragging the rectangle above and to the right of the origin.

3. Place the four dimensions, as shown in Figure 4.28. These dimensions describe the size of the rectangle and locate the rectangle relative to the origin. Your dimensions will likely be different. Do *not* edit the numerical dimensions to match those in Figure 4.28.

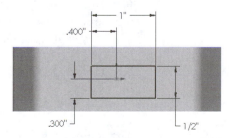

Figure 4.28. Rectangular-hole sketch.

4.3.4 Adding Equations to Dimensions

When dimensioning, it is sometimes useful to describe dimensions using *equations* rather than entering numeric values. For example, one dimension can be set to be two times the value of another dimension. If the first dimension ever changes, the second dimension will be updated accordingly. In this sketch, you will add equations to the rectangle's dimensions to ensure that the rectangle is always centered about the origin.

1. Activate the **Select** tool. Then, click **Tools ⇒ Equations**. The ***Equations*** dialog box appears.

2. Click on the numerical value for vertical dimension, which happens to be .300" in the sketch shown in Figure 4.29. Click ***Add*** in the ***Equations*** dialog box to add the dimension to the new equation. "**D2@Sketch2**" or something similar appears in the ***New Equation*** dialog box, as shown in the figure. In the example that is shown, the "D2" means that it is the second dimension placed in **Sketch2**. Since the "2" reflects the order in which the dimensions were placed, your number may be different.

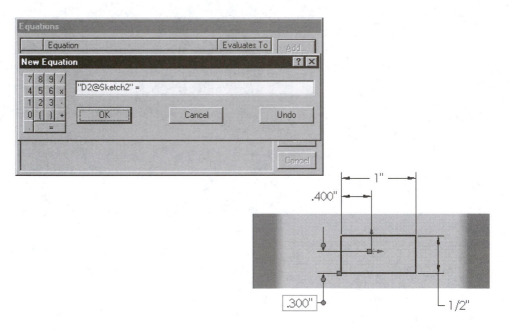

Figure 4.29. *New Equation* dialog box.

3. Click on the other vertical dimension in the sketch, which happens to be 1/2" in Figure 4.29. This adds ***"D1@Sketch2"*** to the equation. (Again, your number may be different.)

4. Type in "***/2***" (without the quotes) at the end of the equation by using the keyboard, or by clicking on items on the keypad in the ***New Equation*** dialog box. This sets the smaller vertical dimension to be half of the larger vertical dimension. The entire string should look something like this:

$$\text{"D\#@Sketch2"} = \text{"D\#@Sketch2"}/2$$

The pound symbols represent different dimension numbers specific to your sketch.

5. Click **OK**. The equation is listed in the dialog box, and the value of the smaller vertical dimension is shown in the ***Evaluates To*** column. Be sure that the smaller dimension is half the value of the larger vertical dimension. The dimension on the sketch will not yet update. If you need to edit an equation, click the ***Edit All*** button.

6. Repeat Steps 2 through 5 to create an equation that makes the value of the shorter horizontal dimension half of the longer horizontal dimension. Click **OK** in the ***Equations*** dialog box when you are done. Now, the dimensions on the sketch update to the values prescribed by the equations.

7. Since there are two "free" dimensions and two dimensions with which equations are associated, you only need to define two of the four dimensions in this sketch. With the **Select** tool, double click the larger vertical dimension. Set the value to **.096** and click on the green check mark. The smaller vertical dimension value should automatically update to **.048**.

8. Set the larger horizontal dimension to be **1/2**. This sets the value of the smaller horizontal dimension to **1/4**. The rectangle should be centered at the origin. Note that, if you attempt to adjust a dimension driven by an equation, SolidWorks will warn you that the value cannot be changed.

9. Exit the sketch by clicking on the <u>**Sketch**</u> button in the <u>**Sketch**</u> toolbar or by clicking on the **Exit Sketch** icon in the upper right Confirmation Corner of the Graphics Window. Because **Cut-Extrude1** is defined to cut the sketch through the part (regardless of the shape of the cut), the guard rebuilds with a rectangular hole.

10. Before returning to the assembly, save the guard with the same name by selecting **File ⇒ Save**, or by using the <u>**Save**</u> toolbar button.

4.3.5   Rebuilding the Pizza Cutter Assembly with the New Guard

Now you can rebuild the pizza cutter assembly with the modified guard.

1. Select **pizza cutter** from the **Window** menu to return to the assembly. The dialog box shown in Figure 4.30 appears, asking if the model should be rebuilt or updated to reflect the changes in the guard. The assembly should be updated with the modified guard, so click **Yes**.

Figure 4.30.   Assembly Rebuild dialog box.

2. The assembly updates the guard component to reflect the changes that were made. Rotate the assembly to be sure that the rectangular hole is in the right position with respect to the handle. Change the display to **Hidden Lines**

Visible, if necessary. To see the rectangular hole in the guard more easily, hide the cutter sub-assembly by *right clicking* on it in the FeatureManager design tree and selecting **Hide components**. When satisfied that the rectangular holes in the guard and the handle align, *right click* on the cutter sub-assembly in the FeatureManager design tree and select **Show components**.

3.   Now, check again to be sure that there is no interference within the assembly. Click on **pizza cutter** in the FeatureManager design tree to select it. Select **Tools ⇒ Interference Detection**. The pizza cutter assembly should be listed in the *Selected Components* field. Click the *Check* button. The result should be *0 Interference*, indicating no interference. Close the *Interference Volumes* dialog box.

4.   Save the pizza cutter assembly. If a dialog box appears about saving the referenced models, click *Yes*, so that the updated models are saved. In the **Window** menu, click on **guard** and **Close** the guard window.

Congratulations! The final pizza cutter assembly should look like the one shown in Figure 4.15. You have successfully assembled the pizza cutter and resolved interference errors.

4.4   CREATING AN EXPLODED VIEW OF THE ASSEMBLY

Exploded views are helpful to see how parts of the assembly fit together and to visualize the assembly procedure. Each component is separated from the components with which it mates, usually along the assembly axis, as shown in Figure 4.31. The pizza cutter can be returned to its assembled configuration, once the exploded view is created.

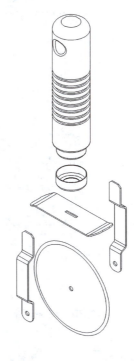

Figure 4.31.   Exploded view of the pizza cutter.

4.4.1   Exploding the Cutter Sub-Assembly from the Handle

First, the cutter sub-assembly is exploded from the handle. Later, the rest of the assembly will be exploded.

1. Before exploding the assembly, **Zoom To Fit** and use the **Hidden Lines Removed** display. Click anywhere on the background in the Graphics Window, so that nothing is selected.

2. Select **Insert ⇒ Exploded View**. The *Assembly Exploder* dialog box shown in Figure 4.32 appears. To see the full dialog box, which is shown in the figure, click on the *New* button (a staircase). This opens a new step of the exploded view. One or more components are exploded in each step. An exploded view can contain several steps.

Figure 4.32. *Assembly Exploder* dialog box.

3. The *Assembly Exploder* dialog box guides you through each stage of a step by highlighting (in pink) the current field that requires an input. The *Direction to explode along* field should be highlighted now. If it is not, click on this field. Use the **Front** view of the assembly. Click on the handle. An arrow appears, indicating the direction of the explosion, as shown in Figure 4.33. **Face of handle <1>** appears in the field.

4. The *Components to explode* field is now highlighted. Click on the blade to select the cutter sub-assembly. *cutter sub-assembly<1>/blade<1>* appears in the field. Leave the *Entire sub-assembly* button checked, so that the entire sub-assembly will be exploded.

5. In the *Distance* field, enter **3**. Click *Apply* (the green check mark) in the *Assembly Exploder* dialog box in order to see the explosion step. If the sub-assembly exploded in the wrong direction, click *Reverse Direction*. Click the **Isometric** button in the **Standard Views** toolbar. The screen should look similar to that shown in Figure 4.34.

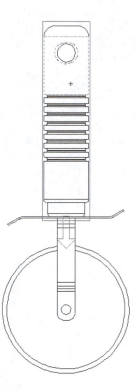

Figure 4.33.   Cutter explode direction.

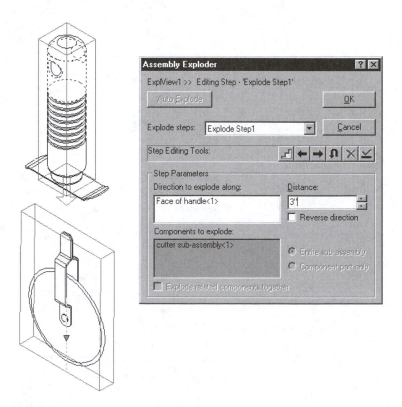

Figure 4.34.   First explode step: cutter exploded.

4.4.2   Exploding an Arm

Next, you will explode one of the arms in the cutter sub-assembly.

1. Click the **New** button (a staircase) in the **Assembly Exploder** dialog box to start a new step.

2. To have the arms explode outward away from the blade, a direction to explode along must be defined. You can use the circular hole at the top of the handle, as shown in Figure 4.35, to indicate the direction for the arm to be exploded. If necessary, move the dialog box to better see the hole. Select the inside surface of the circular hole. The face should be listed in the **Direction to explode along** field. The arrow should be pointing along the axis of the hole.

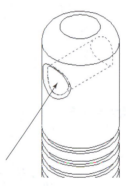

Figure 4.35.   Inside surface of hole.

3. Click on the **Component part only** button so that only the arm will be exploded, rather than the entire cutter sub-assembly. Click on the arm to be exploded in the direction indicated by the arrow at the top of the handle, as shown in Figure 4.36. This adds the arm to the **Components to explode** field. This is probably the arm on the near side of the blade.

4. Set the **Distance** to **2** and click the **Apply** button (a green check mark). The arm moves outward from the blade. Click the **Isometric** button. The screen should look similar to that shown in Figure 4.36.

4.4.3   Exploding the Other Components

The other components can be exploded in a similar manner. Before each step, click the **New** button to start a new explosion step. Use the **Delete** button (a red X) in the **Assembly Exploder** if you make a mistake. There will be six explode steps in all. Two have already been completed.

1. Explode the other arm in the other direction away from the blade. Use the same surface of the circular hole in the handle used to explode the first arm, but be sure to check the **Reverse Direction** checkbox in order to explode the second arm to the opposite side. Also, be sure to click the **Component part only** button. Use a distance of **2** inches.

2. Explode the rivet **4** inches to the side of the blade toward the head of the rivet. It may be necessary to zoom in to see which end of the rivet is on the near side of the blade. Use the inside surface of the circular hole in the

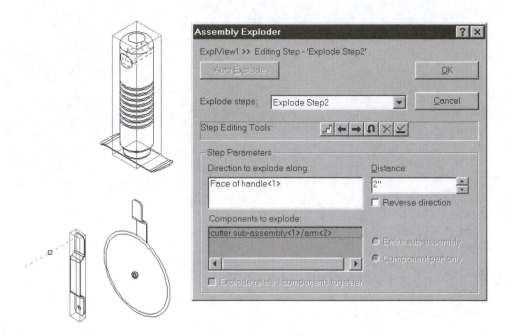

Figure 4.36. Second explode step: arm exploded.

handle as the ***Direction to explode along***. Since the exploded view indicates assembly direction, the rivet should be exploded to the side of the assembly that the rivet's head is on. Click the ***Component part only*** button, then select the rivet.

3. Explode the guard downward **2.5** inches, using the handle as the direction to explode along.

4. Explode the cap downward **1.25** inches.

5. Note that the explode steps are listed in the ***Explode steps*** pull-down menu. Clicking on any particular step in the menu causes that step to be highlighted. Each step can be modified. For instance, the distance that a part is exploded can be changed. When the ***Apply*** button is clicked, the modifications are applied. Make any necessary adjustments to the exploded view. When you are satisfied with the results, click ***OK***. Click anywhere on the background, so that nothing is selected. The complete exploded view should look similar to that shown in Figure 4.31, although the rivet could be on the opposite side, depending on how your pizza cutter was assembled.

6. Click the ConfigurationManager tab (the rightmost tab), below the Feature-Manager design tree near the bottom of the window. Then, click the plus sign next to **Default [pizza cutter]** in the ConfigurationManager. To collapse the assembly, *right click* on **ExplView1** and select **Collapse**. If you want to change any parameters of the exploded view, you can *right click* **ExplView1** and select **Edit Definition**, which will activate the **Assembly Exploder** dialog box.

Congratulations! The pizza cutter assembly is now complete. Save the assembly and close the window.

Problems

1. Assemble the pizza cutter, beginning with the blade and working toward the handle. Do not use a sub-assembly.

2. Assemble the pizza cutter, beginning with the guard and working toward the handle and then toward the blade.

3. Assemble the handle, the cap, and the guard into a sub-assembly. Then, assemble the handle sub-assembly to the cutter sub-assembly.

4. Starting with the completed pizza cutter assembly, modify the hole in the cap to be rectangular instead of circular. This will require removing the hole from the original sketch of the cap. Then, create a new sketch plane in the plane of the flat surface of the cap. Make a rectangular cut like the one in the guard. When assembling the revised cap, a new assembly constraint must be added in order to rotate the cap to align properly with the arms and the rectangular hole in the handle. One possible constraint is to make the long side of the cap's rectangular cut parallel to the long side of the rectangular cut. It may help to hide the guard and the cutter sub-assembly. Do an **Interference Detection** check to be sure that the revised cap fits in properly with the rest of the assembly.

5. Model a wooden pencil. Most pencils have three parts: a hexagonal wooden portion with embedded lead (extruded hexagon with a cut at one end to form the point and a cut at the opposite end to fit the cylindrical eraser holder), a metal eraser holder (thin revolve), and the cylindrical eraser. Assemble these three parts to model a pencil.

6. Model a plastic butter tub and cover. Model the tub as a thin revolve. Model the cover as a thick revolve, so that the lip at the bottom edge of the cover can be included.

5

Creating Working Drawings

OVERVIEW

Working drawings are the traditional means of graphically displaying a part or assembly. These drawings must provide all of the information necessary to manufacture a part or assembly. Drawings in SolidWorks are based on parts and assemblies that have already been modeled. Views of the models are placed in the drawing and then dimensioned. Notes and a title block are added to the drawing to include other pertinent information. Section views and detail views are also used in drawings to better describe the part or assembly.

5.1   DETAIL DRAWINGS IN SOLIDWORKS

Now that you have learned how to model parts and assemblies, you must learn how to put this information into an engineering drawing, or working drawing—the standard engineering graphics format. The engineering drawing presents the details of the part or the assembly in a formal manner. There are many variations of the format of engineering drawings. However, one key guideline is that *a drawing should clearly convey all of the information necessary to fabricate the part*. In this chapter, you will learn the common SolidWorks commands for generating engineering drawings.

Prior to solids modeling software like SolidWorks, engineering drawings were laboriously created by draftsmen and designers translating the three-dimensional visual image, either from their minds or a physical model, into detailed orthographic projections. The process was slow and changes were difficult. Using SolidWorks, the designer or

SECTIONS

OBJECTIVES

After working through this chapter, you will be able to

- Create a new drawing,
- Modify a drawing sheet format,
- Place and arrange views on a drawing,
- Add dimensions to a drawing,
- Add tolerances to a drawing,
- Display an exploded view in a drawing,
- Add a section view to a drawing,
- Add a detail view to a drawing,
- Label parts and add leader lines to a drawing, and
- Create a bill of materials.

engineer first creates a three-dimensional virtual model of a part. Based on this model, the SolidWorks drawing mode quickly extracts the two-dimensional orthographic information. Any changes to the three-dimensional model are automatically transferred to the drawing, because of the associative nature of SolidWorks.

In this chapter, you will create drawings of the arm and the pizza cutter assembly. The drawing in Figure 5.1 shows three two-dimensional orthographic views and one three-dimensional isometric view of the arm. Details such as dimensions, tolerances, and material specifications are also displayed on the drawing. The title block, which contains drawing control information, is in the lower right corner of the drawing.

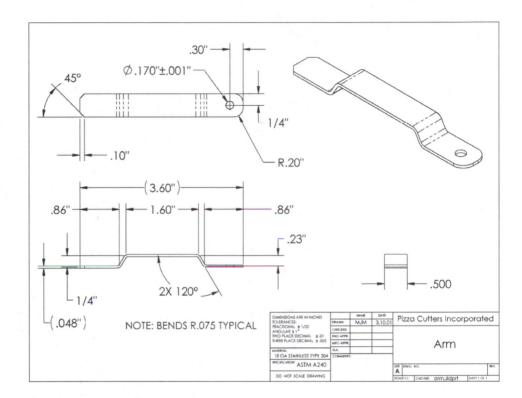

Figure 5.1. Finished arm drawing.

5.2   EDITING A DRAWING SHEET FORMAT

In this section, a drawing sheet format that can be used in future drawings will be created. The format can be thought of as the template for all of the drawings that will be created. It includes a border for the drawing and a title block. The completed drawing sheet format is shown in Figure 5.2.

5.2.1   Creating a New Drawing Document

Creating a drawing in SolidWorks begins by opening a drawing document, which is different from a part or an assembly document. In addition to specifying the file type, it is necessary to specify the drawing size. Several standard drawing sizes are available, as indicated in Table 5.1. In this case, an *A*-size drawing will be used for the arm of the pizza cutter.

1. To open a new drawing file for the arm, click the **New** button in the **Standard** toolbar, or **File** ⇒ **New**.

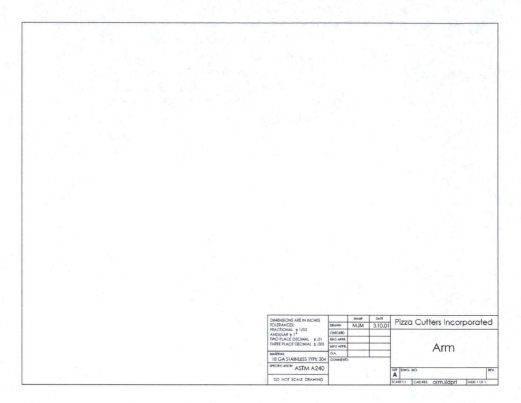

Figure 5.2. Finished sheet format.

TABLE 5.1 Standard drawing sizes

	ANSI (in inches)	ISO (in millimeters)
A	8.50 × 11.00	A4 210 × 297
B	11.00 × 17.00	A3 297 × 420
C	17.00 × 22.00	A2 420 × 594
D	22.00 × 34.00	A1 594 × 841
E	34.00 × 44.00	A0 841 × 1189

2. Choose **Draw** from the dialog box and click **OK**.

3. A new drawing using the SolidWorks standard A size sheet format opens, as shown in Figure 5.3. The drawing size is indicated just below the large box in the title block in the lower right corner of the sheet. (If a different drawing size is necessary, the size can be changed by *right clicking* in any open space in the drawing, clicking **Properties,** and selecting the **Paper size,** followed by **OK**.)

4. Notice that an icon that looks like a drawing appears next to the cursor when the drawing is opened. This means that the cursor is above the sheet of the drawing. As you will see later, the icon will change when the cursor is over a particular view or other entity (such as a dimension) of the drawing.

5. In the **View ⇒ Toolbars** menu, be sure that **Annotation, Drawing, Line Format, Sketch, Sketch Relations, Sketch Tools, Standard,** and **View**

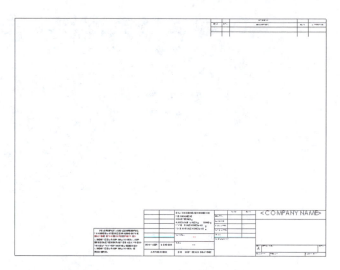

Figure 5.3.   Standard-sheet format.

are checked. If any item appears as a dialog box, drag it to the side or top of the window so it becomes a toolbar.

5.2.2   Checking the Options Settings

Before modifying the drawing sheet format, be sure that the SolidWorks settings match the following ones:

1. Select **Tools ⇒ Options** and then select the *System Options* tab, followed by the *Default Display Type* item. In the *Default display mode for new drawing views* section, select *Hidden visible*. This causes hidden lines in the drawing to be displayed as dashed lines in the printed output. In the *Default display of tangent edges in new drawing views* section, select *Visible* to show tangent edges as solid lines. The settings should match the ones shown in Figure 5.4.

2. Click the *Document Properties* tab. In the *Detailing* section, set the *Dimensioning standard to ANSI*. Click on the *Center marks* check box to turn off this option in the *Auto insert on view creation* field. In the *Units* section, be sure that the options are the same as those used to create the parts. Use *Inches, Fractions, 3* for *Decimal places, 8* for *Denominator,* and *0* for *Decimal places* of angles.

3. Select the *Annotations Font* item, and click on the *Note/Balloon* item in the *Annotation type* field. In this window, both the font type and font size for the notes on the drawing are specified. In the *Height* section, click on the *Points* button, and then set the size to *8,* as shown in Figure 5.5. This causes the font size to be eight points. Be sure that the font is set to **Century Gothic** to match this tutorial. Click *OK*.

4. Select the *Dimension* item in the *Annotation type* field to set the font size for dimensions in the drawing. In the *Height* section, click the *Units* button, if it is not already activated. Then, type *3/16* inches as the height. Be sure that the font is set to **Century Gothic** to match this tutorial. Click *OK.*

5. Click *OK* at the bottom of the *Document Properties* dialog box to apply all of the settings.

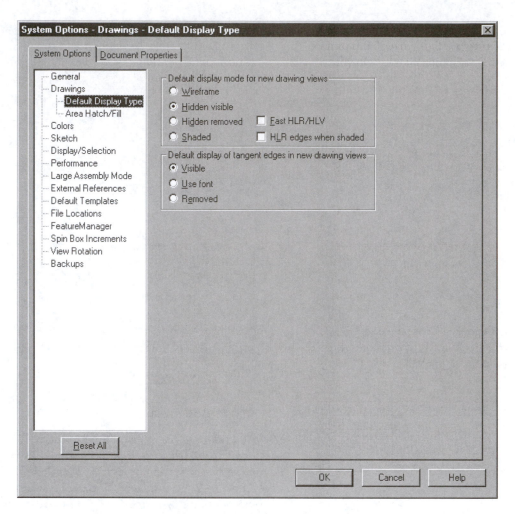

Figure 5.4. *System Options* dialog box.

5.2.3 The Drawing Environment

The drawing environment in SolidWorks is very similar to the part and assembly environments. Both the FeatureManager design tree and the tools in the **View** toolbar are still active. This section describes the elements and the tools used to create drawings from either part or assembly files in SolidWorks.

1. The drawing consists of two layers: a format and a sheet. Think of the sheet as a transparent page lying over the format. The format contains items that appear in every drawing, such as the title block, general tolerances, a border, and the scale of the drawing. The sheet contains the drawings, notes, and details specific to a particular part. One drawing can have several sheets, all using the same format.

2. The **Drawing** and **Annotations** toolbars, shown in Figure 5.6, contain the tools both for inserting views of parts onto the sheet and for adding details to the drawing. The toolbars may be vertical, as shown in Figure 5.6, or horizontal. A toolbar can be moved to a different position by clicking on the parallel lines at the end of the toolbar and dragging it to a new location. Hold the cursor over the buttons in the toolbars to display the names of the tools.

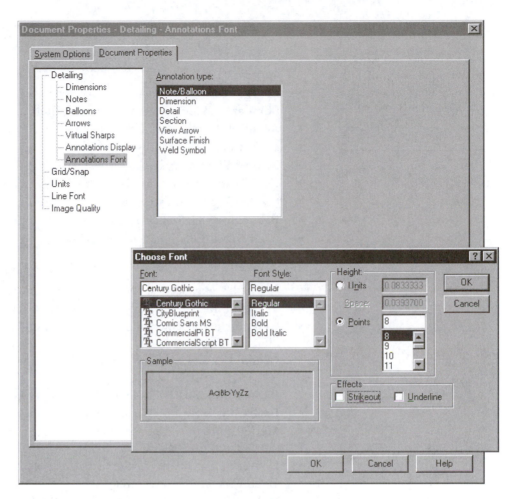

Figure 5.5.   *Document Properties* dialog box: *Annotations Font*.

Figure 5.6.   <u>**Drawing**</u> and <u>**Annotations**</u> toolbars.

Each of the tools is also available from either the **Insert ⇒ Annotations** menu, the **Insert ⇒ Drawing View** menu, or the **Tools** menu.

The **<u>Drawing</u>** toolbar contains the following tools:

* **Projected View** creates a new projected view from an existing view.
* **Standard 3 View** creates standard top, front, and right views of a part.
* **Auxiliary View** creates a view of an inclined plane.
* **Predefined View** creates a named view that can be saved.
* **Named View** creates a chosen view (e.g., an isometric view) of a part.
* **Detail View** displays an enlarged portion of an area.
* **Section View** creates a cross-sectional view of a part.
* **Broken-out Section** creates a partial section view.
* **Area Hatch/Fill** fills a sketched area with a predefined pattern.

The **<u>Annotation</u>** toolbar contains the following tools:

* **Note** adds a textual description to a selected portion of the drawing.
* **Surface Finish** displays the symbol used to specify the surface finish of a part.
* **Geometric Tolerance** displays the symbols that describe tolerances on both dimensions and constraints.
* **Datum Feature Symbol** attaches a symbol that indicates a datum plane to a selected edge or surface.
* **Balloon** attaches a balloon note to the selected edge.
* **Insert block** creates or inserts custom symbols for standard drawing items.
* **Model Items** imports dimensions, annotations, and reference geometry from the part or the assembly.
* **Center Mark** creates a center mark for a selected circle or arc.
* **Centerline** creates a centerline.
* **Hole Callout** inserts text related to a hole.

5.2.4 Modifying the Format's Text

The standard SolidWorks format can be customized to suit project or company needs. In this section, the standard format, shown in Figure 5.3, will be modified into a custom format, shown in Figure 5.2.

1. With the drawing symbol next to the cursor, *right click* on the sheet and select **Edit Sheet Format**. Or, in the **Edit** menu, select **Sheet Format**. If **Sheet** is in black letters and **Sheet Format** is shaded, then SolidWorks is already in the **Edit Sheet Format** mode. The text, the boxes, and the text within the boxes can now be edited.

2. Use the **Zoom To Area** tool to zoom to the bottom right corner of the drawing in order to view the title block.

3. With the **Select** tool, *right click* **<COMPANY NAME>** and then click **Properties,** or select it and use **Edit ⇒ Properties**. A *Properties* dialog box appears, as shown in Figure 5.7. Change **<COMPANY NAME>** to **Pizza Cutters Incorporated**. While still in the dialog box, be sure that the *Use document's font* is *not* selected, because the font that was specified in the *Options* dialog box is too small for this item. Click the *Font* button. In the window that appears, the *Font,* the *Font Style* (e.g., plain or bold), and the *Height* can be changed. Set the *Height* of this text to be *12 Points*. Click *OK* twice.

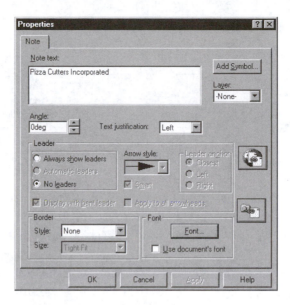

Figure 5.7. *Properties* dialog box.

4. To move the text to the center of the box, click on the text to select it, and then, drag it to the center of the box. It might help to use **View** ⇒ **Redraw** to clean things up.

5. On the left side of the title block, double click on the text **FINISH**. Change the text to **SPECIFICATION** by typing it in. Click outside of the text box. This is an alternate method to change text in drawings.

6. In the **MATERIAL** field, use the *Properties* dialog box to change the dash to **18 GA STAINLESS TYPE 304.** Modify the font size to seven points by using the *Font* button and typing in **7** followed by *OK*. Center the text in the box by changing *Text justification* to *Center*. **GA** refers to the gauge, or thickness, of the sheet metal. For stainless steel sheet metal, 18 gauge is .048 inches thick. After clicking *OK,* use the **Select** tool to drag the text to reposition it.

7. In the **SPECIFICATION** field, change the dash to **ASTM A240,** a stainless steel specification, and position the text in the box.

8. Change the text **WEIGHT:** at the bottom of the title block to **CAD FILE:**.

9. Click the **Note** button in the **Annotations** toolbar, or select **Insert** ⇒ **Annotations** ⇒ **Note**. Place the box that appears by the cursor just to the right of the text **CAD FILE:**. Be sure that the leader line or arrow is not visible when the box is placed. Type **arm.sidprt** in the box. Click OK in the *Note* PropertyManager and reposition the text, if necessary. It may help to zoom in to place the text.

10. Create a **Note** with the text *Arm* in the box below Pizza Cutters Incorporated. Set the font size to *18 Points* in the *Note* PropertyManager by unchecking *Use document's font,* clicking the *Font* button, and changing the *Height* to *18* points, Click *OK* and move the text to the center of the box.

11. **Zoom to Fit** and the **Zoom to Area** are on the left end of the title block. With the **Select** tool, click the **PROPRIETARY AND CONFIDENTIAL** line of text. Remove the text using the Delete key. Likewise, remove the text block remaining in the box. Normally, a note like this is used to protect proprietary information, but it is not necessary for this tutorial. When you are finished removing the text, the title block should look similar to that shown in Figure 5.8.

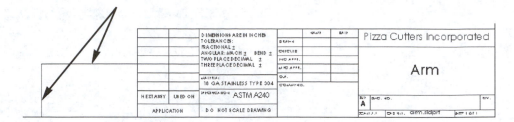

Figure 5.8. Text placed in title block. (Arrows indicate lines to delete.)

5.2.5 Modifying the Lines of the Sheet Format

Now, extra lines in the title block will be removed. When modifying the lines, keep in mind that the format can be used for other parts, so there will be some blank boxes.

1. Be sure that you are still editing the format (and not the sheet) by clicking the **Edit** menu. If **Sheet Format** is grayed out, then you are still editing the format. Do *not* click on **Sheet**. This will toggle the edit to the sheet.

2. Zoom to the left end of the title block. *Control click* and delete the two lines in the title block shown in Figure 5.8. Selected lines are highlighted in green. If you accidentally select the sheet format, instead of the lines, the **Confirm Delete** dialog box will appear. In this case, click **No** to avoid deleting the format.

3. The boxes above **APPLICATION** on the left side of the title block need to be removed. Using control-selection all of the lines and text would be tedious. Instead, use the **Select** tool to drag a box similar to the one shown in Figure 5.9. This selects all of the lines and text within the box. Hit the Delete key on the keyboard to remove them.

4. Sketch entities can be added to the sheet format just as they were added to parts. Click the **<u>Line</u>** button in the **<u>Sketch Tools</u>** toolbar. Draw a vertical line to close the left end of the title block, as shown in Figure 5.10. Reactivate the **Select** tool.

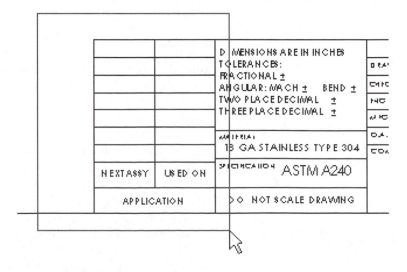

Figure 5.9. Selected lines to delete.

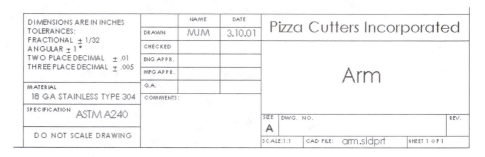

DIMENSIONS ARE IN INCHES		NAME	DATE	Pizza Cutters Incorporated		
TOLERANCES: FRACTIONAL ± 1/32 ANGULAR ± 1° TWO PLACE DECIMAL ± .01 THREE PLACE DECIMAL ± .005	DRAWN	MJM	3.10.01			
	CHECKED					
	ENG APPR.					
	MFG APPR.		Arm			
MATERIAL 18 GA STAINLESS TYPE 304	Q.A.					
	COMMENTS:					
SPECIFICATION ASTM A240				SIZE	DWG. NO.	REV.
				A		
DO NOT SCALE DRAWING				SCALE:1:1	CAD FILE: arm.sldprt	SHEET 1 OF 1

Figure 5.10. Finished title block.

5.   Figure 5.10 indicates the values of the drawing's general tolerances. A dimension that has two digits after the decimal point indicates that the tolerance is plus or minus .01 inches. In other words, the dimension of the actual part can be .01 inches larger or .01 inches smaller than the specified dimension and still be acceptable. Update the tolerance note to reflect the tolerances of the drawing, as shown in Figure 5.10. Right click the tolerances text block and select **Properties**. In the ***Note Text:*** field the text ***<MOD-PM>*** is equivalent to a ± symbol. Type ***1/32*** after ***FRACTIONAL <MOD-PM>***. Delete ***MACH*** and ***BEND<MOD-PM>***. Type ***1*** after ***ANGULAR <MOD-PM>***. Then add the degree symbol by clicking the ***Add Symbol*** button in the ***Properties*** dialog box to activate the ***Symbols*** dialog box, as shown in Figure 5.11. These symbols are in the ***Modifying Symbols*** symbol library. Be sure that the ***Use Symbol*** button is on. Click ***OK*** to insert the symbol. Move up or down in the ***Note text:*** field by moving the cursor while depressing the left mouse button. Add ***.01*** after ***TWO PLACE DECIMAL <MOD-PM>*** and add ***.005*** after ***THREE PLACE DECIMAL <MOD-PM>*** to match Figure 5.10. Then click ***OK***.

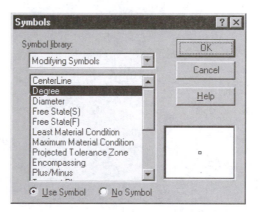

Figure 5.11. ***Symbols*** dialog box.

6.   Using the **Note** tool, add your initials in the **DRAWN** box of the format. Be sure the ***No leader*** button (an arrow with an X) is selected in the ***Arrows/ Leaders*** field of the ***Note*** PropertyManager. Turn off ***Use document's font*** and set the font size to ***8 point***. Repeat this process to add the date. The final title block should look like Figure 5.10.

7. **Zoom to Fit** and then zoom in on the upper right corner of the sheet format. Delete the Revisions block and **Zoom to Fit**.

8. *Right click* on any open space on the sheet format and select **Properties**. The **Sheet Setup** dialog box appears. In the **Type of projection** section, be sure **Third angle** is selected. This is the standard projection system used in North America. Click **OK**.

Once you are satisfied with the sheet format, save it for future use. Select **File ⇒ Save Sheet Format** and click the **Custom Sheet Format** button in the dialog box. Click **Browse** to locate the folder or device in which you want to save the format. Save it as **tutorial format**. Click **OK** in the **Save Sheet Format** dialog box. This format can be used for any new drawing. Since this drawing will be used for the arm, also save it as **arm drawing** using **File ⇒ Save** or the **Save** button.

5.3 CREATING A DRAWING OF THE ARM

In this section, several views of the arm will be inserted into the drawing that is currently open. You will also add the dimensions of the arm, to fully describe its geometry. The finished drawing of the arm is shown in Figure 5.12.

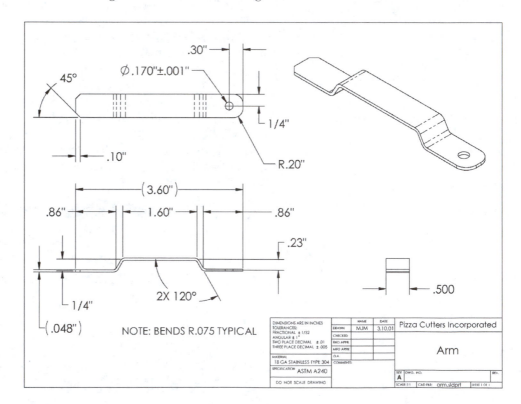

Figure 5.12. Finished arm drawing.

5.3.1 Placing Orthographic Views

Three orthographic views are customarily used in engineering practice to describe the geometry of a part. These views—the top, the front, and the right views—can be placed into a SolidWorks drawing directly from a part with just a few clicks of the mouse. Be sure that the drawing sheet format that you created in the previous section is still open.

1. To begin, open the file of the part that will be depicted in the drawing. Click **File ⇒ Open**, and open the *arm* part file that you saved earlier. Be sure that the ***Files of type:*** is set to ***Part Files*** or to ***SolidWorks Files*** in the ***Open*** dialog box. A new window that contains the model of the arm opens. Return to the drawing window by selecting **Window ⇒ arm drawing-Sheet1**. If necessary **Zoom to Fit** to show the entire drawing.

2. Select **Edit ⇒ Sheet**, so that you will edit the sheet and not the sheet format. The bottom right corner of the Status bar displays *Editing Sheet1* indicating that the sheet, not the sheet format, is being edited.

3. Click on the <u>**Standard 3 View**</u> button (three views) in the <u>**Drawing**</u> toolbar, or select **Insert ⇒ Drawing View ⇒ Standard 3 View**. Notice that the cursor includes a three-dimensional box, indicating that a part should be selected. The PropertyManager displays different methods of selecting a model for the drawing.

4. Activate the **arm** window by selecting **Window ⇒ arm**. The cursor should still have a box next to it.

5. Click anywhere on the arm to select it. Upon selecting the arm, SolidWorks automatically returns to the drawing window. If the ***Tangent Edge Display*** dialog box appears, select ***Visible*** so that the views show tangent lines. Check ***Don't ask me again*** and then click ***OK.*** The top, the front, and the right views are placed on the sheet, as shown in Figure 5.13.

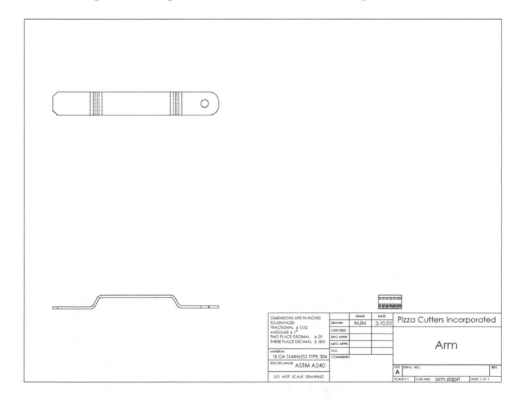

DIMENSIONS ARE IN INCHES TOLERANCES: FRACTIONAL ± 1/32 ANGULAR ± 1° TWO PLACE DECIMAL ± .01 THREE PLACE DECIMAL ± .005		NAME	DATE	Pizza Cutters Incorporated
	DRAWN	MJM	3.10.01	
	CHECKED			
	ENG APPR.			
	MFG APPR.			Arm
MATERIAL 18 GA STAINLESS TYPE 304	G.A.			
SPECIFICATION ASTM A240	COMMENTS:			SIZE DWG. NO. REV. A
DO NOT SCALE DRAWING				SCALE:1:1 CAD FILE: arm.sldprt SHEET 1 OF 1

Figure 5.13. Orthographic views placed.

6. Bring the cursor over one of the views in the drawing. Notice that a box appears surrounding the view. When the cursor is inside this box, but is not over the part itself, the cursor icon is a component surrounded by the corners of a

box. In this mode, the cursor will select the view of the component. When the cursor is over the features of the component (such as faces, lines, or points), an icon of that feature appears next to the cursor. In this mode, the cursor will select the feature.

5.3.2 Adding a Named View

Named views are preset orientations of the part from the part document. The most commonly used named view is the isometric view. Including an isometric view helps the person reading a drawing to visualize a three-dimensional image of the part.

1. Click the **Named View** button (a view with an N) in the **Drawing** toolbar, or select **Insert** ⇒ **Drawing View** ⇒ **Named View**. Notice that the cursor changes to a three-dimensional box, indicating that a part should be selected.

2. Click one of the views of the arm in the drawing. The *Named View* PropertyManager appears. Any view of a part can be placed in a drawing. In this case, you want to place an isometric view, so click *Isometric* from the *View Orientation* list.

3. When the cursor is brought over the drawing, it changes to a cross. Click on the upper right portion of the drawing to place the isometric view. The isometric view should look similar to that shown in Figure 5.14.

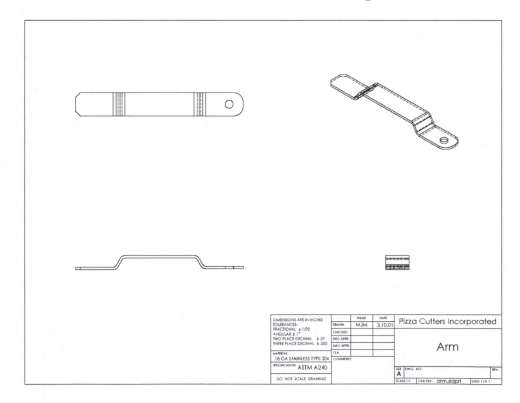

Figure 5.14. Isometric view placed.

5.3.3 Adjusting the Views on the Sheet

Views can be moved or modified in several ways. The positions of the views can be changed either to clarify the drawing or to make room for more views on the drawing. The scale of a view can be changed to see more detail. The display for each view can be set to **Wireframe, Hidden Lines Visible,** or **Hidden Lines Removed,** depending upon which display is optimal.

1. To ensure that the views do not overlap the sheet format (or other views), the views may need to be moved. Click on the box that surrounds the front view (the bottom left view), but not the arm itself. The box around the view becomes highlighted in green. To move the view, click and drag the green bounding box. Be sure *not* to click on one of the eight green squares. The icon next to the cursor must appear as perpendicular lines with arrows at the ends in order to move the view. Notice that the other two orthogonal views are forced to move with the front view, since they are projections of this principal view. Move the front view to match that shown in Figure 5.14.

2. The right view (lower right) is somewhat difficult to move, because the box enclosing this view is very close to the part. Zoom in on the right view. Select the box enclosing it, so that it is highlighted in green. Then, position the cursor over a corner of the box until the cursor changes into a diagonal arrow. Drag the cursor to make the box larger and **Zoom To Fit**. Now, it should be easier to move the larger box. Move the views to match that shown in Figure 5.14. Notice that both the right and top views are constrained to stay aligned with the front view. You can preview the printed drawing at any time by clicking the **Print Preview** button in the **Standard** toolbar, or by selecting **File ⇒ Print Preview**. Click *Close* to return to the drawing.

3. Click within the box surrounding the isometric view (but not on the arm itself) to select this view. Zoom in on the isometric view of the arm. The hidden lines are somewhat confusing in this view. Click the **Hidden Lines Removed** button in the **View** toolbar to remove the hidden lines. Repeat this for both the top view (upper left) and the right view (lower right).

4. The current display of the drawing shows tangent edges between a curved surface and a flat surface as a solid line. This occurs at the bends and the filleted corners of the arm. There are three ways to display tangent edges: **Tangent Edges Visible** (solid line), **Tangent Edges With Font** (dashed line), **Tangent Edges Removed** (no line). To change the display of tangent edges for the isometric view, *right click* on the view, and then, select **Tangent Edge**. Click on **Tangent Edges With Font** in this case. The isometric view should look like that shown in Figure 5.15. Repeat this for the top view. For the front and the right views, use **Tangent Edges Removed** for clarity.

5. Each view within a drawing can have its own scale. To make the isometric view larger, select the isometric view to activate the *Named View* Property-Manager. Check the box next to *Custom Scale.* Set the scale to *3 : 2,* as shown in Figure 5.16. (Note that the ToolTip that appears when the cursor is over the green check mark indicates *Close Dialog* instead of *OK.* For convenience, we will continue to refer to the green check mark as *OK.*) Click *OK.* The isometric view enlarges to be 1.5 times larger than the other views. The drawing should look like the one in Figure 5.15.

5.3.4   Adding Dimensions to Orthographic Views

The dimensions that were used during the creation of the part may automatically be placed on the views of the drawing. Dimensions placed in the drawing are the current dimensions of the part. If the part geometry is changed later, the drawing will automatically

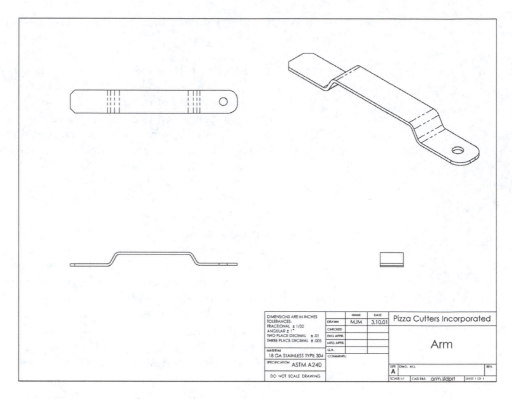

DIMENSIONS ARE IN INCHES
TOLERANCES:
FRACTIONAL ± 1/32
ANGULAR ± 1°
TWO PLACE DECIMAL ± .01
THREE PLACE DECIMAL ± .005

MATERIAL
18 GA STAINLESS TYPE 304
SPECIFICATION ASTM A240

DO NOT SCALE DRAWING

DRAWN MJM 3.10.01
CHECKED
ENG APPR.
MFG APPR.
Q.A.
COMMENTS:

Pizza Cutters Incorporated

Arm

SIZE A DWG. NO. REV.
SCALE:1:1 CAD FILE: arm.sldprt SHEET 1 OF 1

Figure 5.15. Isometric view enlarged on drawing.

Figure 5.16. *Named View* PropertyManager.

update to reflect the changes. Likewise, if the dimensions on the drawing are changed, the part will be updated automatically.

1. Select the top view (upper left), so that it is highlighted in green. Click the **Model Items** button in the **Annotations** toolbar, or select **Insert ⇒ Model Items**. In the *Insert Model Items* dialog box shown in Figure 5.17, be sure

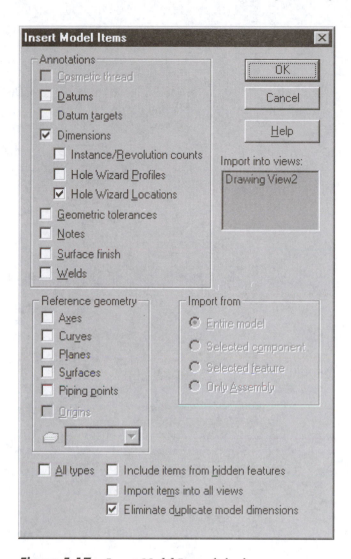

Figure 5.17. *Insert Model Items* dialog box.

that the ***Dimensions*** box is checked. Click ***OK***. The dimensions for the view are displayed. Do not worry if the dimensions are hard to read. They will be cleaned up shortly.

2. In a similar manner, place dimensions on the front view. If you try to place dimensions on the right view, none will appear, because all of the necessary dimensions have already been shown in the other two views. In fact, this view is not even necessary in this drawing. All of the details of the arm are shown in the front and top views. Nevertheless, the right view will be retained for completeness.

3. Clean up the dimensions by dragging them just as you did when creating parts. In placing dimensions, the most important thing to remember is that they should be both clear and in a logical order. A dimension can be moved between views by holding down the Shift key on the keyboard and dragging it to another view. It is necessary to drag the dimension all the way onto the new view before releasing the mouse button. Once the dimension is in the

new view, drag the dimension to the desired location. If a dimension is in a plane perpendicular to the plane of the view, the dimension cannot be moved to certain other views. Move the dimensions to the positions shown in Figure 5.18. If a dimension is off the edge of the drawing, select the front view and move the view on the sheet, or use *Zoom to Area*. Then, adjust the position of the dimension. The dimensions for the chamfer and fillet on the top view may be placed differently than those shown in the figure.

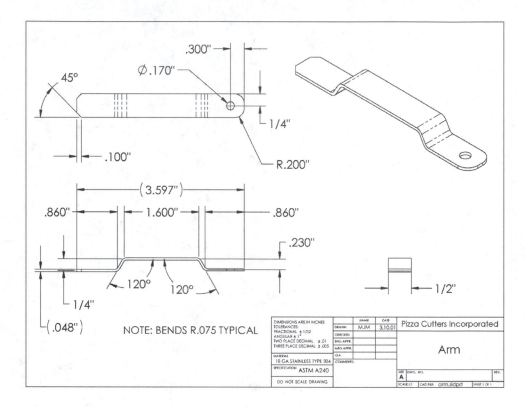

Figure 5.18. Dimensions placed.

4. Some dimensions flip when they are moved. To see this, horizontally move the **1/4** dimension on the front view. The dimension should flip as it passes the left end of the arm. To make this dimension appear as it does in Figure 5.18, move it so that the arrows are positioned as in the figure. While the dimension is still selected, click the green circle where the lower arrow makes a right angle. This flips the position of the **1/4** dimension to that shown in Figure 5.18. Repeat this for other dimensions as necessary.

5. The arrowheads on some dimensions may not appear as shown in Figure 5.18. To change the arrowhead positions, select the dimension and then click one of the buttons in the *Arrows* field of the PropertyManager, as shown in Figure 5.19. Change the 1.600 dimension to *Inside*.

6. On a drawing, center marks should be added to circles. To do this, click on the **Center Mark** button in the **Annotations** toolbar. The icon next to the cursor turns to a cross. Click on the .170 hole in the top view to add center marks to the hole. It may be necessary to zoom in to see the center marks.

Figure 5.19. *Dimension* PropertyManager.

7. Sometimes, the dimensions used to model the part are inadequate to clearly represent its dimensions on the drawing. For instance, the overall length of the arm is not evident in the drawing. However, a *reference dimension* can be displayed on the drawing to indicate the overall length. Reference dimensions cannot be used to "drive" the model of the part. In other words, changing a reference dimension on the drawing cannot change any dimension on the part model. To add a reference dimension for the overall length of the arm, zoom in on the front view and activate the **Dimension** tool. In the front view, click on the left end of the arm, followed by the right end of the arm, and place the dimension as usual. The dimension will have parentheses around it, indicating that it is a reference dimension.

8. Because the text "**18 GA**" in the title block defines the arm's thickness to be .048 inches, the .048 dimension in the drawing should be displayed as a reference dimension, that is, with parentheses. To do this, activate the **Select** tool, *right click* the **.048** dimension, and select **Display Options** ⇒ **Show Parenthesis** in the menu that appears. Parentheses now surround the dimension, indicating that it is a reference dimension. Unlike the previous reference dimension, this dimension "drives" the model of the part. Changing it will change the part.

9. The radius of the bends did not appear when dimensions were automatically placed on the views because the *Auto Fillet* option was used when the arm was extruded. To add a note specifying the bend radius, click on the **Note** toolbar button. Place the note box and type **NOTE: BENDS R.075 TYPICAL** in the box. Change the font to 16 points and click **OK** twice. Then, adjust the position of the note. Your drawing should look similar to the one shown in Figure 5.18. If any origins appear on the views, click **View** ⇒ **Origins** to turn them off.

5.3.5 Modifying a Dimension's Text

Text can be added to dimensions in order to better describe a part. For example, if two (or more) dimensions refer to similar features they are often combined. In this case, one of the dimensions can be removed, and a "**2X**" or a "**2 PLACES**" description can be added to the other dimension, indicating that the dimension occurs two times. This saves space and simplifies drawings of parts with several similar features.

1. One of the two **120°** dimensions can be removed, if the dimension of the remaining angle indicates that the angle occurs twice. Delete the left dimension by selecting it and then hitting the Delete key on the keyboard.

2. Select the other **120°** dimension. The **Dimension** PropertyManager appears. In the **Dimension Text** field, type "**2X**" (without quotes), followed by a space in front of **<DIM>,** as shown in Figure 5.20. The **<DIM>** refers to the numerical value of the dimension.

Figure 5.20. *Dimension Text* field.

3. Click **OK** to accept the change. The **120°** dimension is shown in Figure 5.21.

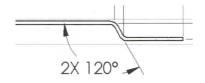

Figure 5.21. 2X dimension added.

COSMETIC THREADS

Cosmetic threads are schematic representations of a threaded feature, such as a threaded hole. Instead of displaying the actual threads, a hidden line and a **Thread Callout** are placed on both the drawing and the part. The hidden line shows the minor diameter for an external thread (e.g., a bolt) or the major diameter for an internal thread (e.g., a nut). Both internal and external threads can be created in SolidWorks, depending upon the edge that is selected. If the circular edge of a hole is selected, then an internal thread is created. If the edge of a cylinder is selected, then an external thread is created.

To create a cosmetic thread, select the circular feature on the drawing that is to be threaded. Then, use **Insert ⇒ Annotations ⇒ Cosmetic Thread**. In the **Cosmetic Thread** dialog box, specify the depth of the thread, the major or minor diameter, and the **Thread Callout**. The **Thread Callout** is the specification for the thread. For instance, "1/4–20 UNC" indicates a thread with a major diameter of .25 inches, a pitch of 20 threads per inch, and the United Course standard thread series. Cosmetic threads can be placed in either parts or drawings.

For an internal thread, the hole should be the size of the tap drill diameter, and the major diameter should be the thread's nominal diameter. For an external thread, the cylinder should be the nominal diameter of the thread. The minor diameter should be the same as the tap drill diameter. Tap drill sizes and nominal diameters of standard threads can be found in any machinist's handbook.

5.3.6   Specifying Tolerances

The tolerance for a dimension is specified according to the number of digits it has past the decimal point. However, the number of digits of the dimensions must be changed to denote the correct tolerance.

1.   The radius of the round at the right end of the arm is not a critical dimension and does not need a tight tolerance. To change the number of digits after the decimal, select the **R.200** dimension. In the **Dimension** PropertyManager, click on the **Primary Unit Precision** pulldown menu with **.XXX(Default)**. Select **.XX**. The text on the dimension updates to reflect the change.

2.   Repeat Step 1 to update the other dimensions, so that the dimensions look similar to those shown in Figure 5.22. Close the **Dimension** PropertyManager by clicking the green check mark.

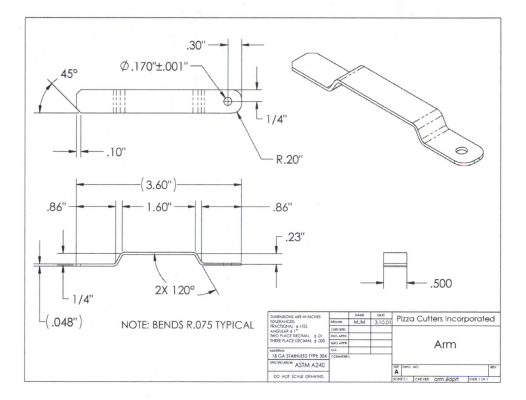

Figure 5.22. Tolerances added.

3.   The width of the arm is critical. Its dimension must be accurate so that it fits snugly into the handle. Right now, the dimension is specified as **1/2,** indicating that the tolerance should be ±1/32 inches. To make this tolerance tighter, *right click* on this dimension and select **Properties**. Uncheck **Use document's units** and click the **Units** button. In the **Dimension Units** dialog box, click the **Decimal** button. Click **OK** two times. The dimension updates to become a decimal with three places of precision.

4.   The tolerance on the .170 hole in the arm should be ±.001. But the general tolerances in the title block only call for a tolerance of ±.005 for a dimension with three digits past the decimal point. To add the tolerance to the dimension, select the **.170** dimension. At the top of the PropertyManager window,

click on **None** in the *Tolerance Type* pulldown menu, and then, select *Symmetric*. Type **.001** in the *Maximum Variation* box. Then, click anywhere in the Graphics Window to show the tolerance. The drawing with these changes should look like that shown in Figure 5.22.

GEOMETRIC DIMENSIONING AND TOLERANCING

Geometric Dimensioning and Tolerancing symbols can be added to parts, assemblies, and drawings. For instance, to specify a flatness-form tolerance, select a face of a part, assembly, or drawing. Then, click **Insert ⇒ Annotations ⇒ Geometric Tolerance** or activate the **Geometric Tolerance** button in the **Annotations** tool-bar. In the dialog box that appears, several items must be set in order to apply the geometric tolerance. Click on the **GCS** (Geometric Characteristic Symbol) button. Then select *Flatness,* followed by **OK**. Set the tolerance value in the *Tolerance 1* field and click **OK**. The annotation that appears can be moved using the **Select** tool.

Geometric Dimensioning and Tolerancing symbols are some of many annotation items found in SolidWorks. Other examples include Notes, Cosmetic Threads, Surface Finish, and Datum Feature symbols. Unlike dimensions, annotations have no bearing on the actual model of the part and are usually used to present more detailed information of the manufacturing process on the drawing.

5.3.7   Changing Dimensions in Both the Drawing and the Part

Dimensions changed in the drawing change the geometry of the solid model, because of the associative nature of SolidWorks. Likewise, dimensions changed in the part are reflected in the drawing. The length of the arm in the drawing will be modified and then changed back in the part, to demonstrate the codependence between the drawing and the model in SolidWorks.

1. *Double click* the **1.60** dimension in the front view of the arm. In the **Modify** dialog box, set the value to **3** inches and click on the green check. The part will not update until the document is rebuilt. Click the **Rebuild** button (a stoplight) in the **Standard** toolbar, or **Edit ⇒ Rebuild**, to update the document. All of the views change, including the isometric view. For now, it is acceptable if the drawing extends past the borders of the sheet. You will be changing the arm back to its original length shortly.

2. Select **Window ⇒ arm** to activate the **arm** window. The arm reflects the dimension change and is now longer.

3. *Double click* the arm to show all of the dimensions. Set the view to **Front**. *Double click* the **3** dimension and change it back to **1.6**. Click the **Rebuild** button in the **Standard** toolbar.

4. Return to the drawing window. The drawing has changed to reflect the changes made in the part document. The associative character of both the part and the drawing is a powerful feature and should be used carefully. A small change in a drawing document could adversely affect the assembly that contains that part.

Congratulations! This completes the drawing of the arm. The drawing should look like that shown in Figure 5.22. Check the preview of the drawing by clicking **Print Preview** in the **Standard** toolbar. Print the drawing by selecting **File ⇒ Print**, or by clicking the **Print** button in the **Standard** toolbar. Save the drawing and close both the drawing window and the arm window. Answer **Yes** to the dialog box warning about the referenced models.

To fabricate a sheet metal part, a flat piece of sheet metal, called a *blank,* is formed to create bends. This process is represented in SolidWorks with a feature called *sheet metal bends*. The four bends of the arm can be flattened to represent the blank for the arm. The sheet-metal tools are displayed in the **Sheet Metal** toolbar, activated using the **View ⇒ Toolbars** menu. Before flattening a sheet metal part, an edge or face must be selected that will remain fixed in the part window with respect to the origin before and after bending. For the **arm,** select the top flat face of the arm to remain fixed in the part window. Then, click the **Insert Bends** button in the **Sheet Metal** toolbar. In the **Bends** PropertyManager set the **Bend Radius** to **.075,** which was the bend radius used in the **Auto Fillet** option of the **Extrude Thin Feature** dialog box when the base feature for the arm was extruded. In general, the **Auto Fillet** feature is not needed to create sheet metal bends. The **Fixed Face or Edge** field indicates **Face<1>,** the top face of the arm, which was selected as the face to remain fixed with respect to the origin upon flattening the part. The **Bend allowance** provides several methods for calculating the unbent length of the part. Setting the **Use k-factor** option to a value of **.5** places the neutral bending surface (which is neither stretched nor compressed during the bending process) at the center of the arm's thickness. In this way the unbent length for this gentle bend will be based on the length of the bend at the center of the arm's thickness.

Softer materials or sharper bends require a smaller k-factor to account for the shift of the neutral surface toward the center of curvature. Finally, the **Auto Relief** checkbox should be unchecked, so that there will be no automatic insertion of cuts to facilitate the bend.

Upon clicking **OK**, three features are added to the FeatureManager design tree: **Sheet-Metal1** defines the part as a sheet metal part, **Flatten-Bends1** is the feature of the flattened sheet metal part in its unbent, blank state, and **Process-Bends I** is the feature that forms the part to its bent shape. To see the blank of the part, click the **Flattened** button in the **Sheet Metal** toolbar. Clicking the **Flattened** button again returns the arm to its bent state.

A view of the unbent blank of a sheet metal part can be inserted into a drawing. In the drawing, click the **Named View** button in the **Drawing** toolbar. Select one of the views of the arm in the drawing and choose **Flat pattern** from the **View Orientation** field of the **Named View** PropertyManager. The view of the blank can then be inserted in the drawing just like any other named view. Dimensions can be added to the blank using the **Dimension** tool. The dimensions appear as reference dimensions, because they are not the dimensions used to model the original bent part. The parentheses can be removed by *right clicking* on the dimension with the **Select** tool and making modifications in the **Properties** dialog box.

5.4 CREATING A DRAWING OF THE PIZZA CUTTER ASSEMBLY

Assembly drawings are useful in showing how parts fit together to create the entire assembly and in labeling individual parts in an assembly. In the next few sections, you will create the assembly drawing of the pizza cutter, as shown in Figure 5.23. Drawings of assemblies are created in a manner similar to drawings created from parts. In this section, you will also create both a section view and a detail view of the pizza cutter assembly.

5.4.1 Setting Up the Pizza Cutter Drawing

1. Open a new drawing by clicking **New** in the **Standard** toolbar. Select **Draw** from the dialog box. Click **OK**.

2. *Right click* on an open space on the drawing and select **Properties**. The **Sheet Setup** dialog box appears. Be sure **Third angle** is checked. In the

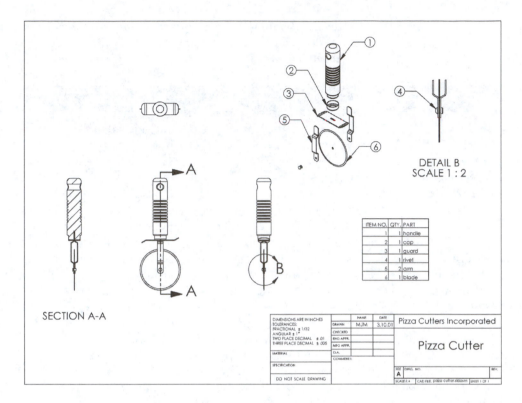

Figure 5.23. Finished assembly drawing.

Sheet Format pulldown menu, select *Custom*. Click the *Browse* button, and open the **tutorial format** file that you saved earlier. Click *OK* in the *Sheet Setup* dialog box once you have selected the format. Normally, a larger drawing size should be used for this assembly drawing to show adequate detail. But to save the effort of making a new template and to allow printing on standard printers, you will use an *A* size drawing.

3. Click **Tools** ⇒ **Options**. In the *Document Properties* tab, activate the *Detailing* item and set the *Dimensioning standard* to *ANSI* and uncheck *Center marks*. Activate the *Notes* item. Turn the *Bent* button on in the *Leader style* field. Click the *Annotations Font* list item and set the *Note/Balloon* font height to 8 points. Activate the *Units* item and set the *Linear units* to *Inches*. Click *OK*.

4. Use the **Zoom To Area** tool to zoom in to the bottom right corner of the drawing. With the **Select** tool, *right click* on an open area on the drawing and select *Edit Sheet Format* from the menu, or select **Edit** ⇒ **Sheet Format**.

5. Remove the text "**18 GA STAINLESS TYPE 304**" and "**ASTM A240**" by selecting the text and hitting the Delete key on the keyboard.

6. Change the text "**Arm**" and "**arm.sldprt**" to "**Pizza Cutter**" and "**pizza cutter.sldasm**", respectively. To do this, *right click* on the text, select **Properties,** and change the text in the **Properties** dialog box. To reduce the size of the **pizza cutter.sldasm** to fit it into the field, unselect *Use document's font* in the *Properties* dialog box and change the font size to *6* points. Move the text to an appropriate position. Note that text can also be modified by *double clicking* the note and entering the text directly.

7. Now that the format is modified for the pizza cutter assembly, return to the sheet by *right clicking* on an open area of the drawing and selecting **Edit Sheet,** or by clicking **Edit ⇒ Sheet**. This permits the drawing to be edited instead of the format. **Zoom To Fit** to see the entire drawing.

8. Since this is an assembly drawing, you can set all of the views to **Hidden Lines Removed** to produce a drawing that is easier to read. Select **Tools ⇒ Options**. Activate the *Default Display Type* item and set the *Default display mode for new drawing views* to *Hidden removed*. Click *OK.*

9. Turn off **Origins** in the **View** menu, if it is checked.

10. In the **View ⇒ Toolbars** menu, be sure that **Annotation, Drawing, Line Format, Sketch, Sketch Relations, Sketch Tools, Standard,** and **View** are checked.

5.4.2   Adding Orthographic and Isometric Views to the Drawing

Adding views of an assembly to a drawing is similar to adding views of a part to a drawing. You will be adding the front, top, right, and isometric views of the pizza cutter to this drawing. The isometric view will be exploded to show the assembly procedure for the pizza cutter.

1. Select **File ⇒ Open** to open the pizza cutter assembly file. Find the file named **pizza cutter**. Remember to set *Files of Type* to *Assembly Files* or *SolidWorks Files,* so that the file can be seen in the dialog box. SolidWorks will probably need to rebuild the assembly once it is opened. This is because of the modification to the arm's length that was previously made. Click *Yes* to rebuild.

2. Hold down the Control key on the keyboard and press the Tab key once to quickly switch back to the drawing window. Be sure that you are editing the sheet and not the sheet format in the drawing window. Click the **Standard 3 View** button in the **Drawing** toolbar. Then, return to the pizza cutter window using Ctrl–Tab. Select **pizza cutter** in the FeatureManager design tree to place the orthographic views into the drawing. Selecting **pizza cutter** in the FeatureManager design tree rather than in the Graphics Window ensures that the entire pizza cutter is selected, instead of a single part.

3. The *1 : 4* on the right side of the Status bar at the bottom of the screen signifies that the drawing of the pizza cutter will be one-quarter its full size. Zoom in on the title block to see how it automatically indicates the scale.

4. **Zoom to Fit** and click the **Named View** button in the **Drawing** toolbar to insert an **Isometric** view into the drawing. Select one of the views (the box around the pizza cutter, not the pizza cutter itself) in the Graphics Window. Choose *Isometric* and place the view on the drawing.

5. *Right click* on the isometric view and select **Properties**. In the *Drawing View Properties* dialog box, check the *Show in exploded state* box to display the view as an exploded assembly. Click *OK*.

6. To make room for more views that will be added to this drawing, move the orthographic and isometric views, as shown in Figure 5.24.

5.4.3   Adding a Section View

Cross-section views are often useful to show how parts fit together. Cross sections can help avoid part interference in assemblies and ensure that interior regions of the parts are correct. "Slicing" a part or assembly along a plane results in a section view. A section

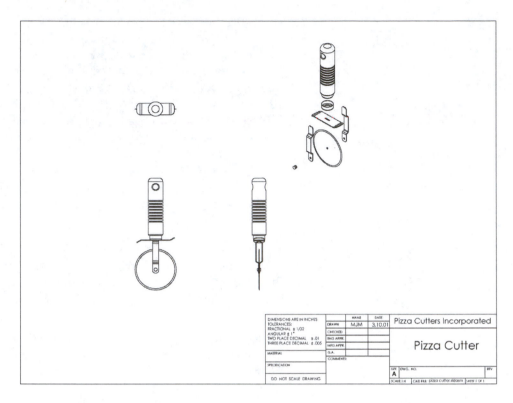

Figure 5.24. Orthographic and isometric views placed.

view is created by sketching a line to indicate the plane at which the part or assembly is to be sliced and by adding a new view of the sliced section. You will create a section view that slices the pizza cutter in half by cutting the front view of the model along a vertical plane.

1. **Zoom To Area** on the front view.

2. Select the **Line** tool in the **Sketch Tools** toolbar. Bring the cursor just above the upper end of the handle in the front view of the pizza cutter. A light bulb will appear next to the cursor when the cursor is aligned with the centerline of the pizza cutter. With the light bulb visible, click and drag to draw a vertical line downward past the bottom of the blade. Look for the "V" next to the cursor before releasing the mouse button. The front view should look similar to the one shown in Figure 5.25.

3. Be sure that the line is selected (highlighted in green) and click the **Section View** button (two arrows pointing left) in the **Drawing** toolbar, or select **Insert** ⇒ **Drawing View** ⇒ **Section**. A dialog box warning about partial sections appears. Partial sections permit only a portion of the view to be sectioned. Since all of the view should be sectioned, click *No*. The *Section View* dialog box appears, which allows some parts of the assembly to be excluded from the section cut. This feature can make the section clearer. In this case, all of the components should be included in the section view, so click *OK* to the *Section View* dialog box. **Zoom To Fit** in order to see the entire drawing. Move the cursor toward the left side of the drawing and click once to place the section view to the left of the front view as shown in Figure 5.23.

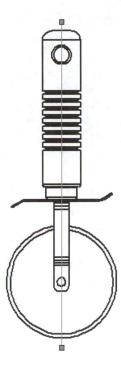

Figure 5.25.   Line on the front view.

The section view appears, named **SECTION A–A,** as shown in Figure 5.26. Notice that the line that was drawn on the front view has changed to a section line with "A"s near the arrows, linking it to the section view. It may be necessary to zoom in to see these details. Move the views, if necessary.

4.   The cutting line arrows in the front view should point to the right for the section positioned to the left of the front view. If necessary, click the ***Flip direction*** checkbox in the ***Section View*** PropertyManager to change the arrow direction. Then click ***OK***.

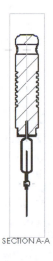

SECTION A-A

Figure 5.26.   Section view.

5.4.4   Adding a Detail View

A detail view is an enlarged view of a small portion of the drawing. A detail view can be particularly useful to show small details, such as the rivet of the pizza cutter. The detail view is dependent on the parent view, but it has a scale that is independent of the rest of the drawing. This scale is usually larger than the rest of the drawing, so that the detail can easily be seen. To create a detail view, a circle or a rectangle is sketched around the area to be shown in detail, and a new view of the enclosed area is added to the drawing. You will create a detail view of the lower portion of the pizza cutter (where the rivet holds the blade between the two arms), so that the detail of the rivet can be seen.

1. Zoom in on the blade in the right view. Activate the **Circle** tool in the **Sketch Tools** toolbar. Draw a circle centered on the rivet and similar in size to the circle shown in Figure 5.27. Although a circle was used in the figure, any closed sketch could be used to create a detail view.

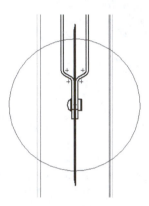

Figure 5.27.   Circle for detail view.

2. With the circle selected, click on the **Detail View** button (a circle with an "A" in it) in the **Drawing** toolbar, or select **Insert ⇒ Drawing View ⇒ Detail**. **Zoom To Fit** and place the view in the upper right corner of the drawing as shown in Figure 5.23. A detail view is placed, with the name **DETAIL B**.

3. Be sure that the detail view is selected and set the scale to *1:2* in the *Custom Scale* field of the *Detail View* PropertyManager to enlarge the detail view, if it is not already set at 1:2. Click *OK*. The text "**SCALE 1:2**" appears below the detail view.

4. Set the font size to **16** points on both **DETAIL B SCALE 1:2** and **SECTION A–A** by *right clicking* on the text and changing the size in the *Properties* window or by using the *Note* PropertyManager. The drawing should look similar to that shown in Figure 5.28. Move the views to match the figure.

5.4.5   Adding Numbers to the Components of the Assembly

In order to identify components in an assembly drawing, each component can be named with or referenced by a number. In this section, numbers will be added to each of the parts of the assembly. A bill of materials referencing these numbers will be created in the next section.

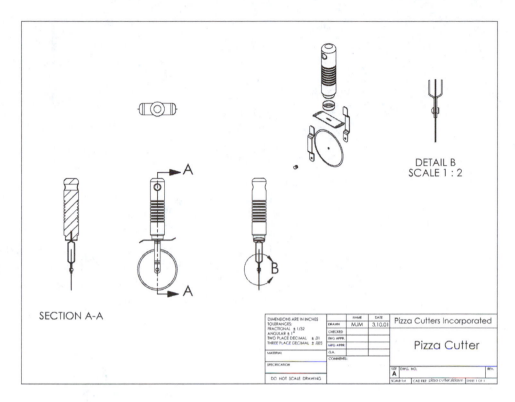

DETAIL B
SCALE 1 : 2

SECTION A-A

DIMENSIONS ARE IN INCHES TOLERANCES: FRACTIONAL ± 1/32 ANGULAR ± 1° TWO PLACE DECIMAL ± .01 THREE PLACE DECIMAL ± .005		NAME	DATE	Pizza Cutters Incorporated
	DRAWN	MJM	3.10.01	
	CHECKED			
	ENG APPR.			
	MFG APPR.			Pizza Cutter
MATERIAL	Q.A.			
	COMMENTS:			
SPECIFICATION				SIZE DWG. NO. REV.
				A
DO NOT SCALE DRAWING				SCALE:1:4 CAD REF: pizza cutter.sldasm SHEET 1 OF 1

Figure 5.28.   Assembly views arranged.

1. The balloons, or circles, enclosing the numbers must be set up correctly. Select **Tools** ⇒ **Options**. In the **Balloons** item of the **Document Properties** tab, set the **Single balloon Size** to **Tight Fit**. This results in a small balloon around the numbers. Check **Use bent leaders** in the **Bent leaders** field for the lines to the balloons. Click **OK**.

2. Zoom in on the detail view. Click the <u>**Balloon**</u> button (a balloon with the number "1" inside) in the <u>**Annotation**</u> toolbar, or select **Insert** ⇒ **Annotations** ⇒ **Balloon**.

3. Click on the head of the rivet. An arrow and a number surrounded by a circle appear. Click **OK**. It may be necessary to **Zoom To Fit** to see the balloon. The number refers to the item number SolidWorks assigned to the part in the assembly. *Right click* on the number to activate the **Properties** dialog box. Change the font size of the balloon note to **14** points.

4. If an arrowhead does not appear at the end of the leader line, turn off the **Smart** checkbox next to **Arrow style** in the **Properties** dialog box. Choose the filled arrowheads from the pull-down menu. Click **OK** to close the dialog box.

5. Click and drag the balloon note a short distance away from the blade, as shown in Figure 5.29. Your figure may have the balloon on the right side, opposite that in the figure.

6. Add numbers using the **Balloon** tool to the exploded isometric view for the other parts of the assembly: the guard, the arm, the blade, the cap, and the handle. The point that you click on the part is where the arrowhead will be located. Move the labels to convenient locations, so that the arrows clearly point

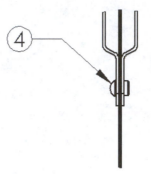

Figure 5.29.   Rivet numbered.

to the parts. The isometric view should look similar to the one shown in Figure 5.30. *Control click* on all of the labels to select them. Then *right click* on one label, select **Properties**, and change the font size to *14* points. This will change the font size for all of the labels.

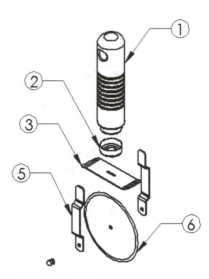

Figure 5.30.   Assembly components numbered.

5.4.6   Adding a Bill of Materials

A bill of materials, or BOM, is a list of the parts in an assembly. Usually, a BOM shows the item number, the name, and the quantity of each item. If Microsoft Excel is installed on your computer, SolidWorks can automatically generate a BOM for you. In this section, you will create a BOM of the parts in the pizza cutter assembly.

1.   Select the isometric view by clicking on the view within the box, but not on the pizza cutter. The view becomes highlighted in green. You can select any view, as long as all of the parts that you want on the bill of materials are present in it.

2.   Select **Insert** ⇒ **Bill of Materials**. The *Select BOM Template* dialog box appears. Open *bomtemp,* a standard SolidWorks template for the bill of

materials. The ***Bill of Materials Properties*** dialog box is shown in Figure 5.31. Be sure that ***Use the document's note font when creating the table*** is checked, so that the font for the bill of materials matches the font of the rest of the drawing. Also, be sure that the ***Show Parts Only*** button is checked. With this button checked, all parts of the pizza cutter assembly will appear in the bill of materials, but the cutter sub-assembly will not. Unselect ***Use table anchor point,*** so that you can drag the bill of materials to any part of the drawing.

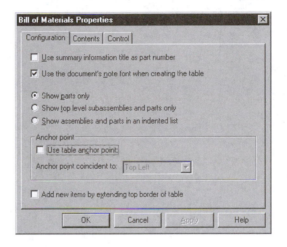

Figure 5.31. *Bill of Materials Properties* dialog box.

3. Click ***OK***. After a short wait, SolidWorks generates an embedded Excel table in the drawing. Click and drag the table to the right side of the drawing, as shown in Figure 5.32. You may need to move some views in order to make room for the BOM.

4. Zoom in on the table. There are four columns, with a row for each of the parts in the assembly. Notice that the numbers created in the balloon notes refer to the same parts in the bill of materials. SolidWorks automatically put a **2** in the **QTY** column for the arm, signifying that there are two identical arms in the assembly. Activate the **Select** tool.

5. The bill of materials can be edited by *right clicking* on the table and selecting **Edit Bill of Materials**. An editable Excel table appears, similar to the one shown in Figure 5.33. You may need to zoom out to see the embedded table. *Right click* on the "**D**" at the top of the fourth column in the Excel window, and select **Hide** from the menu. This removes the Description column.

6. Change the text "**PART NO.**" to "**PART**" by clicking on the field and editing the text at the top of the screen, just as you would in Excel. Hit Enter to accept the change. Click on the SolidWorks portion of the screen to return to the drawing.

7. **Zoom To Fit** and move the items on the drawing to match that shown in Figure 5.23.

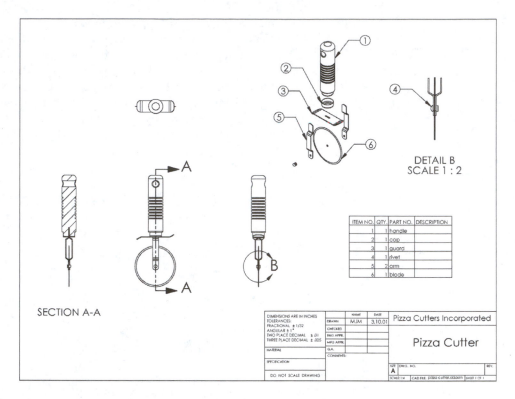

ITEM NO.	QTY.	PART NO.	DESCRIPTION
1	1	handle	
2	1	cap	
3	1	guard	
4	1	rivet	
5	2	arm	
6	1	blade	

Figure 5.32. BOM placed in assembly drawing.

	A	B	C
1	ITEM NO.	QTY.	PART
2	1	1	handle
3	2	1	cap
4	3	1	guard
5	4	1	rivet
6	5	2	arm
7	6	1	blade

Figure 5.33. BOM Excel edit window.

Congratulations! This completes the drawing of the pizza cutter assembly. Save your work as *pizza cutter drawing*. Check the drawing in **Print Preview,** make any necessary changes, and print the drawing using **File ⟹ Print**.

EDRAWINGS

eDrawings is an add-on feature to SolidWorks that allows two-dimensional drawings to be converted to an animated format that is easily understood by nonengineers and is compact enough to be sent by e-mail. Once an eDrawing is published from within SolidWorks, it can be opened on any Windows PC, even if SolidWorks is not installed.

Two types of files can be created when an eDrawing is published. The first type contains the drawing data and a viewer for the drawing in a single file with an .exe extension. The second type, which is smaller in size, contains only the drawing data and can be opened by anyone who already has the eDrawing viewer. This type has an .edrw extension.

To use eDrawings, the eDrawings publisher and viewer must first be downloaded from SolidWorks' Web site: http://www.solidworks.com. Once the eDrawing publisher is installed, an eDrawing can be created from any drawing in SolidWorks by opening the drawing and clicking the **Publish an eDrawing** button in the **eDrawings** toolbar.

The eDrawings program opens and shows the part. In the eDrawing viewer, use the **Save As** button in the **Standard** toolbar, or **File ⇒ Save As**, to save the eDrawing as an .edrw or an .exe file. To send a file directly by e-mail, click the **Send** button in the **Standard** toolbar, or **File ⇒ Send**. This will open a new message in your default mail program with the eDrawing attached. The small file size of eDrawings facilitates sending them by e-mail.

One of the key features of eDrawings is the ability to animate views. A solid model of one view of the part is rotated to another view of the part. This is especially useful to people who are not accustomed to reading engineering drawings. If multiple views exist in a drawing, the viewer can be set to automatically animate from one view to the next by clicking the **Play** button in the **eDrawing** toolbar.

Problems

1. Create a drawing of the guard. Include three orthographic views and one isometric view.

2. Create a drawing of the cap. Include a section view through the cap, in addition to two orthographic views and one isometric view.

3. Create a drawing of the blade. Include a detail section view of the cutting edge, in addition to two orthographic views and one isometric view.

4. Create a drawing of the rivet using a scale of 5:1. Include a section view through the rivet, in addition to two orthographic views and one isometric view. (Note that it is unlikely that a drawing of the rivet after it is deformed would be necessary in a practical situation.)

5. Create a half-scale drawing of the handle. Include a section view through the diameter of the handle and a detail section view of the rectangular cut at one end of the handle, in addition to two orthographic views and one isometric view.

6

Modeling the Handle as a Plastic Injection-Molded Part

OVERVIEW

Many advanced capabilities make SolidWorks an ideal tool for modeling injection-molded parts. In this chapter, several advanced features will be used to redesign the handle to make it suitable for injection molding. The original handle will be cut in half and shelled to create a thin-walled part. Counterbored holes will be added for self-tapping screws to fasten the two halves of the handle together. Ribs will be added for strength and rigidity. Then, sweep features will be used to add an interlocking edge to align the two halves. Finally, the two halves will be assembled to create a new, thin-walled version of the pizza cutter handle.

The handle that was modeled in the earlier chapters would probably be made of wood or molded as solid plastic. However, to save on machining time or on material costs, a thin-walled, injection-molded handle would be advantageous. In this chapter, you will redesign the handle to be a plastic injection-molded part.

Plastic injection molding permits the fabrication of complex parts with relatively low cycle times—usually 10 to 30 seconds. Solid plastic pellets are heated and the molten plastic is injected at a high pressure into a two-part mold. After the plastic solidifies in the mold cavity, the two halves of the mold are separated and the part is ejected. To design a high-quality, injection-molded part, the engineer must account for the shrinkage of the plastic as it solidifies, design the part so that it can be ejected easily from the mold, be sure that air is not trapped in the molded part, and provide a part that is cosmetically appealing. Cosmetic imperfections

SECTIONS

OBJECTIVES

After working through this chapter, you will be able to

- Create a new part from an existing part,
- Shell a solid body to create a thin-walled part,
- Roll back the model to a previous state,
- Create a plane,
- Insert ribs,
- Add draft to features,
- Convert features of a model to sketch entities,
- Create a boss sweep,
- Create a cut sweep,
- Use SmartMates for assembly, and
- View cross sections through the model.

include weld lines (resulting from nonuniform solidification of the plastic as it flows around part features), flash (as plastic is extruded between the two halves of the mold), and sink marks (depressions that result from the slower solidification and shrinkage of a thicker portion of the part). An important rule of thumb in the design of plastic injection-molded parts is to maintain a relatively uniform wall thickness for all sections of the part. A constant wall thickness results in uniform solidification of the molten plastic, yielding a part that is stronger and has fewer cosmetic and internal defects.

The handle will be redesigned to have a uniform wall thickness of about 1/16″, while maintaining the outer geometry of the original handle. This results in a hollow handle that could be quite weak. To overcome this problem, many plastic parts, including the handle, are strengthened with ribs—extrusions of material that prevent deflection and add structural rigidity. The handle modeled in this chapter will consist of two identical plastic injection-molded parts. Each part is one-half of the handle, as shown in Figure 6.1. The identical parts are designed to be held together with screws. Most likely, this is not the optimal design for the handle. However, the design that is modeled in this chapter uses many of the exceptional capabilities of SolidWorks, including shells, ribs, and sweeps.

Figure 6.1.   Injection-molded handle.

6.1   THE DESIGN OF THE PLASTIC INJECTION-MOLDED HANDLE

The half of the handle shown in Figure 6.1 is designed to be fabricated by injection molding. It has a uniform wall thickness to mold well and ribs to enhance the strength. It is designed to be ejected easily from the mold. There are four holes, used to assemble the two parts of the handle. When the two halves are placed together, the holes of one half mate with the holes of the other half. The two identical halves of the handle are attached using self-tapping screws, as shown in Figure 6.2. The resulting handle has the same dimensions as the solid handle created earlier.

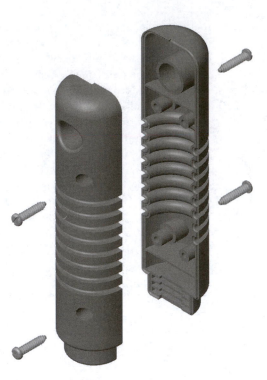

Figure 6.2. Assembly of the handle halves.

The mold that would be used to create the half of the handle is shown in Figure 6.3. One-half of the mold forms the inner surface of the handle, while the other half of the mold forms the outer surface. After the molds are clamped together, molten plastic is injected into the cavity between the two halves and is left to solidify. An inlet channel, or *runner*, is necessary for the plastic to enter the mold cavity. In addition, vents and other items are necessary to assure a high-quality molded part, but these details have been omitted here for simplicity.

To create the part shown in Figure 6.1, you will use the original solid handle as a starting point. First, half of the handle will be removed using an extruded cut. Then, the handle will be shelled, a process that creates a model with a uniform thickness by removing material offset from a surface of a part. The holes used for the assembly of the handle will be modeled next. Ribs will then be added to the model to strengthen the part and provide a surface to which the arms are secured when the pizza cutter is assembled. To prevent the two halves of the handle from slipping past each other, an interlocking profile will be created along the edge of the handle using two sweeps: one that adds material and one that removes material. Once one-half of the handle is modeled, two identical halves will be assembled to create the complete handle. The assembly will be checked for interference to ensure that the halves were modeled correctly.

In practice, the molds to produce the part would be modeled in SolidWorks and the geometry data sent to a numerically controlled machine tool to fabricate the molds. Depending on the material and quality of the molds, thousands, even millions of plastic parts could then be created using an injection molding machine. Since creating the molds is usually an expensive process, plastic injection molding lends itself to high-production parts.

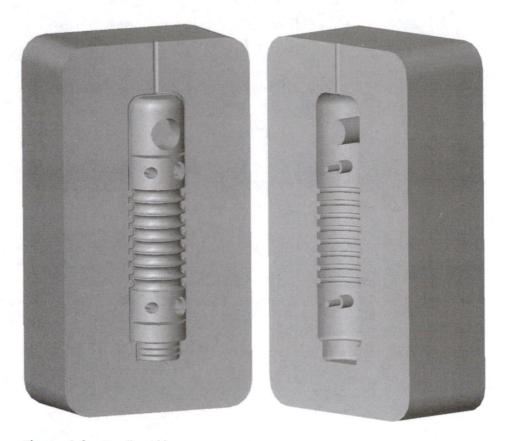

Figure 6.3. Handle mold.

6.2   SHELLING THE HANDLE AND ADDING ASSEMBLY HOLES

The existing solid handle will be modified to create a model suitable for plastic injection molding. Half of the handle will be shelled to create a part of uniform thickness. Then, holes will be added so that the parts can be assembled using self-tapping screws.

6.2.1   Creating a New Part From the Existing Handle

The part file, **handle.sldprt**, will be opened and then saved with a new name. This allows you to work on the new file without altering the original solid handle or disturbing the pizza cutter assembly. Be sure that you have modeled the handle as previously described.

1. Open **handle.sldprt** by selecting **File ⇒ Open**, or by clicking the <u>**Open**</u> button in the <u>**Standard**</u> toolbar. The solid handle opens in a new part window.

2. In the **View ⇒ Toolbars** menu, be sure that **Features**, **Sketch**, **Sketch Relations**, **Sketch Tools**, **Standard**, **Standard Views**, and **View** are checked, so that these toolbars appear on the screen.

3. In the **File** menu, select **Save As**. This opens the *Save As* dialog box, which allows you to save a version of the handle with a new name in a new location. Save the handle as *shelled handle* and click *Save*. The name of the part window changes to reflect the new name.

4. Click the **<u>Grid</u>** button in the **<u>Sketch</u>** toolbar. Select the *Units* list item and set *Decimal Places* to *5* and *Denominator* to *32*, so that the dimensions as small as 1/32 (.03125) are displayed as fractions and not as truncated decimals. Be sure that the other settings match the ones shown in Figure 6.4. Click *OK*. You are now ready to modify the handle to be a plastic injection-molded part.

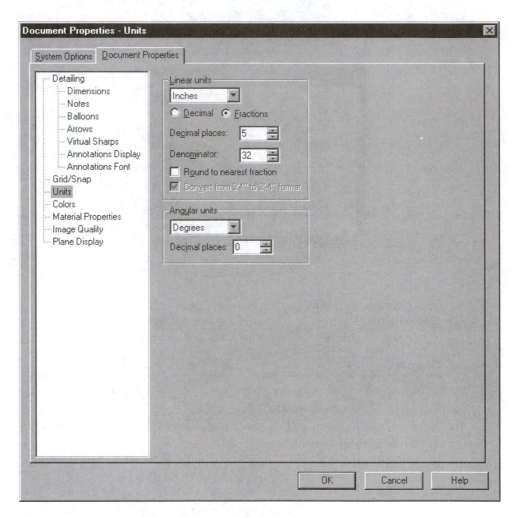

Figure 6.4. ***Document Properties*** dialog box: ***Units***.

6.2.2   Cutting the Solid Handle in Half

To begin, half of the handle will be removed so that the remaining half can be shelled. There are several ways to remove the unwanted material of the handle so that it looks similar to that shown in Figure 6.5. One method would be to create a sketch on the plane through the center of the handle, the **Right** plane, in order to extrude a cut to remove all of the material to one side of the **Front** plane. Instead, you will use a simpler method, in which you sketch a closed semicircle on the top end of the handle and extrude a cut to remove material.

Figure 6.5. Half of the solid handle.

1. Set the view to **Hidden Lines Visible** and **Isometric**. Select the flat circular face at the top end of the handle and open a sketch on it. Be sure to select the face as indicated by the icon next to the cursor, and not the edge. Go to the **Top** view.

2. Select the outer edge of the handle, as shown in Figure 6.6. With the edge selected, click the **Convert Entities** button (a cube) in the **Sketch Tools** toolbar, or **Tools ⇒ Sketch Tools ⇒ Convert Entities**. The **Convert**

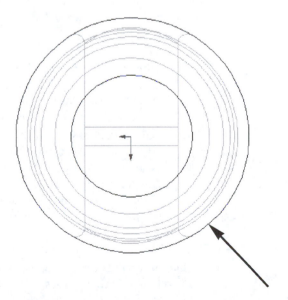

Figure 6.6. Outer edge of the handle.

Entities tool is useful to project geometries that have already been modeled onto the current sketch plane. The edges of the selected feature are transformed into a series of sketch entities, namely lines and arcs. In this case, the selected circular edge is projected onto the sketch plane as a circle. This circle is fully defined and is part of the active sketch.

3.   Draw a horizontal line that cuts the circle in half through the center of the handle's axis. Be sure that both endpoints of the line are touching the arc of the circle. To ensure that the line is horizontal, click the **Add Relation** button in the **Sketch Relations** toolbar, select the line (to list it in **Selected Entities**), be sure that **Horizontal0** is listed in the **Existing Relations** field and click **OK**. If the line does not go through the origin, add a Coincident relation to ensure that the two entities touch.

4.   **Trim** the upper part of the circle to create a closed semicircle, similar to the one shown in Figure 6.7.

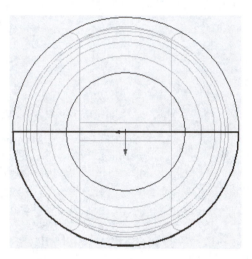

Figure 6.7.   Completed semicircle sketch.

5.   Return to the **Isometric** view. The sketch of the semicircle should be above the front half of the handle, as shown in Figure 6.8. If it is not, return to the view that is normal to the sketch, delete the entities, and sketch the semicircle in the correct orientation.

6.   Use an **Extruded Cut** that goes **Through All** to cut away the front half of the handle. The result should look like that shown in Figure 6.5. Although you used a semicircular cut, the sketch for the cut could have any shape, as long as the material to be cut away is within the boundaries of the sketch. For instance, a rectangular cut with one side of the rectangle through the center of the handle would work equally well.

6.2.3   Shelling the Handle

Now that the front half of the solid handle has been removed, the rest of the handle can be shelled to a uniform thickness.

1.   Click the **Shell** button (a hollow cube) in the **Features** toolbar, or **Insert** ⇒ **Features** ⇒ **Shell**. The **Shell** PropertyManager appears as shown in Figure 6.9.

Figure 6.8. Closed semicircle above handle.

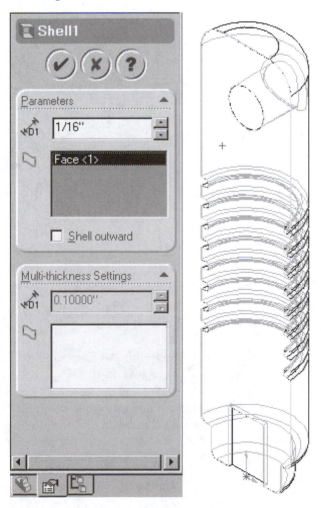

Figure 6.9. *Shell* PropertyManager.

2. Set the ***Thickness*** under ***Parameters*** to ***1/16***. This is the uniform thickness that will be applied to the part.

3. Click the flat face at the front of the handle. ***Face <1>*** appears in the ***Faces to Remove*** field. This face will be "opened" to form an open shell of the handle. SolidWorks will completely remove any material on this face. If this face were not selected, the resulting part would be a closed hollow shell with a flat 1/16″-thick surface on this face, as well as on all of the other surfaces.

4. Click ***OK***. The front face is removed and the rest of the handle is shelled with a constant thickness of 1/16″. The part should look similar to the one shown in Figure 6.10. Use the **Shaded** display and rotate the shelled handle. All of the features created in the original handle are still on the shelled handle, including the grooves and the rectangular slot at the bottom. **Shell1** has appeared in the FeatureManager design tree for the shell feature. Return to **Hidden Lines Visible** and **Isometric**.

Figure 6.10.   Shelled handle.

6.2.4   Removing the Rectangular-Cut Feature

The current model of the handle could not be injection molded using a simple two-part mold. After the plastic solidified, the part would be trapped in the cavity of the mold by the undercut of the rectangular slot at the bottom of the handle. You will delete this feature, but save the sketch that was used to create it. This sketch will be used later to model the slot after the rib features have been added to the shelled handle.

1. In the FeatureManager design tree, click on **Cut-Extrude1** to highlight it. This should be the first Cut-Extrude feature in the FeatureManager design

tree. Verify that the rectangular cut is highlighted in green in the Graphics Window.

2. Hit Delete on the keyboard to remove the feature. Answer **Yes** to the **Confirm Delete** dialog box. Although the cut is removed from the model, the original sketch used to create it remains. The sketch entities appear in gray at the bottom of the handle, as shown in Figure 6.11.

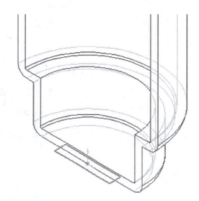

Figure 6.11.   Rectangle sketch entities.

3. Click on the name **Sketch3** (or the appropriate name of your sketch of the rectangle) in the FeatureManager design tree, so that the rectangle becomes highlighted in green. Click again on the name (not the icon) to rename it within the FeatureManager design tree window. A box surrounds the text, which becomes highlighted. Change the text to **rectangle sketch** so as not to confuse this sketch with any other sketches. Hit Enter after typing in the text. It is helpful to use meaningful names for features and sketches in the FeatureManager design tree, especially with complex models. Well-named features allow you and other users of the models to make changes without confusion.

4. Since you will not need the sketch right away, hide it by *right clicking* on **rectangle sketch** in the FeatureManager design tree and selecting **Hide Sketch** from the menu that appears.

6.2.5   Rolling Back the Model

The features are listed in the FeatureManager design tree from top to bottom in the order in which they were created. The FeatureManager design tree can be thought of as a feature-creation time line. The Rollback Bar can be used to return the model to a previous state, suppressing features that were created later. You will roll back the model to a state before the shell was created, in order to add the holes for the self-tapping screws necessary for the shelled handle.

1. Move the cursor over the horizontal yellow line just below **Shell1** in the FeatureManager design tree. This line is the Rollback Bar. The cursor changes to a hand holding the Rollback Bar. Drag the bar from below **Shell1** to just above it, as shown in Figure 6.12.

2. The shell is suppressed (the icon is grayed out in the FeatureManager design tree) and the model is returned to the state before the shell was created.

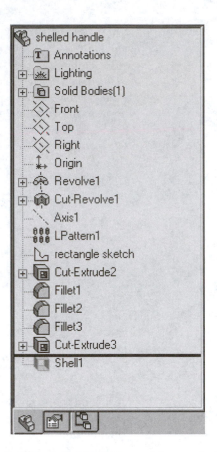

Figure 6.12. Rolled-back FeatureManager design tree.

The only features shown in the Graphics Window are those created before the shell feature.

6.2.6 Creating a Plane

It is now necessary to create a plane that can be used for sketching. A plane is considered to be *Reference Geometry* and does not represent a feature of the part. Like the Reference Geometry axis that was created in the original model of the solid handle, this plane is used to add other features. There are several ways to define a plane from existing features. In this case, you will create a new plane that is offset a specified distance from the plane of the flat surface of the sliced handle, the **Front** plane.

1. Select **Insert** ⇒ **Reference Geometry** ⇒ **Plane**. The *Plane* Property-Manager appears as shown in Figure 6.13. Several choices for the creation of a plane are available. Use the *Offset Distance* button (a double-ended arrow) to create a plane offset from the **Front** plane.

2. Set the *Distance* to *5/8*.

3. Specify the plane to be offset from the **Front** plane by clicking **Front** in the FeatureManager design tree, which is activated with the tab at the bottom of the PropertyManager. **Front** appears in the *Reference Entities* field.

4. Go to the **Right** view to verify that the new plane will be created tangent to the curved side of the handle, as shown in Figure 6.13. If the new plane is on the wrong side of the **Front** plane, check the *Reverse direction* box.

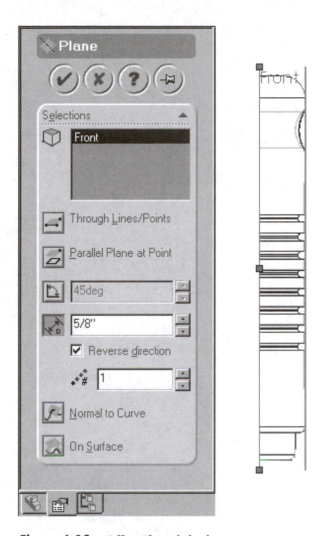

Figure 6.13. *Offset Plane* dialog box.

5. Click **OK**. The new plane, **Plane1**, appears in the Graphics Window. The new plane is inserted into the FeatureManager design tree just above the Rollback Bar, so that it is before (above) the **Shell1** feature.

6.2.7 Modeling the Counterbores

The heads of the self-tapping screws that hold the two halves of the handle together will sit in recesses, called counterbores. Counterbores sink the heads of the screws into the part, so that they do not protrude from the assembled handle. Since the counterbores extend from the outer surface of the handle inward, it is easiest to create them as an extruded cut inward from a plane tangent to the outer surface (**Plane1**).

1. Select the newly created **Plane1** in the FeatureManager design tree, so that it is highlighted in green. Open a sketch on **Plane1**. Click the **Back** button in the **Standard Views** toolbar to view the rounded portion of the handle.

2. Sketch two circles for the holes, as shown in Figure 6.14. After sketching and dimensioning the two circles as indicated, the lower circle should be fully defined (black). The upper circle remains underdefined (blue), because neither its horizontal position nor its diameter have been specified.

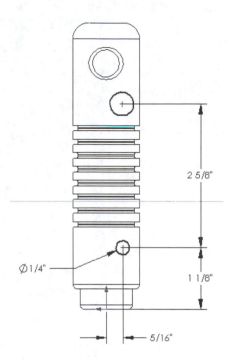

Figure 6.14. Counterbore hole sketch.

3. The upper circle will be fully defined by adding two relations: one Equal relation, which will define the diameter of the upper circle to be the same as that of the lower circle, and one Vertical relation, which will align the centers of the circles to lie on an imaginary vertical centerline. Click the **<u>Add Relation</u>** button in the **<u>Sketch Relations</u>** toolbar, or **Tools** ⇒ **Relations** ⇒ **Add**. Select the arcs of the two circles, so that they appear in the ***Selected Entities*** box. Click the ***Equal*** button. The upper circle adjusts to be the same diameter as the lower circle.

4. With the ***Add Relations*** PropertyManager still open, select the center-points of the circles (zoom in, if necessary) and align them in the ***Vertical*** direction. This fully defines the upper circle to be directly above the lower circle. Click ***OK***.

5. Return to the **Isometric** view and open the ***Cut-Extrude*** PropertyManager, as shown in Figure 6.15.

6. The holes will extend into the handle and terminate at a given distance from the front flat surface at the center of the handle. To do this, set the ***End Condition*** to ***Offset From Surface***. Set the ***Offset Distance*** to ***5/16***. Select the front flat surface of the handle. ***Face<1>*** appears in the ***Face/Plane*** field. This will produce a cut from **Plane1** to a surface 5/16″ away from the front flat face of the handle.

7. Click ***OK***. In the **Right** view, the holes in the handle should look similar to those shown in Figure 6.16. Hide **Plane1** and **Redraw**, if necessary.

6.2.8 Modeling the Through Holes

The next feature to be added is the pair of through holes that are concentric with the counterbores. Two different methods will be used to model these holes.

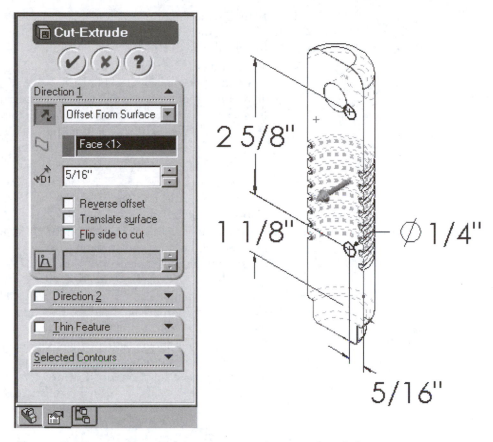

Figure 6.15. *Cut-Extrude* PropertyManager for counterbore holes.

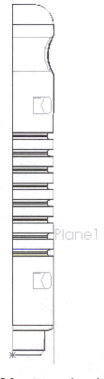

Figure 6.16. Counterbore holes created.

1. Return to the **Isometric** view and open a sketch on the flat face on the front of the handle. Change the view to **Normal To** the sketching plane. Be sure that the display is **Hidden Lines Visible**.

2. The first method is to sketch a circle and use a geometric relation to make it concentric with the counterbore hole. Begin by sketching a large circle just above the upper counterbore. Add a **Concentric** relation, so that the circle is concentric with the upper counterbore. Both the new circle and the counterbore circle should be selected, so that both appear in the **Selected entities** field of the **Add Relations** PropertyManager. Dimension the diameter of the new circle to be **.12**.

3. The second method to make a concentric circle is to offset it from the counterbore. Select **Offset Entities** in the **Sketch Tools** toolbar, or **Tools ⇒ Sketch Tools ⇒ Offset Entities**. The **Offset Entities** Property-Manager appears, as shown in Figure 6.17. Type in an **Offset Distance** of **.065**. Select the circle corresponding to the lower counterbore. A new circle offset from the counterbore circle appears. If the new circle is outside of the counterbore circle, click the **Reverse** checkbox. When the new circle is inside of the counterbore circle, click **OK**. A .065″ dimension appears between the counterbore hole and the new offset circle. By making the offset .065″ from the .250″ counterbore diameter, the diameter of the new circle is .120″, which is identical to the other new circle in the sketch. The **Offset Entities** tool creates a geometry by offsetting it from an existing geometry. This is similar to the **Convert Entities** tool used earlier, which creates a geometry by projecting an existing geometry onto the sketch plane.

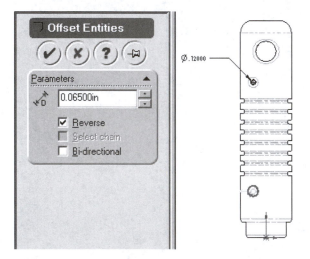

Figure 6.17.   *Offset Entities* PropertyManager.

4. Cut holes of type **Through All** into the handle. The **Isometric** view of the handle with the holes and counterbores is shown in Figure 6.18.

6.2.9   Modeling the Tap Holes Using the Simple Hole Feature

The remaining two holes that need to be created are the holes that the self-tapping screws will "tap" into. The diameter of these holes is smaller than the major diameter of the screws, so that each screw will cut a thread as it is screwed into the hole. To expedite

Figure 6.18.   Counterbored holes created.

the process of making holes, the **Simple Hole** tool will be used to place one hole on the part. Then, the second hole will be added to the sketch. The **Simple Hole** tool is a shortcut to create a circular extruded cut (hole) without a sketch. The locations of the holes are dimensioned after the holes are created.

1. Use the **Select** tool to click to the right of the lower counterbored hole on the front flat face of the handle. A plus sign appears at the selected point on the face. Click **Insert** ⇒ **Features** ⇒ **Hole** ⇒ **Simple**. The *Hole* PropertyManager appears.

2. Set the *End Condition* to *Through All*, so that the hole will go completely through the handle. Set the *Hole Diameter* to *.1*.

3. The arrow shows the direction of the hole cut. Click *OK*. A hole with the specified diameter is placed where the plus sign appeared on the flat face of the handle.

4. Click the plus sign next to **Hole1** in the FeatureManager design tree. The feature expands to show the sketch that was generated automatically when the **Simple Hole** feature was applied. *Right click* that sketch and select **Edit Sketch**. Click **Normal To**.

5. Specify the location of the circle, as shown in Figure 6.19, by adding horizontal and vertical dimensions.

6. Sketch another circle near the upper counterbored hole. Make the new circle **Equal** in diameter to the first one using a relation. It may help to zoom in on the lower circle to select it. Dimension the location to be **2 5/8** vertically above the existing circle by adding a dimension and a relation. The sketch should now be *Fully Defined*.

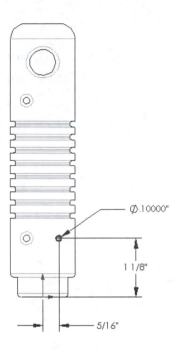

Figure 6.19. Lower circle dimensioned.

7. Exit the sketch by clicking the **Sketch** button in the **Sketch** toolbar or by clicking the **Exit Sketch** icon in the upper right Confirmation Corner of the Graphics Window. The two holes should look similar to the ones shown in Figure 6.20 in the **Isometric** view. It was not necessary to extrude a cut for

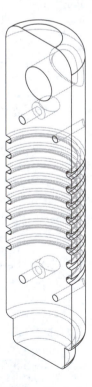

Figure 6.20. Tap holes created.

the second hole. Because it was added to the sketch of the cut for the first hole, it was extruded automatically with the first hole.

6.2.10 Reverting to the Shelled Model

Now that the holes have been added, the model can return to its shelled form. Recall that the holes added in the previous sections were modeled as if the shell feature had not yet been created. As a result, the shelling feature will now include the hole surfaces.

1. Drag the Rollback Bar below the **Shell1** feature in the FeatureManager design tree. The model is rebuilt and the shell feature is applied to all features above it in the FeatureManager design tree, including the new holes. The handle should look like the one shown in Figure 6.21. Notice that each hole has 1/16″ of material surrounding the hole surface.

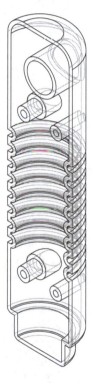

Figure 6.21. Shell feature applied to assembly holes.

2. It was necessary to make the tap holes through holes rather than blind holes, so that the shelling feature would work properly without errors. However, the appearance of the open ends of the through holes on the surface of the handle is not cosmetically appealing. To fill in the ends of the holes, you will create an offset plane and extrude material in the hole from the plane to the outer surface of the handle. Begin by using the **Right** view and clicking on **Front** in the FeatureManager design tree to display the plane. Create a new plane, offset *.435* to the right of the **Front** plane, using **Reference Geometry** in the **Insert** menu.

3. Open a sketch on the new plane and switch to the **Front** view. *Right click* on the new plane, **Plane2**, in the FeatureManager design tree and **Hide** the plane.

4. Select the two tap holes indicated in Figure 6.22, and click the **Convert Entities** button in the **Sketch Tools** toolbar to create two circle sketch entities in the new sketch plane.

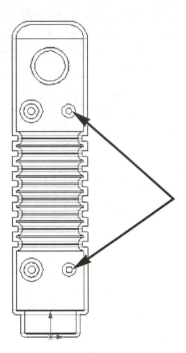

Figure 6.22.   Tap holes.

5. Switch to the **Right** view. Then, extrude material to fill the holes from the new plane outward to the outer surface of the handle. Use *Up To Surface* and select the outer surface of the handle near either hole as the *Face/Plane*. Be sure that the arrow in the Graphics Window points to the right, so that material is extruded from Plane2 to the outer surface of the handle. If the arrow does not point to the right, click the *Reverse Direction* button just under *Direction 1* in the PropertyManager followed by *OK*. After creating the extrusion, set the display to **Shaded**. Rotate the part to be sure that the tap holes no longer extend through to the surface of the handle. The part should look like the one shown in Figure 6.23.

Congratulations! This completes the shelling of the handle. To incorporate the changes, **Save** the part. Leave the window open. In the next section, you will add ribs to the handle.

6.3   ADDING RIBS TO THE HANDLE

Ribs are commonly used in plastic injection-molded parts to add strength while maintaining the requirement of nearly uniform thickness throughout the part. Ribs in Solid-Works require a profile sketch to which thickness is added before extruding it up to an existing surface of the part. You will add several ribs, as shown in Figure 6.24, to the shelled handle. These ribs add strength to the handle and provide a surface to hold the arms at the bottom of the handle.

Figure 6.23.   Tap holes closed.

Figure 6.24.   Ribs added to the shelled handle.

6.3.1 Creating the First Rib

The first rib is located below the lower assembly holes. It is a straight rib with a thickness that is approximately 60% of the thickness of the shelled handle. Ribs are usually thinner than the uniform thickness of the part to avoid surface defects (sink marks) caused by slower solidification time at the intersection of the rib and the wall of the part.

1. Go to the **Front** view and use **Hidden Lines Visible** display. Open a sketch on the **Front** plane.

2. Sketch a horizontal line that goes from one inside edge of the handle to the other, as shown in Figure 6.25. This is the position of the rib.

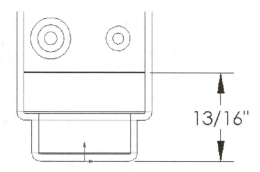

Figure 6.25. Horizontal line dimensioned.

3. Dimension the line to be **13/16** above the bottom of the handle.

4. With the sketch open, click **Insert** ⟹ **Features** ⟹ **Rib**. The parameters of the rib are set in the *Rib* PropertyManager, as shown in Figure 6.26.

5. Click the middle *Thickness* button so the rib is created on *Both Sides* of the sketched line. Set the *Rib Thickness* to *.04*. This will create a rib .04″ thick (about 60% of the 1/16″ wall thickness), with the sketched line as the center of the rib.

6. Set the *Extrusion direction* to *Normal to Sketch* by clicking the appropriate button. This will extrude the rib downward into the cavity of the handle perpendicular to the sketch plane. It is possible to sketch just a portion of a rib and have SolidWorks automatically extend the rib to the sidewall. *Type* is used to define the nature of the rib, if the rib extends beyond the sketched section. For example, consider a semicircular arc sketched so that the ends of the arc do not touch a sidewall. Using *Linear* as the *Type* extends the rib from the end of the arc to the sidewall along a line. Using *Natural* as the *Type* extends the rib along its natural curve to form a circular rib. For the rib sketched in Figure 6.25, the *Type* does not matter, because the rib is defined from sidewall to sidewall.

7. Rotate the handle, so that you can see the direction in which the arrow at the rib points. If the arrow is pointing away from the cavity of the handle, click the *Flip material side* checkbox to change the direction.

8. Click **OK**. The feature **Rib1** appears in the FeatureManager design tree. The new rib should look similar to that shown in Figure 6.27.

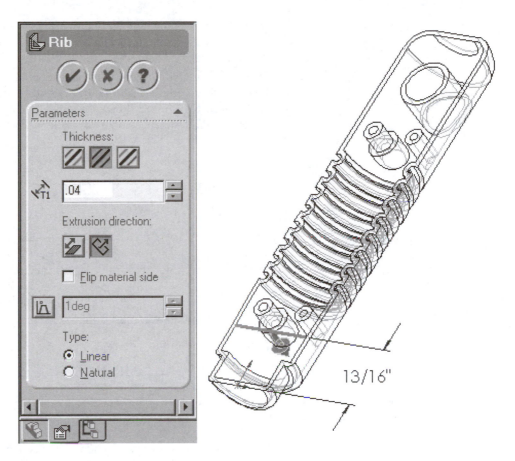

Figure 6.26. *Rib* Property Manager.

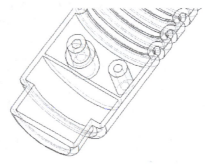

Figure 6.27. First rib created.

6.3.2   Creating the Sketch of the Lower Ribs

Three ribs are located at the bottom of the handle. These ribs not only add strength, but will also serve as a surface to which the arms will be secured when the pizza cutter is assembled. One line will be sketched, and the other two lines will be patterned after the first line.

1. Return to the **Front** view and notice that lines appear at the intersection of curved surfaces and other surfaces. This is most noticeable near the top of the handle—there is a horizontal line between the top and the hole. This line is a

projection of the tangent edge and the point at which the top fillet meets the sidewall of the handle. It is helpful to remove these tangent edges from the display by clicking **View** ⇒ **Display** ⇒ **Tangent Edges Removed**.

2. Open a sketch on the **Front** plane and zoom in on the bottom of the handle. Draw a line for another rib that will extend between the two corner points, as shown in Figure 6.28. Since these points are defined on the handle, the sketch is *Fully Defined* without any dimensions.

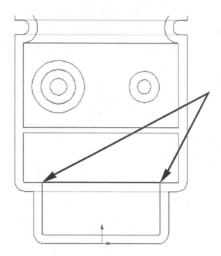

Figure 6.28. Corner points.

3. Two more lines for ribs can be added by making a linear pattern of the first line. Click the **Linear Sketch Step and Repeat** button in the **Sketch Tools** toolbar, or **Tools** ⇒ **Sketch Tools** ⇒ **Linear Step and Repeat**. The *Linear Sketch Step and Repeat* dialog box appears, as shown in Figure 6.29. Notice that this dialog box is different from the *Linear Pattern*

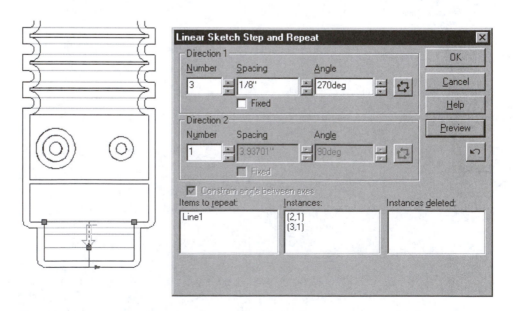

Figure 6.29. *Linear Sketch Step and Repeat* dialog box.

dialog box (used to copy the grooves on the handle), which is used with features, not with sketch entities.

4. Add the line to the *Items to Repeat* field by clicking the line in the Graphics Window, if it is not already selected.

5. In the *Direction 1* field, set the *Number* of instances to *3*, the *Spacing* between instances to *1/8*, and the *Angle* to *270*. The *Angle* refers to the direction in which the pattern will be repeated. In this case, the pattern will be repeated toward the bottom of the screen corresponding to 270°—right would be 0°, upward would be 90°, and so on.

6. Click the *Preview* button. The arrow should point downward (270°) and the lines should be repeated toward the bottom of the handle. If the lines are patterned in the wrong direction, click the *Reverse Direction 1* button (two right-angled arrows) to flip the direction. When you are satisfied with the preview, click *OK*. Two new lines are added to the sketch.

6.3.3   Creating the Lower Ribs

The lower ribs are created on one side of the sketched line, instead of at the mid plane of the line, as was done with the first rib. In this case, one rib feature will be used for multiple sketched lines to create multiple ribs.

1. Click **Insert** ⟹ **Features** ⟹ **Rib**. The *Rib* PropertyManager appears.

2. Set the *Rib Thickness* to *.04*, and click the rightmost *Thickness* button to place material on the lower side of the sketched lines.

3. Zoom in, if necessary, to preview the ribs. If a line appears above the line that was sketched first, the ribs will be created in the wrong direction. If necessary, click the leftmost *Thickness* button to place the ribs below the sketched lines.

4. Return to the **Isometric** view. In the **Extrusion Direction** field, click the **Flip material side** checkbox to see the direction in which the ribs will be created. If necessary, uncheck the **Flip material side** checkbox, so that the ribs will be created in the handle's cavity.

5. Click **OK** to complete the rib feature. Three ribs are created in the lower portion of the handle, as shown in Figure 6.24, and **Rib2** is added to the FeatureManager design tree.

6.3.4   Creating a Rib with Draft

Draft adds a small angle to an extrusion or a cut. Draft is important in plastic injection molding, so that the part can be removed easily from the mold without getting stuck. You will create a rib similar to the first rib, but with a draft angle.

1. Open a new sketch on the **Front** plane, and sketch a horizontal line across the cavity of the handle that is **4 1/16** above the bottom of the handle, as shown in Figure 6.30. Be sure that the line is horizontal and not coincident with any midpoints of existing features.

2. Set up a rib **Normal to Sketch** with a thickness of *.04* with material on *Both Sides* of the line. *Do not* click *OK*.

3. Click the *Draft On/Off* button and set the *Draft Angle* to *5*. Five degrees is a large draft angle. However, the large angle is useful to demonstrate the draft condition more clearly. After creating the rib, you will change the angle to one degree.

4. Click **OK**. The upper rib is created with draft, and **Rib3** appears in the FeatureManager design tree.

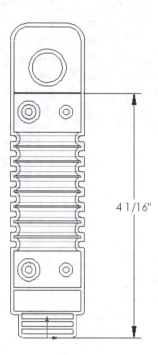

Figure 6.30. Upper rib dimensioned.

5.   Go to the **Left** view and *double click* the last rib in the FeatureManager design tree. The thickness, the position, and the draft-angle dimensions appear in the Graphics Window, as shown in Figure 6.31. Use the **Select** tool to move the .04 dimension, if necessary. Notice the 5° dimension, which represents the draft angle.

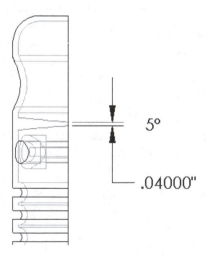

Figure 6.31. Draft on upper rib.

6.   With the **Select** tool, *double click* the **5** and change the value to **1**. Click the **Rebuild** button in the **Standard** toolbar, or **Edit** ⇒ **Rebuild**, to update the model with the new dimension. In the **Isometric** view, the handle should look like the one in Figure 6.24.

7. Although draft was only added to one rib on the handle, it could be added to the other ribs. To add a draft to the first rib, *right click* on **Rib1** in the FeatureManager design tree and select **Edit Definition**. The original definition appears in the PropertyManager window. Click the ***Draft On/Off*** button, set the **Angle** to **3** degrees, and be sure the **Draft outward** box is checked, so that the angle of the draft is outward toward the opening of the cavity. Click **OK** and verify that the rib looks correct. Change the draft angle to **1** degree. Like ribs, boss extrusions, cuts, and holes can also have a draft added to them.

Congratulations! This completes the creation of the rib features. Save the part and leave the window open.

6.4   ADDING SWEEPS TO THE HANDLE

In solids modeling, sweeps are invaluable because they produce relatively complex features that might be impossible to model using other methods. There are two basic elements for a sweep feature: a section and a path. The section, or profile, is "swept" along the path. For example, if a circular section is swept around a circular path, a doughnut shape would be created. Another example is the handle of a coffee mug. It could be modeled using the section and the path shown in Figure 6.32.

Figure 6.32.   Coffee mug handle modeled using a sweep.

There are two constraints to keep in mind when creating sweep features. First, the sweep section must touch the sweep path. This will be demonstrated later in this section. Second, a sweep feature cannot intersect itself. For example, a profile swept along a figure-eight path is not possible.

To allow the two halves of the handle to be perfectly aligned with each other when assembled, an interlocking profile will be created along the edge of the handle using two sweeps: one that adds material and one that removes material. The interlocking edge has a ridge that mates with a groove, as shown in Figure 6.33. A sweep is necessary to add these features, so that the interlocking edges follow the profile of the handle's edge.

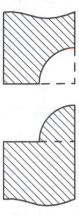

Figure 6.33. Interlocking profile.

6.4.1   Creating the Boss Sweep Path

The boss sweep path is the path along which the protruding profile will be swept. It follows the outer left edge of the handle. The **Convert Entities** tool will be used to transform the existing edge of the handle into a set of sketch entities. These entities will be used for the sweep path.

1.   Show tangent edges by selecting **View ⇒ Display ⇒ Tangent Edges Visible**. Set the display to **Hidden Lines Removed**.

2.   Open a sketch on the **Front** plane and set the view **Normal To** the sketching plane. You should be viewing the cavity of the shelled handle.

3.   *Right click* between the lines forming the upper flat end of the handle, as shown in Figure 6.34. Choose **Select Other** from the menu that appears. SolidWorks will cycle through possible selections. You can accept or reject the proposed selection by clicking either the left mouse button (Yes) or the right mouse button (No). Cycle through the selections by clicking the right mouse button until the entire front face (the 1/16″-thick edge of the handle) is highlighted. Click the left mouse button to accept the selection. Alternatives to using the **Select Other** option are to zoom in or set the **Selection Filter** to **Filter Faces**. Often, the **Select Other** method is quicker.

4.   With the face selected, click the **Convert Entities** button in the **Sketch Tools** toolbar, or **Tools ⇒ Sketch Tools ⇒ Convert Entities**. This transforms the outer edge of the selected face into a series of sketch entities, namely lines and arcs. It may be difficult to see what portions of the edge have been converted to sketch entities. To see the new sketch entities, activate the **Select** tool and drag a box until the entire handle is within it, just as you would if you were creating a box for zooming in on an area. The new sketch entities, which outline the edge of the handle, are displayed in green.

5.   The lines on the right side of the handle will be removed, since the boss sweep will be applied only to the left edge of the handle. In order to trim the horizontal lines that cross over the middle of the handle, a centerline will be used. Draw a vertical **Centerline** that starts at the origin and extends upward past the top edge of the handle.

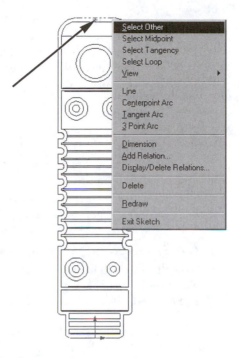

Figure 6.34. **Select Other** menu item.

6.   Trim the side of the two horizontal lines to the right of the centerline, as shown in Figure 6.35.

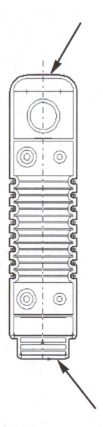

Figure 6.35. Segments to be trimmed.

7. Now that the lines that cross over the middle of the handle have been trimmed, the remaining lines and arcs on the right side can simply be deleted. Activate the **Select** tool, and drag a box until it envelops all of the sketch entities on the right side of the handle. They become highlighted in green. Be sure that none of the lines or arcs on the left side are selected, and hit Delete on the keyboard. This completes the boss sweep path sketch. Verify that only the outline to the left of the centerline remains by drawing a box around the entire handle with the **Select** tool. You will not model any features using this sketch until the section sketch is created. Exit the sketch by clicking the **Sketch** button in the **Sketch** toolbar or the **Exit Sketch** icon in the Confirmation Corner.

8. Rename the sketch you just created to **boss sweep path** in the FeatureManager design tree.

6.4.2 Creating the Boss Sweep Profile

Now that the path has been defined, you must make a profile to be swept along that path. The profile sketch is a closed quarter-circle that will be swept along the path that was just created.

1. Open a sketch on the **Right** plane, set the view to **Left**, and zoom in on the top of the handle.

2. Draw a vertical line on a blank area in the Graphics Window to the right of the handle. From the upper endpoint of the vertical line, draw a horizontal line to the right. Add a relation to set the two lines **Equal**.

3. Activate the **Centerpoint Arc** tool. Bring the cursor over the intersection of the lines that you just sketched and look for the square icon. Click and drag the arc to the endpoint of the horizontal line (again, look for the square icon). Release the mouse button. Click again on the right endpoint of the horizontal line and drag the arc to the lower endpoint of the vertical line. This creates a quarter-circle. Release the mouse button and activate the **Select** tool, so that nothing is selected. The closed quarter-circle should look similar to that shown in Figure 6.36.

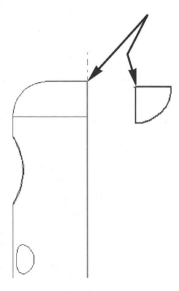

Figure 6.36. Coincident selections for quarter-circle sketch.

4. Open the ***Add Relations*** PropertyManager by clicking the **Add Relation** button in the **Sketch Relations** toolbar. Select the two points shown in Figure 6.36, and click the ***Coincident*** button. The position of the quarter-circle adjusts to satisfy the constraint. Click ***OK***.

5. Dimension the length of the horizontal line of the quarter-circle to be one-half of the wall thickness of the handle, or **1/32**. The sketch should be *Fully Defined*.

6. Rotate the view slightly to see the cavity of the handle. Select **boss sweep path** in the FeatureManager design tree to highlight the path. Notice that the corner of the profile that was just sketched touches the path. This is a necessary requirement for creating sweep features. This completes the section sketch for the boss sweep. Exit the sketch.

7. Rename the sketch that was just created to **boss sweep profile**.

6.4.3   Creating the Boss Sweep Feature

Because both the sweep path and the sweep profile have been sketched, the boss sweep feature can now be created.

1. Click the **Sweep** button in the **Features** toolbar, or **Insert** $\Rightarrow$ **Boss/Base** $\Rightarrow$ **Sweep**. The ***Sweep*** PropertyManager appears, as shown in Figure 6.37.

2. With the ***Profile*** field highlighted, click on **boss sweep profile** in the Flyout FeatureManager design tree to add it to the field, if it is not already there.

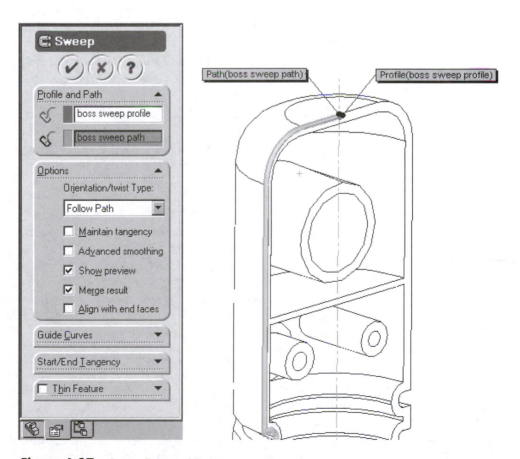

Figure 6.37. *Sweep* PropertyManager.

3. Click in the *Path* field to highlight it and add **boss sweep path** to it.

4. Callouts appear in the Graphics Window indicating the selected components of the sweep feature. Click *OK*. The section is swept along the path, creating a quarter-circle ridge along the left edge of the handle. Be sure that the sweep starts at the top of the handle, follows the left edge, and terminates at the bottom of the handle. The top of the handle with the newly created sweep is shown in Figure 6.38. It may be easier to see the ridge using the **Shaded** display.

Figure 6.38.   Boss profile swept.

6.4.4   Creating the Cut Sweep Path

The groove with which the ridge interlocks will also be modeled using a sweep. However, this sweep will remove material instead of adding it. The path of the cut sweep is similar to that of the boss sweep, except that the cut sweep follows the right edge of the handle.

1. Return to **Hidden Lines Removed** and open a sketch on the **Front** plane. Select the front face (the edge of the shell) using the **Select Other** option, if necessary.

2. Convert the selected geometry to sketch entities.

3. Delete the sketch entities on the left side of the handle. This time, it is not necessary to draw a centerline to trim segments at the top and the bottom of the handle, because there are no lines that cross over the middle of the handle. Your sketch should look similar to that shown in Figure 6.39. Be sure that all of the lines on the left side *and* the small vertical lines at the top and the bottom of the handle have been removed.

4. Exit the sketch and rename it **cut sweep path**.

6.4.5   Creating the Cut Sweep Profile

The last item to create is the cut sweep profile, which is very similar to the sweep profile used to make the boss sweep. It is a closed quarter-circle that will cut a groove along the right edge of the handle. When the two identical halves of the handle are assembled, the ridge on the left side of one-half will fit into the groove on the right side of the other half.

1. **Zoom to Fit** and move the cursor over each of the three main planes in the FeatureManager design tree. It should be evident that the **Right** plane is the logical choice for making the cut sweep profile sketch. Open a new sketch on the **Right** plane and switch to the **Right** view. Zoom in on the top of the handle.

2. Sketch a closed quarter-circle using equal horizontal and vertical lines, as well as a centerpoint arc, as shown in Figure 6.40. Be sure that the intersection of

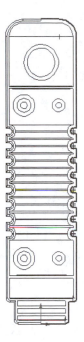

Figure 6.39.   Cut sweep path (outer edge of right side).

the two lines of the quarter-circle touches the top edge of the handle by looking for the square next to the cursor when drawing them, or by using a **Coincident** relation.

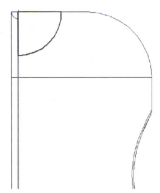

Figure 6.40.   Cut sweep profile positioned.

3. Dimension the length of the horizontal line to be **1/32**. This should fully define the sketch.

4. Exit the sketch and rename it **cut sweep profile**.

5. Click **Insert ⇒ Cut ⇒ Sweep**. The *Cut-Sweep* PropertyManager opens, which uses the same parameters used to create the boss sweep.

6. Add the two cut sweep sketches to the appropriate fields.

7. Click **OK** to finish the sweep. The result is a groove cut along the right edge of the handle. When the two handle halves are assembled, the ridge of one side will fit into the groove of the other, and vice versa. The ridge and the groove at the top of the handle are shown in Figure 6.41.

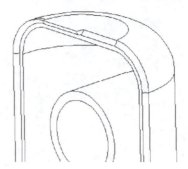

Figure 6.41.   Cut and boss sweeps on handle.

6.4.6   Adding the Rectangular Hole

The rectangular hole at the bottom of the handle that was removed earlier in this chapter must be replaced. The original sketch, which was not deleted, can be used to cut a new hole into the three lower ribs.

1.   Return to the **Isometric** view. Select **rectangle sketch** in the FeatureManager design tree.

2.   Notice that the **Extrude Boss/Base** and **Extruded Cut** buttons are active in the **Features** toolbar. The sketch does not need to be open to create a feature; it only needs to be selected. Click the **Extruded Cut** button. The **Cut-Extrude** PropertyManager opens.

3.   Create a **Blind** cut **3/4** inch into the ribs of the handle.

4.   Click **OK**. The cut into the ribs is shown in Figure 6.42. Unlike the shelled handle, shown in Figure 6.10, the new shelled handle has no undercuts, so that it can be removed from the injection mold.

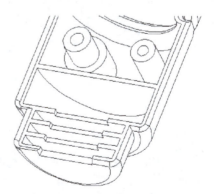

Figure 6.42.   Rectangular hole cut into lower ribs.

Congratulations! This completes the model of the shelled handle. Your part should look similar to the one shown in Figure 6.1. Save the handle but do not close the **shelled handle** window.

An actual injection-molded part would probably have many other features to produce a high-quality molded part. For instance, more ribs might be added for strength; small fillets might be added at the intersections of the ribs and the shelled section, so that the molten plastic could flow more easily around the corners and to minimize stress concentrations; draft could be added to both the holes and the ribs to make the part easier to eject from the mold. These details would be quite easy to add using the features discussed earlier.

3D SKETCHER

Sketches in SolidWorks are usually defined on a two-dimensional surface, either a plane or the face of an existing part. However, the **3D Sketch** tool allows entities to be sketched in three-dimensional space rather than on a single plane. 3D Sketches are often useful for creating guide curves for loft features or sweep paths. For example, imagine that it is necessary to model a pipe system with a path that is not in a single plane. Using two-dimensional sketches, it would be necessary to create several sections of the pipe with each section in a different plane. But in a **3D Sketch**, the full path of the pipe could be sketched in three-dimensional space using lines and fillets. Then, the pipe section could be swept along that path.

To open a 3D Sketch, select **Insert** ⇒ **3D Sketch**. It is not necessary to choose a sketching plane. Generally, the orientation should be set to **Isometric** so that the three axes, X, Y, and Z, may be seen. Lines, points, fillets, and several other sketch entities are available in 3D Sketches. As lines are sketched, axes appear to show the orientation of the line. The plane in which the line is sketched (XY, XZ, or YZ), or the axis parallel to which the line is sketched (X, Y, or Z), is indicated next to the cursor as the line is being sketched. Clicking the Tab key on the keyboard switches the plane in which the line is sketched. Once entities are created, dimensions can be added, and the properties of the entities (positions, angles, length, etc.) can be edited in the PropertyManager.

6.5 USING SMARTMATES TO ASSEMBLE THE HANDLE HALVES

Using SmartMates is a quick way to assemble parts based on the logical relationship between features of the assembled parts. To create a mate in previous chapters, two mating surfaces were selected and a mate type was chosen in the *Mate* PropertyManager. With SmartMates, the PropertyManager is avoided, because SolidWorks infers the type of mate that is needed. For example, if two cylindrical surfaces are selected, SmartMates will create a concentric mate between the features. Likewise, two planar surfaces will be mated to be coincident. The mates are still listed in the FeatureManager design tree, so that they can be edited after they are created.

In this section, you will mate two identical halves of the shelled handle to create a complete handle. This new handle is interchangeable with the solid handle modeled earlier. The assembled handle is shown in Figure 6.43.

6.5.1 Setting Up the Assembly Document

The new assembly will contain two instances of the the shelled handle.

1. Open a new assembly window using either the toolbar or menu commands. Use the **View** ⇒ **Toolbars** menu to display the **Assembly** toolbar, if it is not already displayed. Turn on the origin using **View** ⇒ **Origins**. Use the **Grid** button to set the *Units* to *Inches.*

2. Be sure that the **shelled handle** window is still open. If it is not, open it now. Click **Window** ⇒ **Tile Vertically** to display both the assembly and part windows simultaneously.

3. Drag the **shelled handle** icon from the FeatureManager design tree of the part window to the origin of the assembly window. Look for the set of right-angled arrows before releasing the mouse button. This ensures that the planes of the part are coincident with the planes of the assembly.

Figure 6.43. Assembled handle halves.

4. Maximize the assembly window and set the view to **Isometric**.

5. To create a new instance of the shelled handle in the assembly document, hold down the Control key and drag (**f**) **shelled handle<1>** from the FeatureManager design tree to a blank area in the Graphics Window. Release the mouse button before releasing the Control key. A second shelled handle appears and (−) **shelled handle<2>** is listed in the FeatureManager design tree.

6. Set the view to **Shaded**, if it is not set already.

6.5.2 Changing the Color of the Second Shelled Handle

To avoid confusing the two parts, the color of the second handle in the assembly will be changed temporarily.

1. *Right click* (−) **shelled handle<2>** in the FeatureManager design tree and select **Component Properties** from the menu that appears.

2. In the ***Component Properties*** dialog box, click the ***Color*** button. This brings up the ***Assembly Instance Color*** dialog box, shown in Figure 6.44.

3. The assembly document defaults to the color for the part that you chose when you originally modeled the handle. Here, you will override the color so that the two shelled handles can be differentiated from one another. Click the ***Change Color*** button.

4. Choose a new color in the ***Color*** dialog box. Usually a light color works best to see the details of the part. After choosing a suitable color, click ***OK*** *three* times to return to the assembly window. The color could also be changed using the **Edit Color** toolbar button.

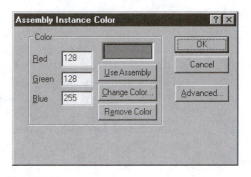

Figure 6.44. *Assembly Instance Color* dialog box.

6.5.3   Creating a Coincident Mate Using SmartMates

The inner faces of the shelled handles will be mated, so that they are coincident.

1. Open the **Selection Filter** toolbar in the **View ⇒ Toolbars** menu, if it is not already visible. Click the **Filter Faces** button, so that only faces can be selected.

2. Click the **SmartMates** button (a paperclip with a star) in the **Assembly** toolbar. The cursor changes to two perpendicular arrows.

3. The face shown in Figure 6.45 is the edge of the circular hole of the second shelled handle. *Double click* this face. The part becomes translucent with the face highlighted in green. This is the face that will be mated.

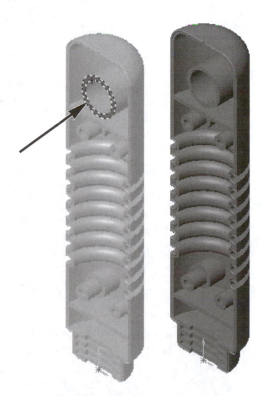

Figure 6.45.   Face of second shelled handle.

4.   Notice that the cursor has become a pointer with a paperclip icon. Click and drag the selected face to the similar face on the fixed handle, *but do not release the mouse button*. The face on the fixed handle that will be mated becomes highlighted in green and a preview of the mate is shown. The icon changes to show two planes, indicating that a coincident mate will be created. Before releasing the mouse button, click the Tab key on the keyboard to see the different orientations that can be created with this mate. Be sure the inner faces of the handles are facing each other as shown in Figure 6.46, and release the mouse button.

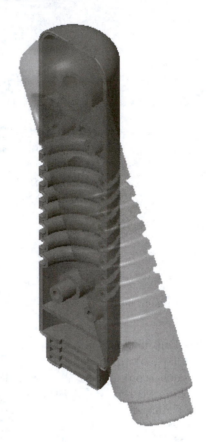

Figure 6.46. Coincident SmartMate applied.

5.   The cursor should change back to perpendicular arrows, indicating that the **SmartMates** tool can be used to move components without activating the **Move Component** tool. Move the second handle. The inside faces of the two handle halves should remain coincident. If they do not, or if the mate is backwards, click **Edit** ⟹ **Undo SmartMates** and redo the previous two steps.

6.5.4   Adding the Concentric Mates

Concentric mates will be added for the two sets of holes, completely constraining the location of the second handle with respect to the first.

1.   The **SmartMates** button should still be active. In the **Isometric** view, drag the second handle so that it is oriented similar to that shown in Figure 6.47.

2. *Double click* the cylindrical surface of the counterbore hole on the second handle, as shown in Figure 6.47. The surface becomes highlighted and the handle becomes translucent.

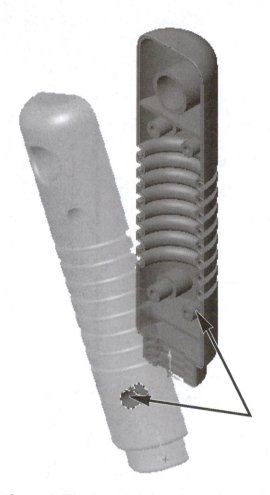

Figure 6.47.   Assembly hole surfaces to be mated.

3. This mate will be slightly different than the previous mate. In that case, you dragged the feature of the first part to the mating feature of the second part. This allowed you to choose between two possibilities for the mate. This time, you will not drag the part. Bring the cursor (a pointer with paperclip) over the outer cylindrical surface of the assembly's screw hole in the fixed handle, as shown in Figure 6.47. Click on the surface. The mate is created to make the two holes concentric.

4. If necessary, rotate the second handle using the **SmartMates** tool, so that it is similar to the orientation shown in Figure 6.48. Add a concentric mate between the two cylindrical surfaces, as shown in Figure 6.48.

5. Click the **Smart Mates** button to deactivate the **SmartMates** tool. The dash in front of **shelled handle<2>** in the FeatureManager design tree has been removed, indicating that the second handle is fully constrained with respect to the first handle. The assembly should look similar to the one shown at the beginning of this section.

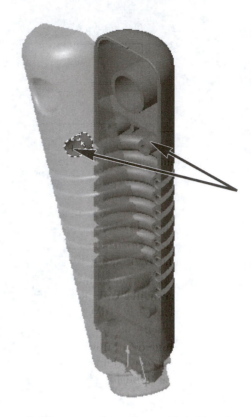

Figure 6.48. Second set of assembly holes to be mated.

6. Click the plus sign next to **Mates** in the FeatureManager design tree. Three mates were created: one coincident mate and two concentric mates. These mates can be edited in the same way that other mates previously created were modified.

7. Click the **Clear All Filters** button in the **Selection Filter** toolbar to deactivate the face filter.

6.5.5   Finishing the Handle Assembly

The handle assembly can be checked for interference using the **Interference Detection** tool. It is also helpful to section the handle to look at the interior of the assembly. In addition, the color of the second handle will be returned to the original color defined in the part document.

1. Check for interferences by clicking **Tools ⇒ Interference Detection** and clicking **Check**. After a short wait, *0 Interference* should appear, signifying that there are no interfering volumes in the assembly. If interference is detected, check the mates and the geometry of the shelled handle for errors. *Close* the *Interference Volumes* dialog box.

2. In addition to an interference check, it is helpful to view a cross section through the handle assembly to verify the alignment of the holes, the interlocking edges, and the interior of the assembly. To do this, it is necessary to define a location for the section with respect to a plane. Return to the **Right** view.

3. Click on the **Top** plane in the FeatureManager design tree. Note that a section through the assembly holes would be parallel to this plane. Switch to a **Bottom view**, which is parallel to this plane.

4. To view a section through the lower set of holes, select **View** ⇒ **Display** ⇒ **Section View**. In the ***Section View*** dialog box, ***Top*** should appear in the ***Section Plane(s)/Face(s)*** field. If necessary, delete the item in the field and select ***Top*** in the FeatureManager design tree. Set the ***Section Position*** to ***1.125***, which is the distance from the **Top** plane to the lower assembly holes. Click **OK**. The section should look like the one shown in Figure 6.49 using the **Hidden Lines Removed** display.

5. Return to the **Shaded** display and rotate the part slightly to see the interlocking edges, the assembly screw holes, and the inside of the handle.

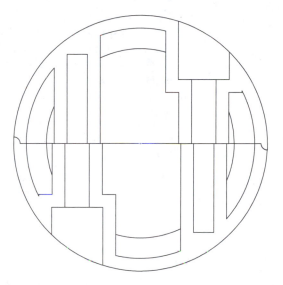

Figure 6.49.   Section view of handle.

6. Toggle off the section view by selecting **View** ⇒ **Display** ⇒ **Section View**, and return to the **Isometric** view.

7. To change the half of the handle back to its original color, *right click* **shelled handle<2>** in the FeatureManager design tree. Select **Component Properties** from the menu that appears. Click the ***Color*** button. Click the ***Remove Color*** button to return to the color specified in the part document. Click **OK** twice to return to the assembly window. The two halves of the handle should now be the same color.

Congratulations! This completes the handle assembly. This handle could easily be substituted for the solid handle in the pizza cutter assembly. Save the assembly as **handle assembly**. Close both the **handle assembly** and the **shelled handle** windows.

Problems

1. Add 8 to 10 more ribs to the **shelled handle**. Locate the ribs based on the dimensions of the existing features of the shelled handle. Ribs can be modeled to extend between the screw holes, between the screw holes and the sidewalls,

between the large hole at the top of the handle and the sidewall, and between the sidewalls at the narrowest section of the grooves. Use a two-degree draft angle for each rib. Add .02 fillets between the ribs and the sidewalls.

2.   Starting with the original solid handle, redesign the shelled handle with two different halves. One-half should have a boss sweep all the way around its edge. The other half should have a mating cut sweep around its entire edge. Use just two holes—one at the top and one at the bottom—for attaching the two halves using self-tapping screws, counterbored on one-half only. Assemble the two halves to form a new version of the shelled handle.

3.   Model the cap as a shell. Begin by extruding a solid cylinder and adding a fillet to round one end. Then, shell the model and cut the hole for the arms.

4.   Model a coffee mug. Begin by extruding a solid cylinder for the cup. Shell the cylinder using a 3/16″ wall. Round the top edge of the cup. Sweep a rounded rectangle along a semicircular path to create a handle. You may need to create a new plane for the rounded rectangle sketch. Add a fillet between the handle and the cup.

7

Redesigning the Handle

OVERVIEW

Sophisticated modeling capabilities in SolidWorks permit the creation of smoothly contoured features that enhance the style or ergonomics of a part. In this chapter, a new ergonomic handle will be designed. Using a loft base feature, the handle will be designed so that it is contoured to fit the user's hand. A surface will be radiated and thickened to create a stylized flange on the handle, replacing the sheet metal guard. After engraving text in the handle, it will be assembled with the cutter sub-assembly. Then, the interference between the cutter sub-assembly and the handle will be used to create a cavity in the handle to accept the arms of the cutter sub-assembly.

In this chapter, a new version of the handle will be modeled, incorporating the guard into the handle to create a simpler and more ergonomic design, as shown in Figure 7.1. The new contoured handle will be modeled with a loft base feature, which makes a transition between two or more cross-sectional profiles. The redesigned handle includes a flanged end that is modeled as a thickened surface. This replaces the guard and the cap, eliminating two components from the final pizza cutter assembly. Once the principle features of the handle are modeled, two configurations based on the common base model will be created: one with the text engraved on the side and one without text. The model of the new handle will be completed, omitting the rectangular hole at one end for the arms of the cutter sub-assembly. The new handle will be assembled with the

SECTIONS

OBJECTIVES

After working through this chapter, you will be able to

- Create sections and guide curves for loft features,
- Create spline curves,
- Create loft features,
- Create dome features,
- Radiate surfaces,
- Knit surfaces,
- Determine the mass properties of a part,
- Engrave text in a part,
- Create multiple configurations of a part, and
- Create cavities based on the interference of two parts.

cutter sub-assembly, resulting in an interference between the handle and the arms of the cutter sub-assembly. Then, a cavity to form the rectangular hole for the arms will be added based on the interference. This is called top-down component modeling.

Figure 7.1.   Finished lofted handle.

7.1   CREATING THE HANDLE'S BASE FEATURE USING A LOFT

Loft features are used to model components with smooth transitions between either sketched profiles or irregular surfaces. A simple example of a loft is an air duct that has a gradual transition from a rectangular cross section to a circular cross section, as shown in Figure 7.2. In general, loft features can form a transition between two or more cross-sectional profiles.

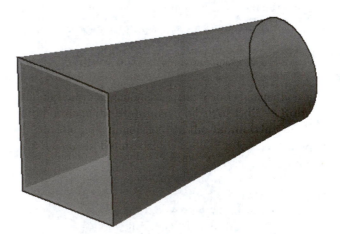

Figure 7.2.   Air duct transition from square to circle using a loft.

Guide curves are used to define the shape of the transition between the profiles for a loft. Guide curves are similar in concept to sweep paths in that the loft "follows" the guide curve just as the sweep profile "follows" the sweep path. With lofts, the shape of the cross-sectional profile transforms as it follows the guide curve, whereas the shape of the sweep profile remains the same as it follows its path. The key requirement for guide curves is that they touch each profile at a single point. Loft features do not require guide curves, but they are often useful to create the subtle contours in the model.

The lofted feature of the handle, shown in Figure 7.3, uses two profiles and two guide curves, which are shown in Figure 7.4. The left profile is a rectangle with rounded corners, and the right profile is an ellipse. The loft feature produces a smooth transition between the two profiles following both the top and the bottom guide curves. The upper guide curve is a straight line, whereas the lower guide curve is a subtle spline to contour the transition.

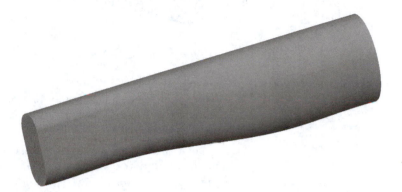

Figure 7.3.   Base feature of the redesigned handle.

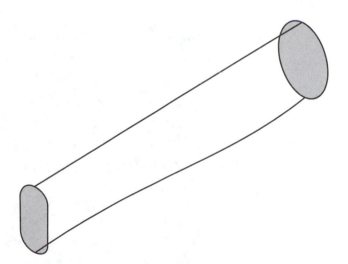

Figure 7.4.   Loft elements used in the base feature.

A dome feature will be added to the right end of the handle to create a rounded end on the flat elliptical face. Finally, a circular hole will be added to the base loft feature. After completing this section, the handle will look like the one shown in Figure 7.5.

7.1.1   Setting Up the Document and Customizing the Interface

Since the **Ellipse** tool will be used to sketch one of the profiles, the **<u>Ellipse</u>** button will be added to the **<u>Sketch Tools</u>** toolbar. The following steps will enable you to customize the toolbar buttons in SolidWorks (once you have completed the tutorial, you can customize the toolbars so that your most commonly used tools are readily available):

Figure 7.5.   Dome and hole added to the base feature.

1.   Open a new part using the **tutorial part** template. Be sure that the **Features, Sketch, Sketch Relations, Sketch Tools, Standard, Standard Views**, and **View** toolbars appear on the screen.

2.   Open a new sketch on the **Front** plane. Examine the tools that are available in the **<u>Sketch Tools</u>** toolbar by bringing the cursor over the buttons, so that the ToolTips appear. You will remove the **<u>Polygon</u>** button and replace it with the **<u>Ellipse</u>** button. Select **Tools** ⇒ **Customize**, or *right click* any toolbar button and select **Customize** to activate the ***Customize*** dialog box. Click the ***Commands*** tab, as shown in Figure 7.6.

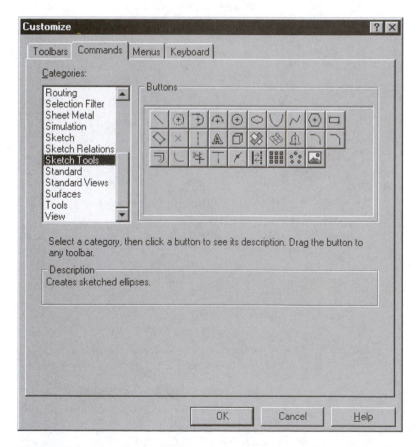

Figure 7.6.   *Customize* dialog box.

3.   Bring the cursor over the **<u>Polygon</u>** button (a hexagon) in the **<u>Sketch Tools</u>** toolbar and look for the ToolTip. Click and drag the **<u>Polygon</u>** button off of the toolbar and onto the Graphics Window. As you drag the toolbar button, a shadow of its icon appears with the cursor. Release the mouse button somewhere in the Graphics Window. The **<u>Polygon</u>** button is removed from the toolbar and the other toolbar buttons move upward to fill the space. (If the toolbars have been modified by a previous user, the **<u>Polygon</u>** button may already have been replaced by the **<u>Ellipse</u>** button. If so, remove the **<u>Ellipse</u>** button and reinstall it in the step below.) Even though the **Customize** dialog box was not used, it must be open to remove a toolbar button.

4.   In the **Customize** dialog box, click **Sketch Tools** in the **Categories** field to highlight it. All of the buttons that are available for the **Sketch Tools** toolbar appear on the right side of the dialog box. Click on some of the buttons to see an explanation of their function in the **Description** field.

5.   Click the **Ellipse** icon (an ellipse) in the dialog box. The following description appears: **Creates sketched ellipses**. Since you will use this sketch feature to create one of the profiles for the loft, you will add it to the **<u>Sketch Tools</u>** toolbar for convenient access. Click and drag the icon from the dialog box to the location on the **<u>Sketch Tools</u>** toolbar in which the **<u>Polygon</u>** button once was. Release the mouse button to add the **<u>Ellipse</u>** button to the **<u>Sketch Tools</u>** toolbar.

6.   Click **OK** at the bottom of the **Customize** dialog box. The customized toolbar is shown in Figure 7.7. Your toolbar might be vertical or the buttons may be in a different order.

Figure 7.7.   Customized **<u>Sketch Tools</u>** toolbar.

7.1.2   Creating the First Profile Sketch

The first profile for the loft feature is a rectangle with rounded corners. Instead of using the **Rectangle** tool to create the sketch, you will use a horizontal centerline to mirror the top half of the sketch.

1.   Draw a horizontal centerline that goes through the origin.

2.   There are two ways to use the **Mirror** tool when creating sketches. One method is to create half of the sketch on one side of the centerline, and then, mirror that half sketch about the centerline to create the whole symmetric sketch. The other way is to set up the centerline as an active mirroring line. When this is done, every entity sketched *after* the creation of the mirror line will be mirrored. In this sketch, you will use the latter method to mirror entities as you sketch them. Select the centerline so that it is highlighted in green. Click the **<u>Sketch Mirror</u>** button (a bell with a vertical line) in the **<u>Sketch Tools</u>** toolbar, or **Tools** ⇒ **Sketch Tools** ⇒ **Mirror**. A set of hash marks appears at the ends of the centerline, indicating that it is the active mirroring line. Notice that the **<u>Sketch Mirror</u>** button remains depressed in the toolbar, indicating that mirroring is active in the sketch.

3.   To the right of the origin, draw a vertical line that starts on the centerline and extends upward. As soon as you finish sketching the line, it is automatically

mirrored below the centerline. With the **Select** tool, drag the upper endpoint of the line to a new position. The lower endpoint moves to create a mirror image of the upper half. SolidWorks has created a single line with a midpoint relation so that the line is always mirrored about the centerline. Your sketch should look similar to that shown in Figure 7.8 (the grid has been omitted for clarity).

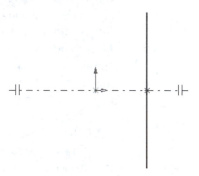

Figure 7.8.   Vertical line mirrored.

4. In a similar manner, draw a second vertical line about the same distance to the left of the origin. In order to make the second line the same length as the first, look for a horizontal dashed line between the upper endpoints of the two lines, which appears when the endpoints are at the same height. This indicates that the lengths of the lines are equal (although no relation has been added automatically).

5. Activate the **3 Pt Arc** tool. Create an arc by dragging the cursor from the upper left endpoint to the upper right endpoint. The arc is dashed, indicating that a third point (the square at the center of the arc) needs to be defined. Drag the square upward until a closed semicircle appears next to the cursor and a dashed horizontal line appears between the two endpoints. Notice that the angle (denoted by **A =** next to the cursor) indicates that the arc is 180 degrees. Release the mouse button. This creates a semicircle that is tangent to both lines. The semicircle is also mirrored about the centerline, since mirroring is still active.

6. Dimension the sketch as shown in Figure 7.9. The vertical 1/2″ dimension defines the distance between the centers of the two arcs. The 1/4″ dimension defines the distance from the *origin* to the right side of the profile. Notice that, as you change the dimensions to the proper value, the entities remain symmetric about the horizontal centerline.

7. Deactivate mirroring by clicking the **Sketch Mirror** button in the **Sketch Tools** toolbar. The hash marks on the centerline disappear.

8. This sketch for the left end of the handle will be needed later when the loft is created. Exit the sketch. **Sketch1** appears in the FeatureManager design tree. Rename it **profile 1**.

7.1.3   Creating the Second Profile Sketch

The profile sketch for the right end of the handle is located in a plane offset from the **Front** plane. The shape for this end of the handle is an ellipse. Ellipses are special sketch entities, like circles or arcs.

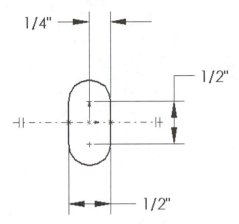

Figure 7.9. Sketch dimensioned.

1. Previously, **Insert** ⇒ **Reference Geometry** ⇒ **Plane** was used to offset a plane. Here, you will use a shortcut to create a plane offset from the **Front** plane. Select **Front** in the FeatureManager design tree and go to the **Isometric** view. Zoom out in order to see the entire plane in the Graphics Window. Deactivate the **Zoom In/Out** tool and be sure that the **Select** tool is active and the **Front** plane is selected in the PropertyManager.

2. Bring the cursor over one of the lines of the plane so that it changes to four perpendicular arrows. Hold down the Control key on the keyboard and drag the plane to the right. Release the mouse button and then release the Control key. Click **OK** in the PropertyManager. A new plane, **Plane1**, is created.

3. *Double click* **Plane1** in the FeatureManager design tree. The dimension between the **Front** plane and **Plane1** is shown in the Graphics Window. This dimension represents the distance that you dragged the new plane. Use the **Select** tool to change the dimension to **5**. Since the dimension was changed after the new plane feature was created, it is necessary to rebuild the model to update the dimension. Click the **Rebuild** button in the **Standard** toolbar, or **Edit** ⇒ **Rebuild**. The model updates to have a plane offset five inches from the **Front** plane, as shown in Figure 7.10.

4. Open a sketch on **Plane1**. Set the view to **Normal To** the sketching plane, so that you are looking at it directly. Notice that the first sketch, **profile1**, is visible. To temporarily hide it, *right click* **profile1** in the FeatureManager design tree and select **Hide Sketch**.

5. Activate the **Ellipse** tool by clicking the newly created **Ellipse** button in the **Sketch Tools** toolbar or by selecting **Tools** ⇒ **Sketch Entity** ⇒ **Ellipse**. After activating the **Ellipse** tool, bring the cursor over the origin, looking for the square next to the cursor. Click and drag the cursor to the right. Release the mouse button to create a dashed circle, as shown in Figure 7.11.

6. Click and hold above the circle. Drag the cursor vertically to elongate the circle vertically into the shape of the ellipse. Release the mouse button when the eccentricity of the ellipse is similar to that shown in Figure 7.12. Do not be concerned if the ellipse is tilted; its orientation will be adjusted next. Activate the **Select** tool.

7. There are four points indicated on the ellipse that define the endpoints of its major and minor axes. The longer (major) axis of the ellipse should be vertical.

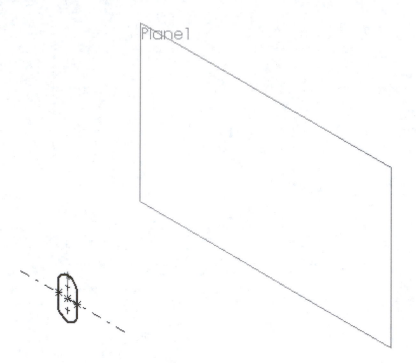

Figure 7.10. Plane1 offset from the initial sketch plane.

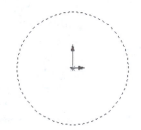

Figure 7.11. Dashed circle.

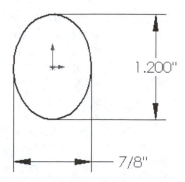

Figure 7.12. Ellipse dimensioned.

To impose this constraint, add a **Vertical** relation for the two points above and below the origin on the major axis of the ellipse. If an error occurs, click the **Undo** button twice to delete the ellipse. Then repeat steps 5 and 6 making sure to drag the dashed circle to the right in Step 5.

8. Dimension the distance between the points by defining the major and minor axes of the ellipse to match Figure 7.12. This fully defines the sketch.

9. Exit the sketch and name it **profile2**. In the FeatureManager design tree, **Hide Plane1** and then *right click* **profile1** and select **Show Sketch**.

In the next sections, guide curves for the loft between the two profiles will be added to the model. However, the two profiles alone are sufficient to create a loft feature with a smooth transition from the rounded rectangle to the ellipse. Without guide curves, the loft made from the sketched profiles would look like that shown in Figure 7.13. In the figure, straight lines connect points on the rounded rectangle to points on the ellipse. Compare this loft feature with the desired loft feature modeled using guide curves, as shown in Figure 7.3.

Figure 7.13. Loft feature with no guide curves.

7.1.4 Creating the First Guide Curve Using a Spline

The third sketch for the loft feature is a guide curve for the lower contour of the handle. A straight line along the lower contour results in the loft feature shown in Figure 7.13, which does not have an ergonomic shape to fit the grip of a person's hand. To create a curved contour on the lower part of the handle, a spline, which is a curved sketch entity, will be used to create a guide curve. The spline has four points that define it: two endpoints and two points to adjust the curvature. A centerline will be used to constrain the tangency of the spline at its endpoints.

1. Open a new sketch on the **Right** plane and set the view to **Normal To**. Since this view is perpendicular to **profile1** and **profile2**, the profiles appear as vertical lines.

2. Draw a centerline that is at an angle (neither horizontal nor vertical) somewhere in an open area of the Graphics Window. Check that an inadvertent constraint has not been applied by selecting the centerline (if it is not already highlighted in green). The *Existing Relations* field in the *Line* PropertyManager should be empty. If any relations (Horizontal, Vertical, or Coincident) exist for the centerline, highlight them and hit *Delete* on the keyboard.

3.   Rotate the view so it appears similar to the one in Figure 7.14. It may help to remove the grid. Select the lower arc of the **profile1** sketch and use the Control key to also select the endpoint of the centerline, as shown in Figure 7.14.

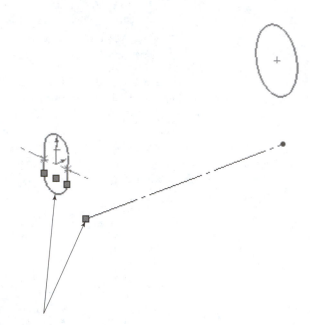

Figure 7.14.   Selections for **Pierce** relation.

4.   This sketch requires that the endpoint of the centerline touches the midpoint of the lower arc of **profile1**. To add this constraint, a relation will be used, so, open the ***Add Relations*** PropertyManager. A **Coincident** relation will not work in this case, because the arc and the centerline do not lie in the same plane. A **Coincident** relation would only constrain the endpoint of the centerline to be in the plane of the arc, but not necessarily intersecting at the midpoint of the arc. Instead, a **Pierce** relation will be used to constrain the endpoint of the centerline to touch the arc at the point where the arc pierces the current sketch plane. Since the lower arc of the **profile1** sketch is in the **Front** plane, it intersects the **Right** plane at a single point, its midpoint. Consequently, the **Pierce** relation constrains the endpoint of the centerline in the **Right** plane to pierce the lower arc at its midpoint. Select the ***Pierce*** button, and click ***OK***.

5.   In a similar manner, add a **Pierce** relationship to constrain the other endpoint of the centerline to touch the ellipse (**profile2**). In this case, select the ellipse rather than the point at the end of the major axis of the ellipse. A **Coincident** relation could be used instead of **Pierce**, by selecting the endpoint of the centerline and the endpoint of the ellipse's major axis, instead of the ellipse itself. For the ellipse, the endpoints of the major and minor axes are sketch entities, so they can be used in a **Coincident** relation. In the case of the lower arc of **profile1**, the midpoint of the arc is not defined as a separate sketch entity. In **Isometric** view, your sketch should look similar to the one in Figure 7.15. Return to the **Normal To** orientation.

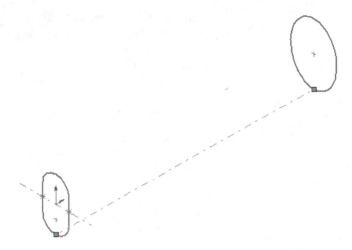

Figure 7.15.   Centerline constrained.

6.   Activate the **Spline** tool by clicking the <u>**Spline**</u> button in the <u>**Sketch Tools**</u> toolbar, or **Tools** ⇒ **Sketch Entity** ⇒ **Spline**. Bring the cursor over the left endpoint of the centerline. When the square is visible next to the cursor, click and drag up and to the right. After dragging about one-third of the distance between the two profiles and a little above the centerline, release the mouse button. A thin line extends between the two points.

7.   Bring the cursor over the right endpoint of the thin line. When a square appears next to the cursor, click and drag the cursor down below and to the right of the centerline, but not as far as the right profile. Release the mouse button. At this point, the spline begins to take shape, as shown in Figure 7.16.

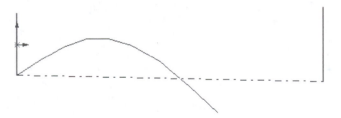

Figure 7.16.   Part of the spline sketched.

8.   Click on the new endpoint of the spline and drag it to the right endpoint of the centerline. This defines four points on the spline, but it is not yet fully constrained.

7.1.5   Constraining the Spline

The two endpoints of the spline are fully constrained, while the two middle points require dimensions to locate them. In addition, the spline will be constrained to be tangent to the centerline at the endpoints. These six constraints (four dimensions and two relations) will completely define the spline.

1.   Activate the **Select** tool and move the cursor over the spline. When it is over one of the two points in the middle of the spline, an asterisk appears. Click

on one of the points. A tangent line and a perpendicular line appear at the point. Drag the point and notice that the entire shape of the spline adjusts to remain smooth as you move the point. Adjust the position of the two middle points so that the spline looks similar to that shown in Figure 7.17.

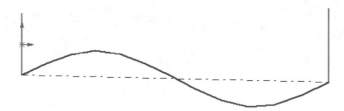

Figure 7.17. Spline sketched.

2. Click on an open space in the Graphics Window, so that nothing is selected. Open the **Add Relations** PropertyManager and select the centerline and the spline. Click the **Tangent** button. One end of the spline adjusts to be tangent to the centerline.

3. Create another **Tangent** relation to make the other end of the spline tangent to the centerline, by clicking the **Tangent** button again. Click **OK**.

4. Four dimensions—two horizontal and two vertical—are needed to define the location of the two points along the spline relative to the origin. Add the four dimensions, as shown in Figure 7.18. In each case, first select the origin. Then, move the cursor over one of the points along the spline. When the cursor is over a point (asterisk), select the point and click again to place the dimension. This fully constrains the spline. Adjust the values of the dimensions to match those shown in Figure 7.18.

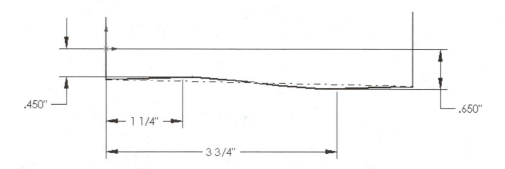

.450"   1 1/4"   3 3/4"   .650"

Figure 7.18. Spline constrained.

5. Exit the sketch and rename it **guide curve1**.

7.1.6   Creating the Second Guide Curve

In Figure 7.13, the loft was shown as it would look if it was created without guide curves. This is the same as using straight lines as guide curves. Figure 7.19 shows the loft feature as it would look if it was created with **guide curve1** only. Notice that the upper contour of the handle defaults to a shape similar to **guide curve1**. In some cases, this would be

Figure 7.19. Loft feature using only the lower guide curve.

fine, but for the pizza cutter handle, the upper guide curve should be a straight line, which will be created in this section.

1. Open a new sketch on the **Right** plane. The lower guide curve should be visible.

2. Draw a line that is at a slight angle to horizontal, somewhere above the other sketches in the model.

3. As before, add two relations so that the two endpoints of the new line pierce the upper portions of the profile sketches. Switch to the **Isometric** view in order to select the profiles. Your sketch should look similar to that shown in Figure 7.20. The two relations fully define the sketch for the upper guide curve.

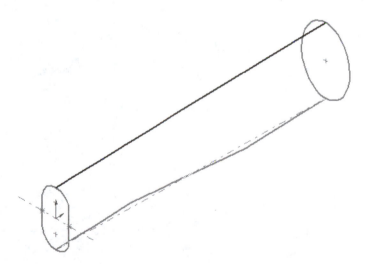

Figure 7.20. Upper guide curve sketch completed.

4. Exit the sketch and rename it **guide curve2**.

7.1.7   Creating the Loft Feature

Now that the four sketches for the loft feature (two profiles and two guide curves) have been created, modeling the loft feature is a relatively simple matter.

1. Click the <u>**Loft**</u> button in the <u>**Features**</u> toolbar, or **Insert** ⇒ **Boss/Base** ⇒ **Loft**. The *Loft* PropertyManager appears, as shown in Figure 7.21.

Figure 7.21 *Loft* PropertyManager.

2. There are two fields in the *Loft* PropertyManager: *Profiles* and *Guide Curves*. Be sure that the *Profiles* field is highlighted in pink and select **profile1** and **profile2** from the Flyout FeatureManager design tree, adding the profiles to the field.

3. Click in the *Guide Curves* field to highlight it. Add **guide curve1** and **guide curve2** to the field.

4. Click **OK**. The loft base feature is shown in Figure 7.22. The loft feature was created with a smooth transition between the profiles that follow the guide curves. Click the plus sign next to the newly created **Loft1** in the FeatureManager design tree. Select each of the four sketches in order to see its role in the loft feature. Hide **profile1** so that its centerline is not visible. Rotate the handle to see how its shape smoothly transforms from a rounded rectangle at one end to an ellipse at the other end. The ergonomic contour of the lower part of the handle is evident from the right- or left-side view.

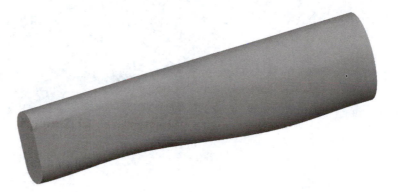

Figure 7.22.   Loft feature created.

7.1.8   Modeling the Rounded End Using a Dome Feature

The dome feature in SolidWorks adds material to round a flat face. The dome feature looks similar to the results of using a fillet feature to round edges. However, a dome adds material to a flat surface, whereas a fillet rounds between two surfaces.

1. Rotate the part so that the flat elliptical end of the handle is visible.
2. Click **Insert** ⇒ **Features** ⇒ **Dome**. The *Dome* dialog box appears, as shown in Figure 7.23.

Figure 7.23.   *Dome* dialog box.

3.   Set the ***Height*** to ***1/2***. This is the distance from the flat elliptical surface to the highest point of the dome feature.

4.   Select the elliptical face of the loft. ***Face<1>*** appears in the ***Dome face*** field and a preview appears in the Graphics Window. If the preview looks like the one shown in Figure 7.24, click **OK**. The dome feature is added and **Dome1** appears in the FeatureManager design tree.

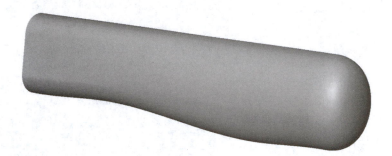

Figure 7.24.   Dome feature added.

7.1.9   Modeling the Circular Hole

Finally, a circular hole, similar to the one on the original cylindrical handle, will be added to the loft feature.

1.   Create a sketch of a circle on the **Right** plane with the dimensions shown in Figure 7.25. The **4 1/2** dimension is referenced to the origin.

2.   Fully define the sketch by making the center of the circle **Horizontal** with the origin.

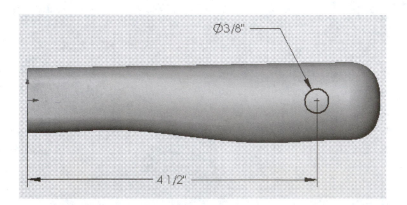

Figure 7.25.   Circle sketch dimensioned.

3.   Extrude a cut that goes through both sides of the handle. Because the **Right** plane bisects the handle, ***Direction 2*** should be checked. The ***End Condition*** has to be set to ***Through All*** for both ***Direction 1*** and ***Direction 2***.

4.   Rotate the handle slightly and select the inside cylindrical surface of the newly created hole to highlight it. Round the edges of the hole using a ***.1*** fillet feature.

5.   Rotate the part to verify that both ends of the hole were filleted. Return to the **Isometric** view.

Congratulations! You have completed the base features of the redesigned handle. Your part should look similar to the one shown at the beginning of this section. Save the part as **lofted handle** and leave the window open. In the next section, a surface will be used to model the flanged end of the handle.

7.2   CREATING THE FLANGED END USING A SURFACE

All of the features created in SolidWorks to this point have been solid features. A different class of features, known as surfaces, are infinitely thin and have no solid properties. Surfaces are useful to produce complex three-dimensional geometries. Often, solid features can be generated from surfaces. For example, the hood of a car could first be modeled as a surface and then thickened to represent the thickness of the material. In a similar manner, you will create a planar surface and then give it a thickness to model the flanged end of the lofted handle. This feature will prevent a user's hand from slipping onto the blade. The handle with the new flanged end is shown in Figure 7.26.

Figure 7.26.   Handle with flanged end.

7.2.1   Creating a Radiated Surface

To create the surface needed, the edges at the left end of the handle will be radiated, or offset radially, from the edge of the surface. The resulting planar surface will have no thickness, but will be used later to add a solid feature.

1.   Click **Insert** ⇒ **Surface** ⇒ **Radiate**. The ***Radiate Surface*** PropertyManager appears, as shown in Figure 7.27.

2.   Use the **Isometric** view so that the face at the left end of the handle can be seen. The surface forming the left end of the handle will be radiated outward. Select the flat face at the left end of the handle. The face is highlighted, and ***Face<1>*** appears in the ***Radiate Direction Reference*** field, signifying that the new surface will be in the same plane as this face.

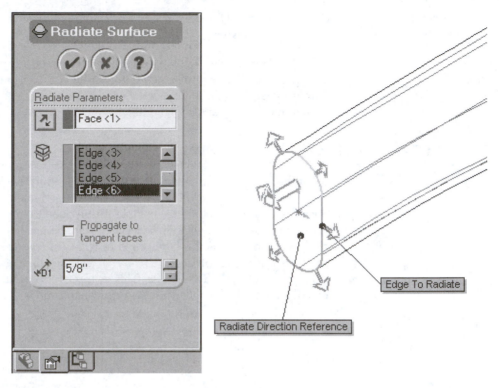

Figure 7.27. *Radiate Surface* PropertyManager.

3. Set the ***Radiate distance*** to **5/8**, so that the surface radiates outward from the edge of the left end of the handle by 5/8″.

4. The six edges (four arcs and two lines) of the selected face will be offset to create the new surface. Set the display to **Hidden Lines Removed** so that the edges of the loft can be seen. Highlight the ***Edges to radiate*** field in the ***Radiate Surface*** PropertyManager, if it is not already highlighted. *Right click* one of the edges of the flat face at the left end of the handle and choose **Select Tangency** from the menu that appears. This selects all six edges (which are tangent to each other) and adds them to the ***Edges To Radiate*** field. An arrow appears for each edge indicating the direction in which the surface will radiate from that edge.

5. Be sure that ***Edge <1>*** through ***Edge <6>*** appear in the ***Edges To Radiate*** field and then click **OK**. The surface is created and **Surface-Radiate1** appears in the FeatureManager design tree.

6. Return to the **Shaded** view. The handle with the radiated surface should look similar to the one in Figure 7.28. To verify that the surface has no thickness, go to the **Right** view. The surface should not be visible. However, the surface can be readily seen when the view is rotated. Return to the **Isometric** view.

7.2.2 Knitting Two Surfaces

Knitting is a function in SolidWorks that produces a single, new surface by combining two or more other surfaces. At this point, two surfaces form the left end of the handle. One surface is the rounded rectangular end of the handle. The other surface is the radiated

Figure 7.28.   Surface radiated.

surface that extends from the rounded rectangle outward. It is necessary to knit the radiated surface with the face of the left end of the handle to create a single surface from the two individual surfaces.

1. Click **Insert** ⇒ **Surface** ⇒ **Knit**. The ***Knit Surfaces*** PropertyManager appears, as shown in Figure 7.29.

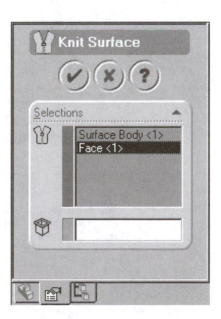

Figure 7.29.   ***Knit Surfaces*** PropertyManager.

2. Add **Surface-Radiate1** from the Flyout FeatureManager design tree to the ***Surfaces and Faces to Knit*** field, if it is not already there. Click any open space in the Graphics Window to close the Flyout FeatureManager. Then, add the face of the left end of the handle by selecting it.

3. Click **OK**. The new knitted surface, which incorporates both the front face and radiated surface, is created, and **Surface-Knit1** appears in the Feature-Manager design tree.

7.2.3 Thickening the Knitted Surface

Now that the surface has been created, it can be thickened to produce a solid feature.

1. Click the **Select** button in the **Sketch** toolbar so that nothing is selected. Select **Insert ⟹ Boss/Base ⟹ Thicken**. The **Thicken** PropertyManager appears, as shown in Figure 7.30.

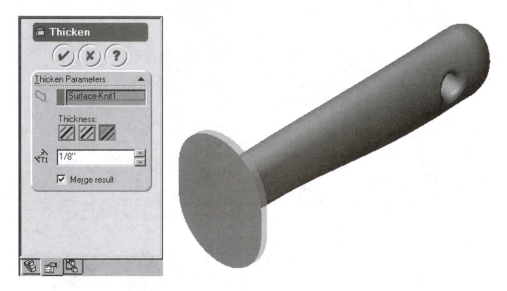

Figure 7.30. *Thicken* PropertyManager.

2. Set the **Thickness** to **1/8**.
3. Select **Surface-Knit1** in the Flyout FeatureManager design tree to add it to the **Surface To Thicken** field. Click any open space to close the Flyout FeatureManager.
4. If the preview in the Graphics Window shows that the surface will be thickened away from the handle, click the **Thicken side 2** button so that the feature is created toward the rear of the handle, as shown in Figure 7.30.
5. Click **OK**. The surface is thickened to create a 1/8-inch thick flange at the left end of the handle, as shown in Figure 7.31.

7.2.4 Filleting the Thickened Surface

The edges of the flange will be rounded using a constant-radius fillet.

1. Open the **Fillet** PropertyManager. Set the view to **Hidden Lines Removed**.
2. Select the face (one of the edges of the flange), as shown in Figure 7.32. If it is difficult to select the face, you can **Select Other** by *right clicking* the face, setting the **Selection Filter** toolbar to **Filter Faces**, or simply by zooming in. **Face<1>** should be listed in the **Edges, Faces, Features and Loops** field.

Figure 7.31.   Flange thickened from surface.

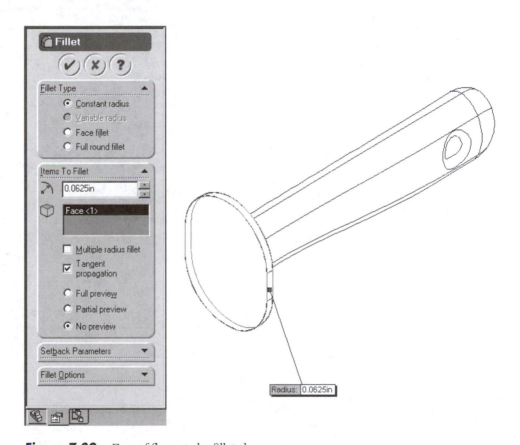

Figure 7.32.   Face of flange to be filleted.

3.   Set the ***Radius*** to *1/16*.

4.   Click ***OK***. The entire edge of the flange is filleted with a 1/16-inch radius. Notice that four faces (two planar and two curved) were filleted, even though only one face was selected in the ***Fillet*** PropertyManager. Because ***Tangent propagation*** was automatically checked, as shown in Figure 7.32,

SolidWorks recognized that the four faces forming the edge of the flange were actually one continuous face.

7.2.5   The Measure Tool

The **Measure** tool is very helpful in determining sizes and distances for a part that are not explicitly defined with dimensions. It can also be used to determine surface areas, arc lengths, and projected distances. You will use the **Measure** tool to find the distance between the fillet on the edge of the flange and the loft feature. With this distance known, an appropriate value for the radius of the fillet between the loft and the flange can be determined.

1. Click **Tools** ⇒ **Measure**. The *Measure* dialog box appears, as shown in Figure 7.33. The cursor changes to a pointed ruler, indicating that edges, faces, and points can be selected to measure.

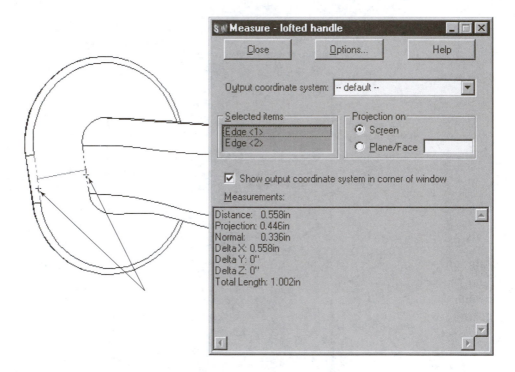

Figure 7.33.   *Measure* dialog box.

2. Orient the model so that the back face of the flange can be seen. Turn off the **Rotate View** tool. Select two edges, as shown in Figure 7.33. The ***Distance*** in inches between these two lines, ***.558***, is computed and displayed in the dialog box. Notice that the distance between the edges is the same value as ***Delta X***, since the shortest line between the edges is in the x-direction.

3. Right click in the Graphics Window, and choose **Clear Selections** to remove the two edges from the ***Selected items*** field. Select any face of the loft feature. The face becomes highlighted and both the surface area and perimeter are displayed. The information provided from the **Measure** tool can be very helpful when calculating areas or distances, such as the surface area of a loft. Often, these areas or distances would be quite challenging to

compute from the dimensions of the part alone. ***Close*** the ***Measure*** dialog box and click the <u>**Select**</u> toolbar button so that nothing is selected.

7.2.6   Adding a Large Fillet between the Loft and the Flange

Using the information from the **Measure** tool, you will create a fillet between the flange and the loft. This incorporates a smooth, ergonomic guard into the handle.

1.   Open the ***Fillet*** PropertyManager.

2.   Set the ***Radius*** to ***1/2***. This dimension is slightly less than the distance measured between the side of the handle and the edge of the flange. A fillet radius larger than .558 inches would not be suitable. An error would result, since SolidWorks cannot construct a fillet that extends beyond the edge of the flange.

3.   *Right click* the edge between the loft and the flange indicated in Figure 7.34. Choose **Select Loop** from the menu that appears. This selects all of the edges that make up the loop. ***Loop<1>*** is added to the ***Edges, Faces, Features and Loops*** field in the PropertyManager. The edge that was selected is actually a part of two different loops, one on the flange and one on the loft base feature. Click the arrow in the Graphics Window to toggle between the two loops. Be sure the rounded rectangular loop between the flange and the loft feature is selected and only ***Loop<1>*** appears in the ***Edges, Faces, Features and Loops*** field before continuing. Select ***Full preview*** to display what the fillet will look like.

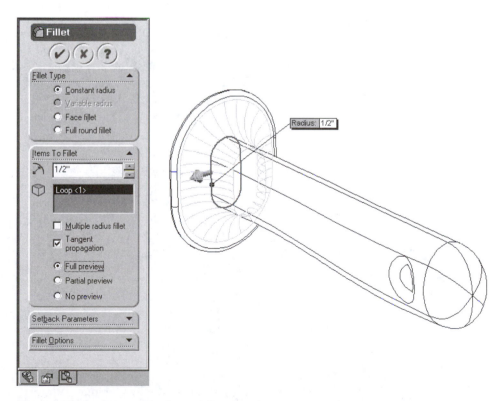

Figure 7.34.   Loop of the flange to be filleted.

4. Click **OK**. After a short wait, the fillet between the loft and the flange appears, as shown in Figure 7.35. Return to the **Shaded** display.

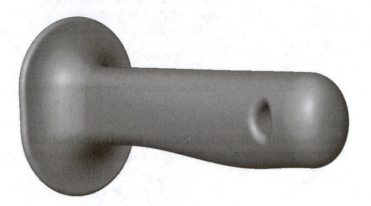

Figure 7.35.   Large fillet added to the handle.

7.2.7   The Mass Properties Dialog Box

There are many advantages to creating a solid model of a part over simply creating a two-dimensional drawing of a part. One of these advantages is the ability to calculate the mass properties of the solid, including the mass, the volume, the surface area, the center of mass, and the inertial properties. The **Mass Properties** tool will be used to calculate these values for the solid model of the handle.

1. Click **Tools ⇒ Mass Properties**. The **Mass Properties** dialog box appears, as shown in Figure 7.36. Three perpendicular arrows appear on the handle (you may need to move the dialog box in order to see them), showing the location of the center of mass. The **Center of mass**, as listed in the dialog box, is defined relative to the origin.

2. Click the **Options** button. The **Measurement Options** dialog box appears. Set the **Density** in the **Material Properties** field to **.284**, the density of steel in lb/in^3.

3. Click **OK**. The **Measurement Options** dialog box closes and SolidWorks recalculates both the weight and the moments of inertia. Take note of the weight (**Mass**) of the steel handle.

4. Change the density to **.042** for nylon, which is a more likely candidate material for the handle. The mass and other properties should match those shown in Figure 7.36. Changing the density of the model does not alter the model itself. The density is only used in the calculation of the mass properties. **Close** the dialog box.

Congratulations! This completes the model of the redesigned handle. Your part should look similar to those shown in Figures 7.26 and 7.35. Note that the rectangular hole that holds the arms of the cutter sub-assembly has not been included in the lofted handle. This hole will be added after the handle is assembled with the cutter sub-assembly. Save the part, but leave the window open. In the next section, you will create two configurations of the handle: one with text engraved on the side and one without text.

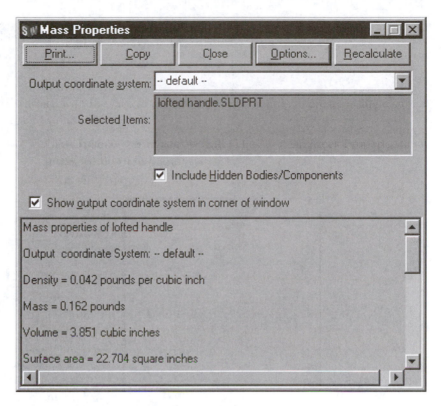

Figure 7.36.   *Mass Properties* dialog box.

7.3   CREATING A CONFIGURATION OF THE HANDLE WITH ENGRAVED TEXT

Configurations are a means to model several variations of the same part or assembly. This can be quite useful in modeling families of parts, or assemblies that vary in only minor respects. Configurations of parts can differ in several ways: Dimensions can be altered, features can be suppressed, and the color can be changed. For assemblies, different configurations can either show or hide particular parts. The lofted handle will have two configurations: one with engraved text and one with the text suppressed.

7.3.1   Adding a Configuration to the Model of the Handle

The ConfigurationManager, which resides in the same area as the FeatureManager design tree, displays the configurations of the part or the assembly. Configurations can be added or deleted, and the properties can be changed in the ConfigurationManager.

1.   Activate the ConfigurationManager by clicking the rightmost tab at the bottom of the FeatureManager design tree. Currently, only the **Default** configuration is listed below **lofted handle Configuration(s)**.

2.   Right click **lofted handle Configuration(s)** and select **Add Configuration** from the menu. The *Add Configuration* dialog box appears, as shown in Figure 7.37.

3.   In the *Configuration Name* field, type *no text*. Add the description shown in Figure 7.37 to the *Comment* field.

4.   Be sure that the *Suppress features* checkbox is checked. With this option checked, new features created in other configurations will be suppressed. In

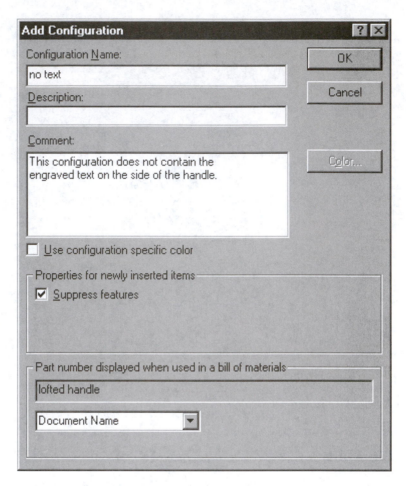

Figure 7.37. *Add Configuration* dialog box.

this case, the text on the handle will be added to the **Default** configuration. Because the text will be a new feature, it will be suppressed automatically in the **no text** configuration.

5. Click *OK* to exit the *Add Configuration* dialog box. The Configuration-Manager now indicates that the **no text [lofted handle]** is the active configuration (yellow). It may be necessary to move the border between the ConfigurationManager and the Graphics Window to the right in order to see the full name. Also, notice that the **Default [lofted handle]** icon is inactive (gray).

6. Double click **Default [lofted handle]** to activate the configuration.

7. Return to the FeatureManager design tree by clicking the left tab at the bottom of the ConfigurationManager window. Note that the top item in the design tree is **lofted handle (Default)**.

7.3.2 Creating the Text Sketch

Once text is created in a sketch, it can be extruded or cut to create a solid feature, just like any other sketched entity. The font and the size of the text can be specified to meet the requirements of the part. You will create a sketch with the words "PIZZA CUTTERS INC.," which will be engraved into the side of the handle. You could add your own text, but for the sake of consistency with this tutorial, use this text.

1. Create a new plane, offset **1/2** to the right of the **Right** plane using **Insert ⇒ Reference Geometry ⇒ Plane**. The new plane, **Plane2**, is shown in Figure 7.38 in the **Top** view.

1/2"

Plane2

Figure 7.38.   Sketching plane offset.

2. Open a sketch on **Plane2** and set the view to **Normal To**.

3. To create text, click **Tools ⇒ Sketch Entity ⇒ Text**. The *Sketch Text* PropertyManager appears as shown in Figure 7.39.

4. Click on the surface of the handle near the left end of the handle. Type "***PIZZA CUTTERS INC.***" (without the quotes) in the *Text* field of the *Sketch Text* PropertyManager.

5. Uncheck *Use Document's Font* and click the *Font* button. In the *Choose Font* dialog box that appears, set the *Font* to *Century Gothic*, the *Font Style* to *Italic*, and the *Height* to *28 Points*. Click *OK*.

6. Note the preview in the Graphics Window. If the spelling is correct and both the font and the size look reasonable, click *OK*.

7. You will position the text using the PropertyManager. Select the small circle at the base of the "P" in the text. The *Point* PropertyManager appears, as shown in Figure 7.40. In the *Parameters* field, set **X Coordinate** to **7/8** and

Figure 7.39.   *Sketch Text* PropertyManager.

Y Coordinate to −*1/8*. This sets the position of the small cross with respect to the origin. The *y*-value is negative, which positions the small cross below the origin.

8.   The sketch is *Under Defined*. The text has been positioned, but it is not yet constrained with dimensions. Instead of adding dimensions, you will simply add a relation to fix the position of the text using the PropertyManager. Click the *Fix* button and click the green check mark. This fully defines the sketch by fixing the text in its current position.

Figure 7.40. *Point* PropertyManager.

7.3.3   Engraving the Text into the Handle

With the sketch for the text completed, the outlines of the letters can be engraved into the handle using an extruded cut.

1. Go to the **Isometric** view. Open the ***Cut-Extrude*** PropertyManager.
2. The text will be cut 1/16″ into the handle. To ensure that the same depth is maintained along the irregular surface of the handle, set the ***End Condition*** to ***Offset from surface***. This results in the extruded cut extending from the sketch plane to an imaginary surface that is offset a specified distance from the selected surface. Material is removed between the sketch plane and the imaginary surface so that the depth of the engraved letters is uniform along the curved surface of the handle.
3. Set the ***Offset Distance*** to ***1/16***.
4. Select the surface, as shown in Figure 7.41. It may help to open the **Selection Filter** toolbar, set it to **Filter Faces**, and view the right side. After a short time, ***Face <1>*** appears in the ***Face/Plane*** field. Turn off the selection filters, so that any item can be selected from now on.

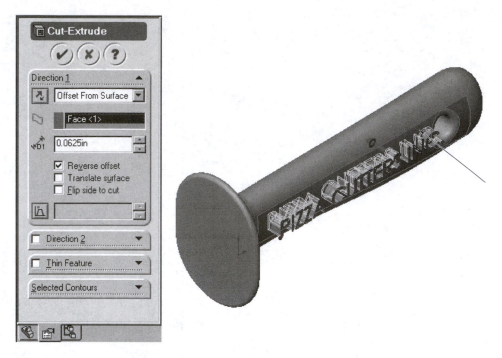

Figure 7.41. Engraving the text with the *Cut-Extrude* PropertyManager.

5. Switch to the **Top** view. Note if the cut goes into the handle from the selected surface. If it is not clear, look for the difference when you click the **Reverse offset** checkbox. Set the **Reverse offset** checkbox, so that the cut goes into the handle from the selected surface.

6. Click **OK**. After a short wait, the text is engraved into the handle. The text might be difficult to see, because it is the same color as the handle. In the next section, you will change the feature color so that the engraving can easily be seen.

7. Hide **Plane2** and switch to the **Isometric** view.

7.3.4 Changing the Color of the Cut-Extrude Feature

Until now, only the color of an entire part has been altered. However, individual features can be distinguished by a change in colors. The color of the engraved text will be changed to show it more clearly.

1. Select **Cut-Extrude2** (the engraved text) in the FeatureManager design tree. Click the **Edit Color** button in the **Standard** toolbar. The **Edit Color** dialog box appears. **Apply To** is currently set to **Feature** so that only the color of the selected feature will be changed.

2. Choose a color for the engraved text by clicking on the desired color button, followed by **Apply**.

3. In a similar manner, choose a color for the entire handle that contrasts the color of the engraved text. First, select **lofted handle (Default)** in the FeatureManager design tree. In this case, **Apply To** is set to **Part** to change the color of the entire part. Choose the desired color.

4. Click **OK** to exit the **Color** dialog box. Examine the engraving more closely by rotating and zooming in to see the individual letters cut into the handle.

Notice that all of the letters have the same depth, even though the surface of the handle is contoured. Return to the **Isometric** view.

7.3.5   Modifying a Configuration Dimension

The circular hole at the end of the handle is too close to the end of the engraved text. To demonstrate the usefulness of the ConfigurationManager, the distance from the origin to the hole will be increased, but only in the **Default** configuration. The **no text** configuration will keep the original dimension for the position of the hole.

1. Double click **Cut-Extrude1** (the circular hole) in the FeatureManager design tree. The dimensions of the hole are now shown in the Graphics Window.

2. Double click the **4 1/2** dimension using the **Select** tool. The *Modify* dialog appears, as shown in Figure 7.42.

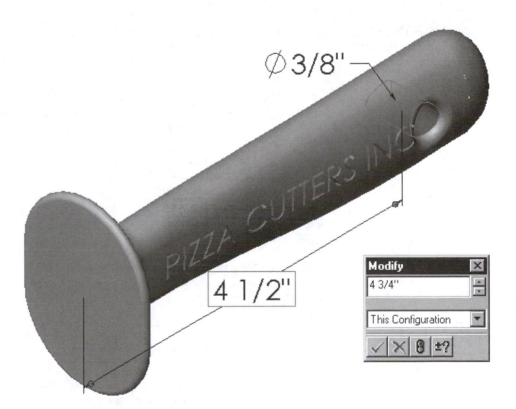

Figure 7.42. *Modify* dialog box with multiple configurations.

3. The dialog box is different from the standard *Modify* dialog box, because more than one configuration exists in the document. The dimension can be set to represent the value for *This configuration* only or for *All configurations*. The new dimension for the hole should be applied to the **Default** configuration only, so select *This configuration*. Set the dimension to *4 3/4*. Click the green checkbox to accept the value.

4. Since the dimension was changed after the hole feature was created, the position of the hole stays the same. **Rebuild** the part to update the dimension. Because the part is fairly complex, it may take a few moments to rebuild.

The position of the hole updates to reflect the new value, most evident in the **Right** view.

5. In the ConfigurationManager, *double click* the **no text [lofted handle]** configuration to activate it. The configuration without the engraved text is shown. This configuration has the original dimension for the circular hole of $4\frac{1}{2}''$, visible by *double clicking* **Cut-Extrude1** in the FeatureManager design tree. Remember that the **no text** configuration's properties were set to suppress new features. The two new features, **Plane2** and **Cut-Extrude2**, were created in the **Default** configuration and suppressed in the **no text** configuration. In the FeatureManager design tree, these two features are grayed out, indicating that they are suppressed.

Congratulations! The model of the lofted handle is now ready to be assembled with the cutter sub-assembly. Save the part and leave the part window open.

7.4 ASSEMBLING THE HANDLE AND CUTTER SUB-ASSEMBLY

A useful feature of SolidWorks is the ability to create and edit parts while they are being assembled. This powerful characteristic allows parts to be defined in the context of the assembly. In other words, the definition of the part can be made partially or completely dependent upon the assembly. This is called top-down modeling, because the details of the part are created (or modified) after the assembly is created. In the case of the **lofted handle**, the rectangular hole for the arms—which was not included in the model thus far—will be defined in the context of the assembly. To do this, the handle (without the rectangular hole) will be assembled with the cutter sub-assembly. Then, a cavity in the handle for the cutter arms will be created while the parts are being assembled. The interfering solid material of the handle—that is, where the arms overlap the handle—will be removed to produce a rectangular hole that holds the arms tightly. The completed assembly is shown in Figure 7.43.

7.4.1 Setting up the Assembly Document

The handle will be the first part brought into the assembly. Be sure that the **lofted handle** window is still open and displays the **no text** configuration of the handle.

1. Create a new assembly document. Display the **Origins**.
2. Click **Window** ⇒ **Tile Horizontally** to show both the assembly and the handle windows.
3. Drag the part icon next to **lofted handle (no text)** from the FeatureManager design tree of the handle window to the origin of the assembly window. Remember to look for the two sets of arrows, indicating that the planes of the part will be coincident with the planes of the assembly. The fixed handle, **(f) lofted handle<1>**, along with its configuration **(no text)** are listed in the FeatureManager design tree.
4. Maximize the assembly window. Go to the **Isometric** view and uncheck **View** ⇒ **Origins**, so that the origin is not visible.

7.4.2 Mating the Cutter Sub-Assembly with the Handle

Three mates will fully define the position of the cutter sub-assembly with respect to the lofted handle. Two planes of the cutter sub-assembly will be mated to the fixed planes of the assembly document. The last mate will constrain an edge of one of the arms to be coincident with the flat face of the handle's flange.

Figure 7.43.   Redesigned handle assembled with the cutter sub-assembly.

1. Bring the cutter sub-assembly into the assembly document by clicking **Insert** ⇒ **Component** ⇒ **From File**. Set the *Files of type* to *Assembly*. *Open* the *cutter sub-assembly* and click anywhere in the Graphics Window to place the component. Recall that the cutter sub-assembly is also a component in the assembly document, **pizza cutter assembly**. Using the cutter sub-assembly in this assembly will not disrupt the relations of the original pizza cutter assembly.

2. **Zoom to Fit** and position the cutter sub-assembly using the **Move Component** and **Rotate Component** tools, so that it is close to its final position with the ends of the arms near the flat face of the handle.

3. Begin by mating the plane of the blade with a plane of the handle. If necessary, click the plus sign next to (−) **cutter sub-assembly<1>** in the FeatureManager design tree to show the components of the cutter sub-assembly. Click the plus sign next to (−) **blade<1>** to show its features. Select the **Front** plane of the blade in the cutter sub-assembly so that it is highlighted.

4. *Control click* the **Right** plane of the assembly document to select it, also. Use the **Mate** tool to create a coincident mate between the two planes to align the blade with the handle. The cutter sub-assembly moves to satisfy the constraint.

5. Click the plus sign next to (−) **arm<1>** to show the features of the arm. Moving the cursor over the planes of the arm or the assembly in the FeatureManager design tree results in each plane appearing in the Graphics Window. It should be evident that making the **Front** plane of the arm coincident with the **Top** plane of the assembly will move the cutter sub-assembly

to its desired position. Create a coincident mate between **Front** of **arm<1>** and **Top** of the assembly. At this point, the cutter sub-assembly can only move along the axis of the handle. Try moving the cutter sub-assembly using the **Move Component** tool. The screen should look similar to the one shown in Figure 7.44. If the cutter sub-assembly is flipped from that shown in the figure, undo the last two mates and reposition the cutter sub-assembly so that the arms are near the face of the handle.

Figure 7.44. Planes of cutter sub-assembly constrained.

6. Move the cutter sub-assembly, rotate the view, and zoom in so that the items shown in Figure 7.45 are visible. Set the display to **Hidden Lines Removed**. If the **Selection Filter** toolbar is not visible, activate it by clicking the **Toggle Selection Filter Toolbar** button in the **Standard** toolbar, and setting it to **Filter Edges**. Activate the **SmartMates** button in the **Assembly** toolbar. *Double click* the edge of the arm, as shown in Figure 7.45. This is the edge between the flat face and the bend—the same edge used for the mate in the original pizza cutter assembly. The edge becomes highlighted and the cursor changes to a pointer with a paper clip icon.

7. Turn off **Filter Edges** and turn on **Filter Faces** in the **Selection Filter** toolbar. Select the front face of the handle, as shown in Figure 7.45. A coincident mate is created between the selected edge of the handle and the face of the flange. Return to the **Shaded** display to see the mate more clearly. The cutter sub-assembly has been mated with the handle so that the arms and the handle interfere. It is this interfering solid that will be removed in the next section. Click the **SmartMates** button to deactivate it.

8. Save the assembly as **pizza cutter2**. Click *Yes* to rebuild the assembly and save the referenced models.

9. Right click **pizza cutter2** in the FeatureManager design tree, and select **Collapse Items** to clean up the FeatureManager design tree. Click the

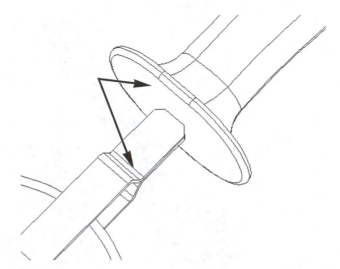

Figure 7.45. Edge and surface selections for a coincident mate.

Clear All Filters button to turn off the selection filter. Return to the **Isometric** view.

7.4.3   Modeling the Rectangular Hole Using the Cavity Feature

The **Cavity** feature is unique to assembly documents. It removes the interfering volumes from one of the components in the assembly. Currently, the arms interfere with the handle. This volume of interference will be removed from the handle. The resulting cavity feature—which will be part of the lofted handle—will be defined in the context of the new pizza cutter assembly.

1.   Return to the **lofted handle** window. The **Default** configuration of the lofted handle is currently set to suppress new features. The cavity should be applied to both configurations. Activate the ConfigurationManager. *Right click* **Default** and select **Properties**. Uncheck the ***Suppress features*** checkbox in the ***Configuration Properties*** dialog box and click ***OK***. The cavity will now be applied to the **Default** configuration as well as to the **no text** configuration. Return to the **pizza cutter2** assembly window.

2.   Click on the lofted handle in the FeatureManager design tree to select it. Click the **Edit Part** button in the **Assembly** toolbar, or **Edit ⇒ Part**. In the original pizza cutter assembly, the guard was edited in its own window. Here, the lofted handle will be edited directly in the assembly window. All components except the handle turn translucent, indicating that the handle is being edited.

3.   Click **Insert ⇒ Features ⇒ Cavity**. This feature is available only if the component to which the cavity is added is in the edit mode.

4.   The ***Cavity*** dialog box appears, as shown in Figure 7.46. Add the two arms to the ***Design component*** field by selecting each of the arms in the Graphics Window. It may be easiest to select the arms in the FeatureManager design tree. Because the lofted handle is being edited, it is understood that the material will be removed from it, and not from the arms.

5.   The ***Scaling Factor in %*** field allows the cavity to be scaled in size relative to the volume of interference. Because material shrinkage in metal castings

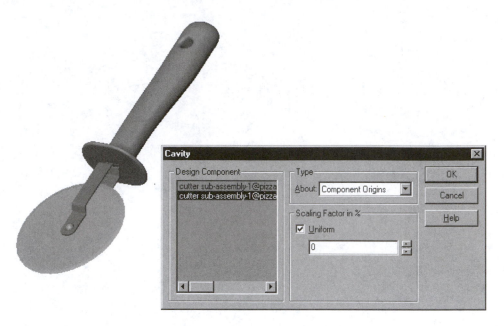

Figure 7.46. *Cavity* dialog box.

and plastic injection molding is common, the ability to scale the mold is a convenient feature to account for the shrinkage. Here, you will assume there is no shrinkage. With **Uniform** checked, set the ***Scaling factor in %*** to ***0***.

6. Click ***OK***. The cavity is created, although it cannot be seen in the assembly window. Click the **Edit Part** button again, to exit the edit mode for the lofted handle. Return to the lofted handle window and set the view to **Isometric** and **Hidden Lines Visible**. The handle should look similar to the one shown in Figure 7.47, which is rotated slightly from isometric. Notice that the cavity created in the handle is perfectly shaped to match the ends of the arms, including the chamfers.

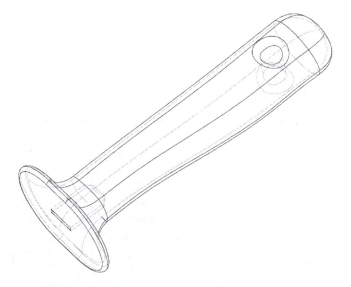

Figure 7.47. Cavity added to lofted handle.

7. **Cavity1** → appears in the FeatureManager design tree for the lofted handle. The →, which appears at the top of the FeatureManager design tree next to **lofted handle (no text)** and next to **Cavity1**, indicates that a feature (**Cavity1**) is defined in a context outside of the part, namely the new pizza cutter assembly document.

8. Save the lofted handle.

7.4.4 Changing the Handle's Configuration in the Assembly Document

Part configurations can be changed in assembly documents. Currently, the **no text** configuration is active in the new pizza cutter assembly. The **Default** configuration will be used so that the engraved text is shown in the assembly.

1. Return to the assembly window. *Right click* (**f**) **lofted handle<1>** → (**no text**) in the FeatureManager design tree. Select **Component Properties** from the menu that appears. The ***Component Properties*** dialog box appears, as shown in Figure 7.48.

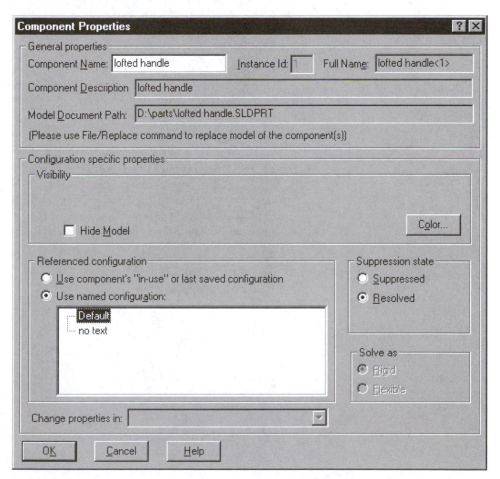

Figure 7.48. *Component Properties* dialog box.

2. In the ***Referenced Configuration*** field, set ***Use named configuration*** to ***Default***.

3. Click ***OK***. The assembly rebuilds with the new configuration. The handle should appear with the engraved text, as shown in Figure 7.43.

Congratulations! This completes the lofted handle and the new pizza cutter assembly. Save the assembly document, close the windows, and exit the program.

Based on what you have learned in this book, it is quite evident that SolidWorks is a powerful, easy-to-use solids modeling CAD system. It allows engineers to evaluate design alternatives, reduce errors, and enhance product quality with sophisticated modeling tools. Having learned the basics of SolidWorks, you are now prepared to model complex parts and assemblies. As you become more proficient with SolidWorks, you will be able to design new and innovative parts more quickly and effectively than ever before.

Problems

1. Starting with the **no text** configuration, create a new configuration with your name embossed (raised lettering) on the side of the lofted handle. The text's sketch should lie on the **Right** plane and extend to a surface offset from the side of the handle. Change the color of the embossed text so that it can be seen easily.

2. Convert the lofted handle into a shelled part with ribs. To begin, change the thickness of the flange to $\frac{1}{4}''$. Then, create a shelled part with a $\frac{1}{16}''$ wall thickness. Add screw holes, ribs, and a cut for the cutter sub-assembly that are similar to those for the shelled handle.

3. Create a new lofted handle with four guide curves that are splines. The guide curves should be on the top, the bottom, and both sides.

4. Model a two-liter soft drink bottle by creating a loft between a circular cross section at the base and a circular cross section at the mouth. Use a fillet to round the bottom of the bottle. Then, shell the bottle. Finally, radiate and thicken a surface just below the mouth of the bottle. (See this feature on an actual two-liter bottle.) Do not include the threads for the cap.

Index